Sociology and the New Testament

SOCIOLOGY AND THE NEW TESTAMENT

AN APPRAISAL

BENGT HOLMBERG

Fortress Press   Minneapolis

To my children
Charlotta, Andreas, Rebecka, and Katarina

SOCIOLOGY AND THE NEW TESTAMENT
An Appraisal

Scripture quotations unless otherwise noted are from the Revised Standard Version of the Bible, copyright © 1946, 1952, and 1971 by the Division of Christian Education of the National Council of Churches.

Cover design: Pollock Design Group

Library of Congress Cataloging-in-Publication Data

Holmberg, Bengt, 1942-
    Sociology and the New Testament : an appraisal / Bengt Holmberg.
        p. cm.
    Includes bibliographical references.
    ISBN 0-8006-2443-2
    1. Sociology, Biblical. 2. Bible. N.T.—Criticism,
interpretation, etc. I. Title.
BS2545.S55H65   1990
225.6′7—dc20   89-78408
                                                                 CIP

The paper used in this publication meets the minimum requirements of American National Standard for Information Sciences—Permanence of Paper for Printed Library Materials, ANSI Z329.48-1984.   ∞™

Manufactured in the U.S.A.   AF 1-2443

94   93   92   91   90   1   2   3   4   5   6   7   8   9   10

Contents

Preface

This book is a result of my first contact with the American theological scene, namely, an invitation from the Seabury-Western Theological Seminary in Evanston, Illinois, to deliver the William C. Winslow Lectures in October 1986. I want to express my gratitude to colleagues and students for their generous reception of the lectures and for the stimulating response I received. The lectures gave me the impulse to reflect further on the relationship between New Testament studies and sociology. I recognized then, and see now, that it is somewhat rash to attempt writing about a subject like New Testament sociology, in which most of the activity takes place in North America. Doubtless the reader will find this work to be marked by its Northern European provenance. A number of works that have been published in English editions (especially those of Gerd Theissen) have been available to me in German editions only; not a few American journals have been practically inaccessible, and the time lag between publication in America and reception in Europe has precluded discussion of some recent work in the field, such as Howard Clark Kee's *Knowing the Truth: A Sociological Approach to New Testament Interpretation* (Fortress Press, 1989). I regret the inconvenience caused by the resulting "European" character of my bibliography.

Sociology and the New Testament has a double aim: first, to present some of the research on the New Testament during the 1970s and 1980s that applied sociological concepts and theories to the biblical texts; and, second, to reflect critically on the value of this type of approach by looking at the actual methodological development of New Testament sociology and by assessing its limits and benefits. In order to give a fuller representation and a more thorough analysis of scholarly work in this discipline, I have limited my discussion to three fields: the social history of first-century Christianity, the use of categories from the sociology of religion, and the application of perspectives from the sociology of knowledge to early Christian beliefs.

One such application that has played an increasingly important part in New Testament studies is the discipline of anthropology. Malina, Moxnes, Neyrey, and other scholars have applied the "group-grid" perspective of the noted anthropologist Mary Douglas to the understanding of New Testament writings in their socioeconomic and cultural context. I have chosen not to include a discussion of this application because anthropology has a scientific tradition and conceptual perspective of its own. In spite of many similarities between the two disciplines, their underlying frames of reference are different enough to merit separate discussion.

As this project developed I have had the privilege of discussing parts of it in the New Testament Research Seminar under Professor Birger Gerhardsson in Lund, where I finished the work in July 1989. I gratefully remember the special interest and help I received from my friend and colleague Professor René Kieffer, now in Uppsala.

Bengt Holmberg
Makumira, Tanzania
All Saints' Day 1989

1 Sociology in New Testament Studies

The need for sociology in New Testament studies

Sociology is not a newcomer in New Testament studies. It was actually introduced almost seventy years ago, as a part of the form critical method.[1] The basic idea of this new approach was an idea from the sociology of literature, namely that types of literature or genres (Gattungen) are bound to and shaped by specific types of social life-settings (Sitz im Leben).[2] This introduction of a social-historical or sociological perspective was a natural continuation of the broad and deep interest in ancient history and the early Christian history as part of it that we can observe in the last few decades before the First World War (1914–1918). One could refer to the names of scholars such as Adolf von Harnack, Eduard Meyer, Ernst von Dobschültz, Emil Schürer, Adolf Deissmann, and Ernst Troeltsch—all of which analysed and described early Christianity as connected in a thousand ways with the social reality of its own world.

But the introduction of sociology made by New Testament form criticism was never fulfilled, because of the fundamental shift in cultural and theological climate that came about as a consequence of the world war. The prevailing optimistic evolutionism and the liberal culture-protestantism was dealt a severe blow, and what came instead was dialectic theology and the existential hermeneutic of biblical texts, and with them a focusing of interest on theology and the individual. Form criticism was directed into finding the social basis of the gospels in the life and faith of the early church: Sitz im Leben became Sitz im

---

[1] Gerd Theissen describes this, and the causes of the following nondevelopment of sociology in his "Zur forschungsgeschichtlichen Einordnung der soziologischen Fragestellung" (*Studien zur Soziologie des Urchristentums*. Tübingen, 1979; ²1983, 3-34), 3-20.

[2] Rudolf Bultmann characterized these two terms as sociological concepts, from the first edition of his *Geschichte der synoptischen Tradition* (1921).

religiösen Leben.[3] This situation prevailed and was even further accentuated in the approach of redaction criticism, which continued the impulse of form criticism in the 1950s and onward: interest was turned toward the individual evangelist and his specific theology, and the social life of the receiving communities was left far aside. And the advent of structuralistic exegesis with its typically text-internal analysis directed the attention of exegetes even further away from concrete historical situations.

This meant that New Testament studies around 1970 suffered from a fifty-year deficit on social history and sociological perspectives. There was a balance that needed to be redressed. After decades of dominance for theology and the history of ideas there existed a certain hunger for renewed contact with and more solid knowledge about the concrete social history of the movement whose thinking had been so diligently studied. And the pendulum has swung: New Testament studies in the last two decades have seen a flood of investigations concerning the social life of the early Christian movement and its contemporary world, books about slavery, the life of women and children, schools, household and family life, poverty and riches, social classes and status stratification, and many similar phenomena.

But there were also mistakes to be corrected, more deep-seated methodological faults than simply leaving some areas of human life unresearched for a long time. Robin Scroggs wrote about the discipline of the theology of the New Testament as operating out of a methodological docetism, as if believers had minds and spirits unconnected with their individual and corporate bodies.[4] I have suggested calling this strongly distorting perspective of early Christian reality the "fallacy of idealism." This is the view, mostly quite unreflected, that the determining factors of the historical process are ideas and nothing else, and that all developments, conflicts, and influences are at bottom developments of, and conflicts and influences between, ideas. Having this view is not simply a philosophical aberration, but regularly leads to the serious methodological mistake of confusing phenomena with the descriptions of them, and a naive fusing of texts and historical

---

[3] "It cannot be denied that even form criticism, with all its talk of the *Sitz-im-Leben* (life-setting) of the text, was a literary and theological discipline which produced hardly any concrete historical, social, or economic information about the traditions which it studied," Thomas F. Best, "The Sociological Study of the New Testament: Promise and Peril of a New Discipline" (*Scottish Journal of Theology* 36, 1983, 181-194), 181 f. Cf. Robert Morgan with John Barton, *Biblical Interpretation*. Oxford, 1988, 145 f.

[4] Robin Scroggs, "The Sociological Interpretation of the New Testament: The Present State of Research" (*New Testament Studies* 26, 1980, 164-179), 165 f.

reality.[5] We need not only studies about the social life of New Testament communities, but the social dimension reinstated into the analysis of New Testament faith and theology. This discipline needs methods of analysis and understanding that take seriously the continuous dialectic between ideas and social structures—and that is why some biblical scholars have experimented in using sociology in their exegesis.

> Interest in the sociology of early Christianity is no attempt to limit reductionistically the reality of Christianity to social dynamic; rather it should be seen as an effort to guard against a reductionism from the other extreme, a limitation of the reality of Christianity to an inner-spiritual, or objective-cognitive system. In short, sociology of early Christianity wants to put body and soul together again.[6]

Robin Scroggs' felicitous metaphor about reuniting body and soul expresses the way I understand the introduction of sociology in New Testament studies: all investigations in this field are, for good or worse, attempts at understanding early Christianity more fully, more as it really was, a flesh-and-blood reality. If we want to understand its "soul," what it means, we must find the "body" it lived as. Nota bene, not the body it lived *in*, as if the individual and corporate bodies of the first Christians were a kind of wrapping, which could be discarded once we had got hold of its contents. As with any human being or reality, the soul is not to be had without the body, i.e., we are not going to see the meaning of early Christianity unless we see the social embodiment of this meaning and the dialectic process between belief and social structure this entails.[7]

How sociology has been used in New Testament studies

To show how this high and golden ambition has been changed into the smaller currency of specific investigations during the last two decades is the aim of this book. But let us start by taking a quick first

---

[5] Bengt Holmberg, *Paul and Power. The Structure of Authority in the Primitive Church as Reflected in the Pauline Epistles* (Lund 1978), 205 f [= Philadelphia, 1980, 201 f].

[6] Robin Scroggs, "State of Research," 165 f.

[7] Cf. the fascinating essay of Wayne A. Meeks, "A Hermeneutics of Social Embodiment" (Nickelsburg—MacRae (eds.), *Christians Among Jews and Gentiles*. Philadelphia, 1986, 176-186).

look at what has been done in this field by turning to some different classifications of work in New Testament sociology.[8]

In 1973 there was held an organizing meeting in Chicago of the study group then called "The Social Description of Early Christianity," and Jonathan Z. Smith delivered a working paper to map out some possible directions for the group's study. This paper was published in September 1975,[9] and has served as a starting point for many subsequent surveys and classifications of work in New Testament sociology. He pointed out four different directions that research in this field had taken and in which it could proceed further:

(1) The description of social realia found in early Christian writings and contemporary materials;

(2) a genuine social history of early Christianity;

(3) investigations in the social organization of early Christianity, meaning

(a) looking at the social forces in society which led to the rise of Christianity, and

(b) analysing the social institutions of early Christianity itself;

(4) understanding early Christianity with the help of (Berger-Luckmann's) sociology of knowledge as a social world, the creation of a world of meaning which provided a plausibility structure for its believers.

It is clear that only the last direction necessitates the application of sociological theory to New Testament evidence, while the first three may be characterized as different approaches of social description, using ordinary historical methods. The difference between these two levels or types of research has become more and more emphasized by other authors in subsequent years.

Philip J. Richter has organized his classification of works within New Testament sociology (the most comprehensive so far) along the same continuum stretching between description of historical facts and sociological theory, and named these two categories of research protosociological and sociological. He defines the latter as follows: "A sociological approach to early Christianity will make use of the explanatory theories and hypotheses of the academic discipline of sociology and will be interested in explaining as well as describing the relevant social

---

[8] Further bibliographical help can be found through the Bibliographical Note at the end of this chapter.

[9] Jonathan Z. Smith, "The Social Description of Early Christianity" (*Religious Studies Review* 1, 1975, 19-25).

data."[10] The important word in this definition is "explain," which means that you proceed beyond description and attempt an understanding of New Testament data from a distinctive analytical and theoretical perspective on human reality—in this case a sociological one. And any fully fledged sociological approach presupposes work at the proto-sociological level.

Richter distinguishes between three different proto-sociological approaches, the first two of which are similar to Smith's. He exemplifies "description of social realia" by pointing to Joachim Jeremias' *Jerusalem in the Time of Jesus* and Martin Hengel's *Judaism and Hellenism,* and as examples of the category "social history" he mentions Abraham Malherbe's *Social Aspects of Early Christianity* (1977), and Gerd Theissen's book on the sociology of the Jesus movement from the same year. Theissen's work is more precise and careful in method and covers much more factual ground, but basically they are doing the same thing, viz., marshalling the relevant data for a sociological treatment.

A third type of proto-sociological work is when you make analytical use of a sociological concept, such as "status" or "power distribution" or "sect," in order to establish and describe the phenomena to which you can then apply an explanation, e.g., a sociological one.[11]

Sociological work proper is when you use sociological theories and models "to explain a particular problem or suggest links between apparently unrelated data in the same or different sources." Perhaps the most well-known example of this is the work of John G. Gager, *Kingdom and Community,* where he applies three theories from the social sciences to the New Testament material. Richter here mentions also Howard Kee's *Christian Origins in Sociological Perspective* (1980), and Bruce Malina's work, partly summarized in *The New Testament World: Insights from Cultural Anthropology* (1981), which, however, as the subtitle indicates, moves over into another of the social sciences. In a footnote Richter lists twenty-five other exegetical works of this truly sociological kind, even subdividing them according to which category of social-science analysis they have used.[12]

[10] Philip J. Richter, "Recent Sociological Approaches to the Study of the New Testament" (*Religion* 14, 1984, 77-90), 78 and passim.

[11] Richter helpfully exemplifies his classifications by giving lists of which works he considers to belong to the categories of realia description (86 note 15), social history (86 f note 18), and the analysis of NT data with the help of sociological concepts (87 f note 32).

[12] Richter, "Recent Sociological Approaches," 88 f note 41. A special type of sociological work is when you use New Testament data to test and perhaps even improve a given sociological theory, 84.

Perhaps a caveat should be entered here. The distinction between proto-sociological and sociological works on which Richter places such an emphasis is certainly useful, because it helps in discerning the scope or ambition of studies in this field, and precludes the easy labelling of any biblical study that touches the social life as "sociological." But on the other hand, one should beware of attaching a too great importance to it, as it can also be misleading. On the practical level of reconstructing early Christian history, it breaks down because no description of phenomena of social life can be made without some idea about what to look for and how to structure phenomena or, in other words, some theoretical frame.[13] This may not have been made explicit by all historical scholars, but that should not lead us into thinking that any fact-finding or historical description can be made without the help of models and theories. Another and more serious effect of the distinction between social history and sociological explanation (as it is usually phrased) is that it can so easily be understood as implying that social description is neutral and objective, while the applying of sociological concepts and models is more theory-laden and precarious.[14]

Is historical sociology possible at all?

As there exists quite an amount of historical sociological work on New Testament material, the question of this heading might seem superfluous. But that there are nonetheless good reasons for putting the question is the contention of Cyril Rodd. In two articles he has scrutinized biblical sociology, first taking on a classic sociologist of towering stature by analysing Max Weber's work on Ancient Judaism against the advances made within Old Testament research since the beginning of the century,[15] and then investigating how John Gager and Robert Carroll have applied a modern sociological theory to biblical material.[16]

In the first article, Rodd finds that Weber was very competent and careful, but that he basically borrowed the optimism of his days concerning the possibility of correctly understanding Israel's past history.

---

[13] Elizabeth Schüssler Fiorenza, *In Memory of Her: A Feminist Theological Reconstruction of Christian Origins.* London, 1983, 71.

[14] John H. Elliott, "Social-Scientific Criticism of the New Testament: More on Methods and Models" (*Semeia* 35, 1986, 1-33), 9.

[15] Cyril S. Rodd, "Max Weber and Ancient Judaism" (*Scottish Journal of Theology* 32, 1979, 457-469).

[16] Cyril S. Rodd, "On Applying a Sociological Theory to Biblical Studies" (*Journal for the Study of the Old Testament* 19, 1981, 95-106).

This kind of confidence is much smaller nowadays. He further notes that Weber reads the evidence backward, i.e., from how he understands later Judaism, in which interpretation he puts two concepts to the fore: rationality and existence as a pariah people. This is inevitably a subtle distortion of the Old Testament evidence, as the Jewish people are not uniformly the same through the centuries. Another remarkable fact in Weber's interpretation of ancient Israel is that he compares it mainly with Indian society and its caste order (to a lesser degree also with Chinese religion), whereas the scholars of today would situate Israel much more firmly against the background of contemporary Near Eastern cultures and societies. The result is that terminology is included that today seems misleading (peasants, plebeians, petty bourgeoisie, caste system).

Finally Rodd turns to the question of the data basis for Weber's reconstructions. The Old Testament is only a surviving selection from a much larger literature, and it is almost silent on the social institutions of Israel. The social life has to be reconstructed from the documents, which means that, unless a close control is kept upon the evidence, the arguments will run the risk of being circular. Rodd's conclusion is that the state of the evidence is such that the sociological programme cannot be carried out. There is simply not enough data to reveal independently of each other the status of institutions and the status of ideas, so that one can then compare them. Rodd concludes as follows:

> This leads me to ask whether the past is ever amenable to sociological analysis, since Weber's attempt to conduct such an analysis of an ancient civilisation set the problem in high relief. The difficulty is not simply a matter of the paucity of data, although for more distant periods this will almost always be a factor. The basic problem lies in the fact that the evidence has 'set' and cannot be forced by the researcher to reveal a choice between two or more options. The sociologist can neither decide what set of empirical facts he will collect nor posit and test hypotheses, both of which operations are central to scientific sociology, if the study of man in society can ever be truly 'scientific'.[17]

---

[17] Rodd, "Max Weber," 469. In the final sentence he adds: "I find it interesting that the most recent attempt to carry sociology into the biblical area, Gerd Theissen's *The First Followers of Jesus* (London, 1978), contains the same weakness that we have seen in Weber's study of Israel."

In his second article two years later, Rodd took a close look at how Festinger's sociological theory of cognitive dissonance had been applied to biblical studies, first by John Gager to understand the missionary drive of the first Christians, and secondly by Robert Carroll to interpret the Israelite prophetic traditions. The weaknesses of the sociological theories themselves (Gager uses Coser's theory concerning the functions of social conflict as well), and especially of Gager's application of them are stunningly demonstrated by Rodd, but will be left aside here. In conclusion he points to three sizable obstacles to historical sociology: (a) the nature of the evidence (faith documents), (b) the differences in culture and the extreme difficulty in transferring theories derived from evidence in one kind of society to a very different society, and (c) the impossibility of testing a hypothesis. He summarizes:

> There is a world of difference between sociology applied to contemporary society, where the researcher can test his theories against evidence which he collects, and historical sociology where he has only fossilized evidence that has been preserved by chance or for purposes very different from that of the sociologist. It is a cardinal error to move promiscuously between the two. Indeed, the weaknesses of sociological studies of historical movements from Max Weber onwards suggests that historical sociology is impossible.[18]

Rodd does not claim that sociology and history are totally different or incompatible disciplines, simply that the difficulties of doing sociology increase steeply as the researcher moves away from our own times. If one but glances at the interplay of the two disciplines, it is clear that they have drawn nearer to each other during the last thirty years. This entails not only that historical sociology is a thriving discipline of its own with a large theoretical literature being written about it, or that each discipline increasingly takes over theory and interpretational modes from the other. Sociologists like Philip Abrams and Anthony Giddens and historians like Ferdinand Braudel and Peter Burke agree that at the bottom the two disciplines are really one. In lieu of demonstrating this more broadly, I simply refer to one scholar, Philip Abrams, *Historical Sociology* (1982):

> In my understanding of history and sociology there can be no relationship *between* them because, in terms of their fundamental preoccupations, history and sociology are and always have been the same

---

thing. Both seek to understand the puzzle of human agency and both seek to do so in terms of the process of social structuring. Both are impelled to conceive of that process chronologically; at the end of the debate the diachrony-synchrony distinction is absurd. Sociology must be concerned with eventuation, because that is how structuring happens. History must be theoretical, because that is how structuring is apprehended.[19]

and

Historical sociology is not, then, a matter of imposing grand schemes of evolutionary development on the relationship of the past to the present. Nor is it merely a matter of recognising the historical background to the present. It is the attempt to understand the relationship of personal activity and experience on the one hand and social organisation on the other as something that is continuously constructed in time. It makes the continuous process of construction the focal concern of social analysis.[20]

Gerd Theissen has likewise argued that sociological analysis is simply a continuation and a deepening of historical research, and that no argument against the legitimacy of the former in exegetical work has been produced that is not fundamentally a questioning of the latter too.[21] It should be clearly recognized that history and sociology are not antagonists but at bottom one and the same scholarly enterprise.

But once this has been recognized, one has to admit the strength of Rodd's objections against biblical historical sociology, and concede that there are a number of questions that can simply not be answered because of the lack of evidence. And as sociological hypotheses concern general, typical behaviour and the commonalities of groups of people, therefore requiring larger data sets, they will receive fewer answers than some other types of questions. The New Testament as a collection of evidence for the social history of the first Christians *is*

---

[19] Philip Abrams, *Historical Sociology.* Near Shepton Mallet, 1982, x. A helpful survey is found in Theda Skocpol (ed.), *Vision and Method in Historical Sociology.* Cambridge, 1984. For a good discussion of what sociologists and historians can learn from one another, see Peter Burke, *Sociology and History.* London, 1980.

[20] Abrams, *Historical Sociology,* 16. Cf. Norman K. Gottwald: "sociology without history is empty; history without sociology is blind. By wedding history and sociology we strive for an understanding of ancient Israel that is both full of content and perceptive of form and meaning." Idem, *The Tribes of Yahweh: A Sociology of the Religion of Liberated Israel 1250-1050 B.C.E.* London, 1981 [=Maryknoll, N.Y., 1979], 17.

[21] In "Zur forschungsgeschichtlichen Einordnung" (*Studien,* 3-34), esp. 15.Cf. also Morgan, *Biblical Interpretation,* 139 f.

a very small data set. Most of the texts do not treat social phenomena at all, and can only be made to yield information about such matters through various processes of inferential reading and interpretation. "The sociologist must read the text as if it were a palimpsest."[22] This means that there are few data that are not modern interpretations of ancient texts. So the New Testament data we have on which to apply sociological interpretations are themselves interpretations, not hard (precise, measurable) data, which could be assembled again or verified through other sources or procedures. This is no doubt a difficult situation, but nonetheless a familiar one, encountering every historian. And the difficulties are not so insurmountable that one cannot discuss ways to grapple with them.

Eliciting sociological information from the New Testament
New Testament sociology, says Gerd Theissen in a much-cited essay, is interested in describing, analysing, and explaining typical social behaviour of the members of early Christian groups.[23] This means that it is not so interested in the individual case as in what is typical, repeated, and general, and that it looks for structural relations that are valid for several situations, rather than analysing the singular and unique circumstances of a particular situation. The first task in this enterprise is to elicit sociologically relevant information from the mostly nonsociological information contained in the New Testament documents, and this has to be done by inferential processes. Theissen distinguishes between three different types of inferential process: constructive conclusions, analytical conclusions, and comparative conclusions.

Constructive conclusions can be drawn from evidence where sociological elements are available on the surface of the text, or in other words, treated directly in the text. *Analytical* conclusions are drawn from material containing indirect information of interest to sociology. Theissen lists as such material (a) historical occurrences, (b) social norms, and (c) religious symbols. When we hear, for example, that it was in Antioch that the believers began to be called "Christians," we can conclude that normally this group was not set off from other Jews by a special designation or nickname—and that, of course, is a sociologically relevant piece of information! What happens repeatedly

---

[22] Another well-found metaphor from Scroggs, "State of Research," 166.
[23] Gerd Theissen, "Die soziologische Auswertung religiöser Überlieferungen: Ihre methodologischen Probleme am Beispiel des Urchristentums" (*Kairos* 17, 1975, 284-299; now in *Studien*, 35-54).

can indicate typical behaviour patterns, and so can conflicts. This is because the individuals engaged in conflict are not seldom representatives of groups and their specific group behaviour. Theissen himself has noted stratum-specific habits of eating in the background of the conflict in the church of Corinth about eating meat from sacrifices. The poor almost never ate meat, except at religious festivals, and therefore the question of whether meat bought in the temple market was tainted by idolatry was a live issue for the poor Christians, but not for the wealthy, who had it every day as an unquestioned part of the way of life in their social stratum.[24] Social norms tell us, although indirectly, what was expected, i.e., typical, behaviour. Of course, we have to reckon with a certain distance between norm and reality— the norm is always more radical than actual behaviour. The method of drawing analytical conclusions from symbols of different kinds will be discussed in chapter 4.

Comparative conclusions are needed because the New Testament sources are generally too fragmentary to give an information basis broad enough to conclude from. We must take in non-Christian sources to learn about what is typical social behaviour for the early Christian movement, and this can be done in two different ways: Either one compares early Christianity with proximate, contemporary movements, looking for the contrasts, that which is unique for the Christian movement. Or one seeks analogies to it in comparable groups or movements from all times and cultures, and here one looks especially for similarities.

Naturally, one has to apply the standard evaluation procedures of the social sciences to the information elicited with the help of all these different approaches, i.e., try to ascertain the reliability, validity, and representativity of the evidence at hand.[25] But when all has been said about the difficulties of research on ancient materials, there remains much truth in the saying that sources are like witnesses: they have to be asked before they begin to speak. And I think nobody who has read Theissen's essay on social stratification in the church of Corinth[26]

---

[24] Gerd Theissen, "Die Starken und Schwachen in Korinth: Soziologische Analyse eines theologischen Streites" (*Evangelische Theologie* 35, 1975, 155-172; now in *Studien*, 272-289). For another example of analysing a conflict as evidence of behaviour patterns of groups in early Christianity, see my "Sociologiska perspektiv på Gal 2: 11–14(21)" (forthcoming in *Svensk Exegetisk Årsbok* 55, 1990).

[25] Theissen, "Die soziologische Auswertung," 37 f.

[26] Gerd Theissen, "Soziale Schichtung in der korinthischen Gemeinde. Ein Beitrag zur Soziologie des hellenistischen Urchristentums" (*Zeitschrift für die neutestamentliche Wissenschaft* 65, 1974, 232-273; now in *Studien*, 231-271).

would deny that clever interrogation can produce a lot of sociologically relevant data that no one had seen before—because no one had asked for it.

In a discussion of the paucity of data, Malina has claimed that this is not such a problem as sometimes stated. The use of social science in biblical interpretation is essentially one of retrodiction, not prediction; we have some idea about how the story turned out, and this important datum acts as a control that is lacking in prediction. Applying social science models to biblical texts is heavily oriented toward efficient causality: "how did this happen?" Sociology, on the other hand, requires a larger data set because of its predictive goals, which means that when looking backward into the past sociology is heavily oriented toward final causality: "for what reason did this happen?" Social sciences on biblical texts seek the probabilities in the past that made the story make social sense and turn out as it did, while sociology is more like a science-fiction novel, trying to describe what will happen. Statistical analysis is, of course, precluded in biblical sociology, but not using social science models for determining how meanings were imposed on people in the past and what those meanings might be.[27]

The use of models

Clifford Geertz has described what he considers to be the task of the social scientific analysis of culture in one well-formulated sentence: "Believing, with Max Weber, that man is an animal suspended in webs of significance he himself has spun, I take culture to be those webs and the analysis of it to be therefore not an experimental science in search of law but an interpretative in search of meaning."[28] This statement, with its distinction between social science as close to the natural sciences with their law-like explanations on the one hand, and social science as close to the humanities with their interpretative approach on the other, evidences a change in the history of sociology. With the reaction against sociological functionalism, and grand theories generally, followed also a distance from viewing the task of sociology as that of finding social iron laws at work in all of human reality.[29] This

[27] Bruce J. Malina, "The Social Sciences and Biblical Interpretation" (in Gottwald (ed.), *Bible and Liberation* (1983), 11-25), 19 f.

[28] Clifford Geertz, *The Interpretation of Cultures. Selected Essays.* New York, 1973, 5.

[29] Halvor Moxnes, "Sociology and the New Testament" (in Erik Karlsaune (ed.), *Religion as a Social Phenomenon. Theologians and sociologists sharing research interests.* Trondheim, 1988, 143-159). On the criticism against functionalism and what has followed it see the article by Ole Reis, "The Uses of Sociological Theory in Theology—Exemplified by Gerd Theissen's Study of Early Christianity" (Ibid., 161-178).

is not merely a change of atmosphere among sociologists, but also the result of deeper analysis of the philosophy of social sciences.[30]

This reserve is found in historical sociology too, where some scholars prefer to downplay explanation as such in favor of the use of theoretical ideas purely as sensitizing devices for case-by-case historical discussions (Bendix), or simply use hypotheses about causal regularities as a starting point in a testing procedure that moves between a set of alternative hypotheses without being committed to any theory of supposedly universal validity.[31] This is a result of the recognition that the concepts and models of sociology are not absolutes, but represent conclusions drawn from the careful observation of particular movements or groups. They are subject to the tests and verification procedures of the scientific method; they are not necessarily built into the structure of creation.[32] This means that the sociological model must not become a die that shapes the ancient materials or a filter that highlights or obliterates textual data in a predetermined way. The non-absolute character of sociological models should also alert the historian to realise that a model that is helpful in one case may not work in another.[33]

But the fact that sociological models are not absolutes or iron laws should not blind us to the more general truth that models are necessary in all understanding. A model can be defined as "an abstract, simplified representation of some real world object, event, or interaction, constructed for the purpose of understanding, control, or prediction."[34] And it is necessary to use models in the unavoidable task of sorting and patterning the welter of phenomena in our daily life to comprehend and grasp them. It is even more necessary in intellectual

---

[30] For example, in his *After Virtue: A Study in Moral Theory* (London, 1981, ²1985), ch. 8, Alasdair MacIntyre has shown that the social sciences cannot formulate laws of real predictive power since they are based on and share in the systematic, logically necessary unpredictability of human affairs.

[31] Skocpol, *Vision and Method in Historical Sociology*, 363.

[32] Daniel J. Harrington, "Sociological Concepts and the Early Church: A Decade of Research" *(Theological Studies* 41, 1980, 181-190), 183.

[33] G. W. E. Nickelsburg, "Social Aspects of Palestinian Jewish Apocalypticism" (in Hellholm [ed.], *Apocalypticism in the Mediterranean World*, 1983, 641-654), 648. Cf. O. C. Edwards, Jr., "Sociology as a Tool for Interpreting the New Testament" *(Anglican Theological Review* 65, 1983, 431-446), 445.

[34] Malina, "The Social Sciences and Biblical Interpretation," 14, following T. F. Carney in his important work *The Shape of the Past: Models and Antiquity.* Lawrence, Kansas, 1975, 1-43.

or scientific analysis of phenomena, in order to avoid being determined by mere feelings or intuitions or those unexamined assumptions about the shape of things that are usually termed "common sense," even if that sense is culture-bound to a high degree.[35]

In sociological terminology a model is "something less than a theory and something more than an analogy. . . . A theory is based on axiomatic laws and states general principles. It is a basic proposition through which a variety of observations or statements become explicable. A model, by way of contrast, acts as a link between theories and observations" (Carney). The difference between a model and an analogy or metaphor lies in the fact that the model *is consciously structured and systematically arranged* in order to serve as a *speculative instrument* for the purpose of organizing, profiling, and interpreting a complex welter of detail.[36] It is not enough, then, for a historian/sociologist to assemble a mass of data, however difficult that may be in itself. "Hard or soft, the data will not furnish answers to our questions unless they are 'fitted', with a greater or less degree of squeezing, into categories."[37] Or into models, which will generate hypotheses that, once verified, may either found or substantiate a theory.[38] A historian who employs sociological theory in understanding the biblical documents must be explicit concerning his use of theories and models, and state his hypotheses clearly (both Meeks and Theissen have been repeatedly criticized for failing to do so in their otherwise impressive work).

---

[35] Esler has some good remarks on the inevitability of models, and specifically of sociological models (such as concern social life), in historical study, in opposition to the criticism of New Testament sociology voiced by E. A. Judge ("The Social Identity of the First Christians: A Question of Method in Religious History" [*Journal of Religious History* 11, 1980, 201-217], 210 and 212). Esler points out that models are not all-encompassing descriptions, but simplifications for research purposes, that they should as much as possible be stripped of temporal and spatial markings, or in other words be truly cross-cultural, and thirdly that Judge's idea of carrying out historical "field work" prior to the use of models betrays an unawareness of his own and any historians use of models, categorizations, and theories; Philip Francis Esler, *Community and Gospel in Luke-Acts. The Social and Political Motivations of Lucan Theology.* Cambridge, 1987, 14-16.

[36] John H. Elliott, "Social-Scientific Criticism of the New Testament: More on Methods and Models," in John H. Elliott, ed. *Social-Scientific Criticism of the New Testament and Its Social World.* Semeia 35 (Decatur, GA: Scholars Press, 1986), 4 f. Elliott's treatment of models and their role in the sociological research process (3-9, and passim) is very readable and clarifying.

[37] Burke, *Sociology and History*, 40.

[38] Esler, *Community and Gospel*, 9. Esler also gives a clear and succinct description of the methodology of the social sciences (6-16), where he underlines the dynamic role of models as compared to mere classification.

If we keep in mind both the non-absolute character of models and the absolute unavoidability of using some models (explicit or implicit), we could perhaps summarize what has so far been said about models by stating that they should be used heuristically, i.e., as a help to frame new questions and look for evidence nobody cared about before. We should not be overwhelmed by models, thinking that they must be right and our data wrong, because they don't fit the model. Nor should we presuppose that our document or data set is so unique or outside ordinary human experience that human, i.e., at bottom social, patterns of meaning can't contribute anything to its understanding. The historian E. P. Thompson's statement that theoretical concepts do not impose a rule, but hasten and facilitate the interrogation of evidence catches something important in how sociological concepts and models are used heuristically. So does his parable of historical discourse as a court proceeding:

> The disciplined historical discourse of . . . proof consists in a dialogue between concept and evidence, a dialogue conducted by successive hypotheses, on the one hand, and empirical research on the other. The interrogator is historical logic; the interrogative a hypothesis . . . ; the respondent is the evidence, with its determinate properties.[39]

Before leaving the subject of using sociological models, I would like to mention one way in which they should not be used. It has been suggested that a model (or ideal type, or theory) could be used as a gap-filler where the data are not sufficient. "If our data evidence some *parts* of the gestalt of a known model, while being silent about others, we *may* cautiously be able to conclude that the absence of the missing parts is accidental and that the entire model was actually a reality in the early church."[40] This is a misunderstanding of what sociological models are. They are simply abstractions, constructed types that do not depict any reality exactly. It is illegitimate to use them as prescriptions or prognoses about what must have happened or been there when there is no evidence to say so.[41]

---

[39] E. P. Thompson, *The Poverty of Theory* (London 1978), 231, quoted from Philip Abrams, *Historical Sociology*, 218.

[40] Scroggs, "State of Research," 166.

[41] Christopher Tuckett, *Reading the New Testament: Methods of Interpreta*tion. London 1987, 149 f; Cyril Rodd, "On Applying" (1981), 104; Esler, *Community and Gospel*, 12. Scroggs suggestion seems to me to go beyond what Thomas Best calls the "interpretive model": that one situation, while not the exact equivalent of another, nevertheless contains an element of comparison that can serve as a guide in explanation. Within limits, comparison allows a causal interpretation to be corroborated or denied. Best, "Promise and Peril," 188, citing Cahnmann-Boskoff, *Sociology and History*. London, 1964, 6-7.

There is no single "sociological method"
Several surveys point to the bewildering variety of sociological approaches, methods, and schools that have been introduced in a few years. This reflects, of course, the same variety within the social sciences, which is not a unified science with one commonly agreed theoretical structure. As a matter of fact, cleavages and national varieties in this field may very well be transferred into biblical scholarship and increase the distance between exegetes of different cultural provenance.[42]

Nonetheless, this diversity of biblical sociology seems to come as something of a disappointment to some scholars who would rather have wanted something more unified and helpful. Thomas Best states:

> Of course there is no single methodology proper to NT sociology. In this it is quite different from older approaches, particularly form-criticism, which sprang virtually full-grown at birth from one book, Bultmann's *History of the Synoptic Tradition*. It is this systematic review of the corpus from a consistent theoretical and methodological perspective which is still lacking in NT sociology. . . . [When reading the work of Theissen one] has the impression of reading a brilliant exegete with a whole new bag of tricks; but the virtuoso performance has not yet been translated into systematic methodology for the workaday scholar.[43]

Naturally, one has a right to hope for an increased clarification of the differing perspectives, and the evolving of tested methodologies in this field. But not enough testing of the many different approaches has been done yet to make possible the sifting and unification of sociological procedures in the biblical field. It is also hard to believe that biblical sociology could become very much more unified than, e.g., theology. And historical sociology itself cannot be bound to only one epistemological, theoretical, or methodological orientation.[44]

Gerd Theissen has demonstrated in his work, and declared in his programmatic essays, that he wanted to use impulses, ideas, and approaches from several different types of sociology: the "verstehende" sociology of Max Weber, Marxist sociology, and functionalistic

---

[42] Ernst Baasland, "Urkristendommen i sosiologiens lys" (*Tidskrift for Teologi og Kirke* 54, 1984, 45-57), 55.
[43] Best, "Promise and Peril," 187 f.
[44] Skocpol, *Vision and Method*, 361.

sociology.[45] Theories are means, not ends, and should be seen as tools that can complement each other. Marxist sociology has a better eye for conflicts, while functionalist approaches are better at explaining different varieties of integration, wherefore both should be used! At the bottom of this methodological pluralism lies an optimistic expectation that if the methods have true heuristic value, they should ultimately prove complementary and contribute to one's confidence in conclusions drawn from them.[46]

The aim and plan of this work

The stated aim of this book is to describe and make clearer what has been done in New Testament sociology during the last twenty years. But as there exists a number of descriptive and classificatory surveys of the field, and I do not aim at writing the history of this line of scholarship, my main interest has been in analysing the work from a methodological perspective. What are the methods used in biblical sociology? Are they good methods? Can one see any development or stabilization of methods during the period I have selected? Such are the questions I have been asking.

Due to the limitations of my time, knowledge, and understanding, and perhaps also of the reader's patience, this book will have to be selective. I am not a sociologist, nor a philosopher, and therefore I cannot offer any deep analysis from the philosophy of historical theology or the social sciences. Anthropology, the neighbouring and fruitful discipline of sociology, has not been left unused by biblical scholars, but I hardly touch on this subject. I have chosen to look closer at just three areas of research. First, I look at the area of social history, concerning the question of the social level of the first Christians. Second, I scrutinize how the church-sect typology from the sociology of religion has been used in interpreting the life of early Christianity; this chapter also has a section about the fairly similar anthropological model of millenarian movement, which is sometimes used together with the sect model. Third, I look at the application of

[45] Gerd Theissen, "Theoretische Probleme religionssoziologischer Forschung und die Analyse des Urchristentums" (*Neue Zeitschrift für Systematische Theologie und Religionsphilosophie* 16, 1974, 35-56; now in *Studien*, 55-76), "Zur forschungsgeschichtlichen Einordnung" (1979), and "Vers une théorie de l'histoire sociale du christianisme primitif" (*Études Théologiques et Religieuses* 63, 1988, 199-225).
[46] Scroggs, "State of Research," 166.

perspectives from the sociology of knowledge made in order to understand correlations between early Christian beliefs and social situations.

In none of these chapters is my interest focused on the material issue under discussion. I do not try to answer the question at what social level the first Christians were situated, or whether this movement can truly be characterized as a sect, even if my analysis of the presuppositions, procedures, and methods of work has some bearing on the answering of such questions. I consider my work as part of the necessary and healthy self-criticism of the discipline of New Testament, or biblical, sociology, which in 1979 Norman K. Gottwald characterized as follows:

> There simply has not been a cumulative biblical-sociological tradition of scholarship in any way comparable to the tradition of higher-critical biblical study rooted in the humanities. We must speak rather of sporadic and isolated upthrusts, abortive and undeveloped explorations, and a glaring absence of disciplined continuity in tackling issues and methods.[47]

Some ten years later Halvor Moxnes summarized what had happened in the same field during the last fifteen years in his opening sentence: "The use of social silences in New Testament studies has come of age." He pointed to a number of connected shifts: away from predominant theological understanding of the texts, from individualism to the collectivity or group, from a history of leaders and elites to a study of the lives of ordinary people.[48] Now the aim of my analysis of New Testament sociology is not just to decide between Gottwald and Moxnes, but I believe the result may be of some help in judging whether the discipline has begun to attain scientific maturity.

A final word about the "use" of sociology in New Testament studies. The word signifies both the application or handling of something, and its usefulness. Also in this study I consider myself mainly as a student of theology looking at sociology from within biblical exegesis which I consider to belong among other theological disciplines. Therefore, I want not only to describe what has been done in biblical sociology, but also try to understand a little clearer what sociology can do and cannot do in theology. That is why a short discussion of the

[47] Gottwald, *The Tribes of Yahweh*, 13.
[48] Halvor Moxnes, "Sociology and the New Testament."

theological usefulness of sociology will be the subject for my final chapter.

Bibliographical Note

There has been so much work done in the sociology of the New Testament that even a short description of it would need a whole book. There are such books: Derek Tidball, *An Introduction to the Sociology of the New Testament*, Exeter: Paternoster Press, 1983 (160 pages), which, however, does not cover the whole ground, and is very basic in its orientation. Carolyn Osiek, RSCJ, *What Are They Saying about the Social Setting of the New Testament?* New York and Ramsey, N.J., 1984 (93 pages), which mainly treats social history, but evidences a clear grasp of the subject.

There are a number of more or less comprehensive surveys of what has been done in New Testament sociology. They are simply listed here in chronological order (for full bibliographical details see the Bibliography):

Leander E. Keck, "On the Ethos of Early Christians" (1974). Treats the contributions from the first decades of this century.

Jonathan Z. Smith, "The Social Description of Early Christianity" (1975). An early, influential outlining of the field.

Gerd Theissen, "Zur forschungsgeschichtlichen Einordnung der soziologischen Fragestellung" (1979). Shows especially the continuity with early form-criticism.

Daniel J. Harrington, "Sociological Concepts and the Early Church: A Decade of Research" (1980). Presentation of Gager, Theissen, and a number of other works.

Edwin A. Judge, "The Social Identity of the First Christians: A Question of Method in Religious History" (1980). Follows up what had been done in social history since his own work in 1960.

Robin Scroggs, "The Sociological Interpretation of the New Testament: The Present State of Research" (1980). Clear classifications, critical discussion of results.

John Howard Schütz, "Introduction" to Theissen, *The Social Setting of Pauline Christianity* (1982). Focus on Theissen.

John G. Gager, "Shall We Marry Our Enemies?" (1982). Discusses the value of the enterprise against background of three selected approaches.

Thomas F. Best, "The Sociological Study of the New Testament: Promise and Peril of a New Discipline" (1983). Lucid presentation, evaluation from inside theology.

O. C. Edwards, Jr., "Sociology as a Tool for Interpreting the New Testament" (1983). Reviews seven major books; summarizes what has been achieved methodologically.

Ernst Baasland, "Urkristendommen i sosiologiens lys" (1984). Covers many important works; classifies the field into six categories; critical discussion.

Philip J. Richter, "Recent Sociological Approaches to the Study of the New Testament" (1984). Groups a large number of articles and books according to the type of sociological work used.

Hermann-Josef Venetz, "Der Beitrag der Soziologie zur Lektüre des Neuen Testaments" (1985). Focuses on form-criticism, and German literature.

Werner Georg Kümmel, "Zur Sozialgeschichte und Soziologie der Urkirche" (1985). Reviews a wide variety of works, critical of most.

Robin Gill (ed.), *Theology and Sociology: A Reader* (1987), "Introduction. Part Three. Implications for Biblical Studies," 13-17; and the separate introductions to the seven readings in this section, 211, 225, 238, 254, 276 f, 293 f, 302 f, with helpful discussions of the readings and some other literature.

Two helpful bibliographies should be mentioned:

Gerd Theissen, "Auswahlbibliographie zur Sozialgeschichte des Urchristentums," in Idem, *Studien zur Soziologie des Urchristentums*, Tübingen ²1983, 331-348.

> The 349 works listed in this wide-ranging bibliography are divided into eight sections that are subdivided into 34 subsections. Focuses on ancient social history.

Daniel J. Harrington, "Second Testament Exegesis and the Social Sciences: A Bibliography" (*Biblical Theology Bulletin* 18, 1988, 77-85).

> This bibliography starts where the author left in his 1980 article, mentioned above. Its 230 different books and articles are divided into eleven divisions. Harrington lists many more articles than Theissen, and focuses on sociology.

2 *The Social Level*
of the First Christians

On measuring social stratification in ancient societies

The question concerning the social level of the first Christians belongs mainly in the field of social description, does not require much use of sociological theory, and in itself entails no attempt at sociological explanation. It can therefore be termed a *proto-sociological question.* Naturally, one has to use some sociologically informed thinking about what defines social level, but basically this question concerns facts at the visible surface of society, ascertainable by an ordinary historical investigation. Once you have decided which criteria determine social level in a given society (say income, power, noble birth), all you have to do is to assemble the data concerning these characteristics in the group you are investigating and summarize the results. This is not to deny that an ordinary historical investigation, even if methodologically simple, may be quite difficult.

The standard criteria for establishing social level, or for measuring social stratification, are three: economic class, status, and power.[1] They usually appear connected to each other, but need not do so. Different times and cultures may evaluate these three types of criteria differently; e.g., in contemporary Western culture income level is considered to be more important as a criterion of social standing than in most other cultures, ancient or modern. Any meaningful discussion of social level therefore has to be related to a specific society and its stratification system, in our case to the first-century Roman Empire generally, and to specific societies within it.

---

[1] E.g. W. G. Runciman, "Class, Status and Power," in J. A. Jackson (ed.), *Social Stratification* (Cambridge, 1968), 25-61, cited from Philip Francis Esler, *Community and Gospel in Luke-Acts. The Social and Political Motivations of Lucan Theology.* Cambridge, 1987, 172 note 26.

The Roman stratification system
Roman society and its social stratification system in the first century have been described as a very steep pyramid.[2] At the very top we find the *imperator* and his family *(domus)*. The rest of society was divided into (1) a very small upper stratum, consisting of the three "estates" or *ordines: ordo senatorius, ordo equester, ordo decurionum,* and (2) the lower stratum, consisting of all other people—free, freedmen, and slaves—both in towns and cities *(plebs urbana)* and in the countryside *(plebs rustica)*. The highest *ordo* comprised no more than 600 senators and their families, the group of *equites, or* "knights," contained a few tens of thousands, and the decurions, i.e., members of the families who made up the local councils and filled magistrate positions in the more than one thousand towns and cities of the empire, probably amounted to around 100,000 persons—together about 0.5 percent of the total population of between 50 and 80 million. The estates were strictly defined as regards entrance requirements, rank, titles, and legal privileges. A general observation of some importance is that noble birth (hereditary status) was the dominant criterion in determining a person's social level in the first-century Roman Empire.[3]

According to Alföldy and other historians, there existed no clearly definable "middle class" in this society. "Class" is a fairly modern concept anyway, referring mostly to a group's income level or relation to the means of production, and it does not distinguish very well between groups in ancient society. The owning of property naturally gave a person some influence, but other social criteria were more decisive: a small-town decurion of moderate wealth, living on his

[2] On social relations and social stratification in ancient Roman society see Géza Alföldy, *Römische Sozialgeschichte.* 3. völlig überarb. Aufl., Wiesbaden, 1984, and idem, *Die römische Gesellschaft. Ausgewählte Beiträge.* Stuttgart, 1986, and Ramsay MacMullen, *Roman Social Relations 50 B.C. to A.D. 284.* New Haven and London, 1974. A useful graphic illustration is found in Alföldy, *Die römische Gesellschaft,* 51. Short, good summaries of information on social stratification in Roman cities are given by David Verner, The *Household of God: The Social World of the Pastoral Epistles.* Chico, California, 1983, 47-54, Wayne A. Meeks, *The Moral World of the First Christians.* London, 1987 (in USA, 1986), 32-39), and by Philip Esler, *Community and Gospel,* 171-175. For a bibliography, see Gerd Theissen, *Studien zur Soziologie des Urchristentums.* Tübingen, 1983, 348.

[3] "Durch die stets entscheidende Bedeutung der Herkunft und der persönlichen Privilegien war das Gliederungsprinzip der römischen Gesellschaft immer aristokratisch. Niedrige Herkunft galt stets als Makel. So waren die sozialen Positionen stets stark durch die Erblichkeit bestimmt, und Bildung z. B. konnte nicht die Rolle spielen wie in einer modernen Gesellschaft." Géza Alföldy, "Römische Gesellschaft: Struktur und Eigenart" (1974) (in idem, *Die römische Gesellschaft,* 41-68), 49.

inherited land, had much higher status, rank, and political power than a freedmen millionaire like Trimalchio (depicted by Petronius).[4] One could point to varying levels of legal privilege between different groups of free persons in the majority of people below the *ordines,* such as the right to enter a legally registered marriage, to own property, conduct legal deals, and take one's case to the court. Slaves, who did not belong even to the *plebs,* of course had very few rights. The difference in status between urban and rural population (below the *ordines)* was very clear, the latter being definitely considered to be at the lower end of society.

Naturally there existed large variations in wealth, power, and status between members of the *plebs:*

> Some of the indices of higher status were these: Roman citizenship, especially in the provinces in the early years of the empire, when it was rare; citizenship in the local polis, compared with resident aliens; among the citizens, the decurions or city councillors of smaller cities; wealth, more and more, preferably inherited rather than worked for, and invested in land rather than trade; family and origin: the older the better, the closer to Rome the better, Greek better than "barbarian"; military office or the status of a veteran in a colony; freedom by birth, though a freedman or even a slave of the emperor or of a senator was better off than many freeborn persons.[5]

On the other hand, obvious as they were, such differences were gradual and not clearly defined. This is why historians like Alföldy and MacMullen consider participation in imperial or local urban political administration to be the only decisive and clearly definable criterion of social level, and only agree to talk about a stratification of Roman society into two strata: upper and lower. Both the application of the term "stratification" and the allowing of only two levels have been much discussed among historians of ancient Rome. Vittinghoff has characterized the division of society into two strata, one comprising 0.5 percent and the other 99.5 percent of the population as "devoid of historical information value and almost absurd."[6] Further, stratification is a sociological concept that presupposes a more modern, market-related society, where all citizens have political and legal equality, and where criteria of grouping them then have to be sought

---

[4] Alföldy, *Die römische Gesellschaft,* "Struktur," 53 f.
[5] Meeks, *Moral World,* 34.
[6] Cited from Alföldy, "Die römische Gesellschaft: Eine Nachbetrachtung über Struktur und Eigenart" (in idem, *Die römische Gesellschaft,* 69-81), 78, my translation.

predominantly in the spheres of economy and prestige. This does not apply to Roman society, where inequality between individuals was legally fixed and did not show any co-variation with differences in wealth (Vittinghoff, Rilinger, et al.).[7]

Alföldy's position may be correct as far as the formulated awareness of the ancient participants themselves goes, but leaves us moderns without much of an instrument to see and understand the social differences within the vast majority of this society. It seems that Alföldy's *honesti/humiles*-distinction needs to be supplemented by a stratificatory classification that allows for a fuller representation of social differences. K. Christ has pointed to the fact that not a few people (like free farmers, merchants, artisans) had a legally protected freedom, citizen's rights, and property, and did not consider themselves as low class people, wherefore it seems adequate to think of them as some kind of middle stratum. Schöllgen follows Christ and Vittinghoff, when he proposes that one should reckon to the upper stratum also persons who answer to the following three additional criteria (preferably present simultaneously): wealth, social prestige, and higher education.[8]

Mediterranean peasant society
Bruce Malina, in his brief survey of the first-century Mediterranean world, states that this world is "a nearly perfect example of what anthropologists call classic peasant society: a set of villages socially bound up with preindustrial cities."[9] This type of society is dominated

---

[7] For the discussion, see Alföldy, "Nachbetrachtung," where Alföldy defends his positions against a number of criticisms.

Bruce Malina considers that the vertical classification and focus on power relations so typical of stratification thinking are misplaced in a preindustrial society. More appropriate would be social differentiation along the dimensions of size, depth assessment, and horizontal space (first/last, relating to commitment, loyalty, precedence, prestige). "It was this last dimension that was salient in the 1st century Mediterranean. Greeks, Romans and Jews were apt to stress the desire for freedom, honor and fame in their explanation of human conduct, not wealth or income or the power preempted by Roman government." Bruce J. Malina, "Review of the First Urban Christians by Wayne A. Meeks" (*Journal of Biblical Literature* 104, 1985, 346-349), 348.

[8] Georg Schöllgen, *Ecclesia sordida? Zur Frage der sozialen Schichtung frühchristlicher Gemeinden am Beispiel Karthagos zur Zeit Tertullians* (Jahrbuch für Antike und Christentum. Ergänzungsband 12). Münster, 1984, 12-15.

[9] Bruce Malina, *The New Testament World: Insights from Cultural Anthropology*. Atlanta, 1981, chapter 4, "The Perception of Limited Good" (71-93); quotation on p. 71. Malina's more anthropologically oriented study supplements the results mentioned earlier, e.g., by explaining why profit and economy were less important in an honour/shame type of society, and how group-focused and non-individualistic were the self-evaluation of

by the city, especially by its elite (perhaps less than 2 percent of the whole city population). The members of this urban elite "are the bearers of the culture's 'Great Tradition', the embodiment of the norms and values which give continuity and substance to the ideals of . . . society," and have political control over the rest of the population by exacting taxes and maintaining order.[10] Below this elite we find the urban nonelite population, mostly engaged in small-scale handicraft manufacturing, living in a symbiotic social relation with the elite, replicating its norms and behaviour in a simplified and often outdated fashion. The third category is the most numerous one, up to 90% of the whole population, and consists of the peasant villagers living outside the city but under its control. These people are even further removed from the centre and top of their society, surpassed in this respect only by the marginal class, beggars and slaves. Applying this picture of peasant society to the New Testament, Malina states that "we deal with peasant communities in the Synoptics and with non-elite, preindustrial urban communities in Paul and the writings of the Pauline school."[11]

Palestinian social stratification[12]

As Palestine politically had been an incorporated part of the Roman Empire for about a hundred years at the time on which we are focusing, some important characteristics of Hellenistic Roman society

---

ancient men and women: idem, ch. 2, "Honor and Shame," and ch. 3, "The First-Century Personality." Cf. also Richard L. Rohrbaugh, *The Biblical Interpreter. An Agrarian Bible in an Industrial Age.* Philadelphia, 1978, esp. ch. 3 with a short comparison of traditional agrarian society with our modern, industrialized one.

[10] Malina, *Insights from Cultural Anthropology,* 73.

[11] Ibid., 74. Malina could be criticized for homogenizing and "ruralizing" first-century society. The many Old Testament examples he uses do not provide self-evident analogies to the cosmopolitan life in great Hellenistic cities like Antioch, Corinth, and Rome. Cf. Ernst Baasland, "Urkristendommen i sosiologiens lys" (*Tidskrift for Teologi og Kirke* 54, 1984, 45-57), 54, and Philip J. Richter, "Recent Sociological Approaches to the Study of the New Testament" (*Religion* 14, 1984, 77-90), 83. Rodolfo Stavenhagen has described the characteristics of agrarian society, and especially the changes connected with the transition to a more complex, eventually industrial society in idem, *Social Class in Agrarian Societies.* New York, 1975, ch. 4. One notes that many of these changes, such as the introduction of a money economy, private ownership of land, migration of workers from rural areas, and urbanization, were already well on their way in the first-century Mediterranean society. This is another reminder that the world of the first Christians may have been less of a "peasant society" than Malina supposes.

[12] The following is of course a sketch, pointing to some important facts of social stratification. For a full bibliography on first-century Jewish society and history, see Gerd Theissen, *Studien,* 346-348.

can also be found in the land where Jesus and the first Jewish Christians lived and worked. The Roman administration looked much as it did in other parts of the empire, even if we encounter the local variation of a system of replaceable Jewish vassal kings together with a High Council (the Sanhedrin) made up of members from different influential groups in the predominantly Jewish parts of Palestine.

Also the economic structure of Palestinian society had been changing for a long time (as part of the Hellenistic influence from 300 B.C. onward), so that it was rather similar to what one could find in Italy or Greece: the ownership of land had gradually become concentrated in the hands of a few rich landowning families (who mostly lived in the cities), and the system of clan- and family-owned holdings was a thing of the past. Many of the rural Jewish population did not own any land and had to find a living by day-to-day labour on the land of others.[13] Jewish Palestine had few large cities, and Jerusalem was a capital that dominated the rest of the land economically, politically, and culturally.[14]

Already Joachim Jeremias, in his invaluable *Jerusalem zur Zeit Jesu*,[15] made it clear that the criteria for social standing are more numerous and complex in Jewish society than in many others. This results from the fact that nobility was reckoned not only or primarily on the grounds of political power and wealth, but also on the grounds of purity in descent and profession, and of "academic" or theologico-juridical proficiency. Jeremias distinguished between priestly and lay nobility, both of which were hereditary. Not all priests were considered to belong to the ruling nobility, "the high priests"; this was a privilege of a few temple-related clans in Jerusalem, highly educated and immensely wealthy through their special relations to the vast economy of the temple. Most of the thousands of priests and levites lived in rural areas, and lived off the work of their own hands, even if they enjoyed a special status also in their local communities because of their priestly, purer descent.

---

[13] This is described in detail in Hans G. Kippenberg, *Religion und Klassenbildung im antiken Judäa. Eine religionssoziologische Studie zum Verhältnis von Tradition und gesellschaftlicher Entwicklung.* Göttingen, 1978.

[14] An instructive description of the differences and tensions between the Jewish urban (Jerusalem) and rural areas is given by Gerd Theissen, "Die Tempelweissagung Jesu: Prophetie im Spannungsfeld von Stadt und Land" (*Theologische Zeitschrift* 32, 1976, 144-158; now reprinted in idem, *Studien*, 142-159).

[15] Joachim Jeremias, *Jerusalem zur Zeit Jesu. Eine kulturgeschichtliche Untersuchung zur neutestamentlichen Zeitgeschichte.* Göttingen, 1923-37; revised ³1969; English trans., Fortress Press.

The landed gentry ruled on much the same grounds as their coun-
terparts in other nations, while the scribes formed an influential group
that can hardly be parallelled in Greek and Roman culture. Their social
background varied: one finds scribes from the high and ordinary
priestly and levitical families, but also scribes who were traders, artisans, and even a poor dayworker (the famous Hillel).[16] Their only
title to influence and status in society lay in their education and knowledge of the law. In the time of Jesus and the early church, the scribes
formed an influential part of the highest Jewish authority, the Sanhedrin, and after the catastrophe of A.D. 70 this body was reconsti-
tuted as a purely scribal council.

To complicate things a bit further, Jeremias mentions that there
existed a difference in status between honourable and not so honourable professions, the honour usually being related to lack of contact
with defiling matters or occupations. To be a fisherman or carpenter
was a "clean" type of work, while being a seller of perfumes, an actor,
or a taverner brought about undesirable contacts, and shepherds and
tax collectors were considered to be almost necessarily dishonest.[17]
Thus, in Jewish society there existed several intersecting criteria of
social status, and it is easy to see that "social level" consequently
must have been a multidimensioned phenomenon, very difficult to
define even to contemporary viewers.[18]

One conclusion from this very brief overview of social stratification
systems in the first century is the recognition that there is no such
thing as one universal stratification system, comprising all the different cultures and nations of the empire. If seen from within the
religiously dominated stratification system of the Jews, even the emperor himself would be an insignificant person, just as would a high-
ranking Jew like Josephus in the eyes of Roman nobility. One practical
conclusion follows: we have to make distinctions when we think and
speak about "the first Christians," a wide term that could cover all

---

[16] Jeremias, *Jerusalem* (1969), 264 ff.

[17] Ibid., 337 ff.

[18] Cf. the case of Jesus: Joseph belonged to the tribe of Judah, and therein to the house
of David, while Mary may have been of priestly descent. But they lived in low-status,
rural Galilee. To judge from the offering in Luke 2:24 (cf. Lev 12:8) the family was poor,
but carpenter was an honourable profession. Jesus seems to have had more than
ordinary learning in the Scriptures, and was regarded as something of a teacher, but
he was also a man outside social conventions: no homestead or family, did not work
for a living but lived off gifts—clearly a deviant person. Sometimes, it is reported, he
was called rabbi, but he cared nothing for his own purity but kept disreputable company.
It is difficult to add this up to one social level.

Christians of the first century. The social level of any Christian individual or group can be measured only against the status system of
the society they are living in, whether Jewish or Gentile, Eastern or
Western, rural or urban, provincial or imperial. Consequently, it is
necessary to distinguish between Christians from different times and
places and social contexts in treating the question concerning the social
level of the first Christians.

The old consensus: The first Christians were on a low social level

From at least the end of the nineteenth century past the middle of
our own there reigned a scholarly consensus, which placed the first
Christians among the lower classes. In a short article, where he described and confronted this consensus, Heinz Kreissig has pointed
out that many scholars (from Baur and Renan, over Ramsay, Wend-
land, Lütgert, Lohmeyer, Foakes Jackson and Lake, to Kittel, Preisker,
Knox, Dibelius, Goppelt, Hartke, and Egger) simply have ignored the
social question.[19] They do not even discuss the problem concerning
which social stratum the early Christians belonged to, nor the question
whether social position was a factor of any importance in the life of
the first Christians.[20] Scholars who do take this aspect into consideration may differ in the weight they accord to it, but both "liberals"
(here Kreissig places Hausrath, Bigelmair, Pfleiderer, Hauck, Lietz-
mann, Winterswyl, and Leipoldt) and Marxist scholars (e.g., Engels,
Kautsky, Alfaric) agree that Christianity was a religion of the slaves
and the oppressed, made up of poor peasants and workers, although
the Marxists consider them more revolutionary than the liberals do.

   Adolf Deissmann is a good representative of this consensus, when
he writes:

> The social structure of early Christianity points us throughout to the
> lower and middle strata. In the beginning relations with the higher

---

[19] Heinz Kreissig, "Zur sozialen Zusammensetzung der frühchristlichen Gemeinden
im ersten Jahrhundert u. Z." (*Eirene. Studia Graeca et Latina* 6, 1967, 91-100).
[20] An interesting illustration of this neglect is that not even S. J. Case and Shailer
Mathews, leading members of "the Chicago School," which already in the early part
of this century advocated a "socio-historic" approach to early Christianity, actually did
attempt any detailed description of early Christian social history, as Leander E. Keck
points out in his essay "On the Ethos of Early Christians" (in *Journal of the American
Academy of Religion* 42, 1974, 435-452; translated as "Das Ethos der frühen Christen"
and published in Wayne A. Meeks (ed.), *Zur Soziologie des Urchristentums*. München,
1979, 13-36), 15 f.

stratum are quite rare. Jesus of Nazareth was a carpenter, Paul of Tarsus a tentmaker, and the word of the tentmaker concerning the provenance of his congregations from the lower strata of the big cities belongs to the historically most important informations from early Christianity about itself. Early Christianity teaches us what every other springtime teaches: the sap rises from below. To the ancient higher culture early Christianity stood in a natural opposition, not primarily as Christianity, but because it was a movement of the lower social strata.[21]

Deissmann found the evidence for this placing of early Christianity in a comparison between the language of the New Testament and the *koine of* the newly found papyri from Egypt. The two groups of texts seemed to him to belong largely to the same vulgar literary level, and therefore constitute evidence for the "folk" (volkstümliche) character of early Christianity.[22] He had to make exceptions for the language of Paul (and naturally also for that of Luke and James and the writer of Hebrews) but this did not alter the general picture.

This consensus was widespread, but not homogeneous. At one extreme one could find a Marxist like Karl Kautsky, describing the first Christians as originally a proletarian and revolutionary movement among the lower classes, characterized by wild class hate, intense egalitarianism, contempt for work, and destruction of family life.[23] The leading elite were radically poor, spirit-filled "apostles and prophets." Only gradually and as a consequence of spreading into a non-Jewish environment, the new movement received a few educated and socially higher placed converts. These became increasingly important as providers to and organizers of the churches' organization for mutual care and support. Eventually people from this cultured middle-class stratum became the leaders, who finally adapted the movement to become a church in peace with its host society.[24]

---

[21] Adolf Deissmann, *Licht vom Osten. Das Neue Testament und die neuentdeckten Texte der hellenistisch-römischen Welt.* 4. Aufl., Tübingen, 1923, 6 f [my translation].

[22] "Ohne sie [die Volkstümlichkeit des Urchristentums] zu kennen und stark zu unterstreichen, können wir den Erfolg der Werbekraft des Evangeliums historisch nicht verstehen. Die Mission des Paulus war Handwerkermission, nicht Mission eines Studierten" (ibid., 329). "Was Kautsky instinktiv gesehen hat, ist richtig: der enge Zusammenhang des Urchristentums mit den volkstümlichen Schichten" (ibid., 405).

[23] Karl Kautsky, *Der Ursprung des Christentums: Eine Historische Untersuchung.* Stuttgart, 1910. See Part IV, ch. 1, "Die urchristliche Gemeinde" (338-373).

[24] Ibid., 432-492 (ch. 5, "Die Entwicklung der Gemeindeorganisation").

At the other end we find Ernst Troeltsch, who begins his description of the social teaching of the Christian churches and groups with the following programmatic statement:

> For the understanding of the whole fundamental direction of Christianity in relation to the social problems it is decisive to realize that the preaching of Jesus and the creation of the new religious community *was not the creation of a social movement*, which means that it did not evolve from or adapt to any class struggle, and actually never relates directly to the social upheavals of ancient society.[25]

Leaning on the work especially of Harnack, Troeltsch considered the social location of the Christian groups of the first century to have been a fairly low, predominantly urban, middle stratum of society, and the members of these groups to have been artisans, house slaves, freedmen and free workers, but not belonging to any real proletariat.[26]

If we try to summarize some common features characteristic of this broad consensus,[27] we may first note that early Christianity is seen as being one homogeneous entity ("das Urchristentum"). When Paul speaks about the social provenance of the Corinthian Christians (1 Cor 1: 26 f), this is taken as evidence concerning all first-century Christians. Even Kautsky, who allows of a differentiation between an originally lower and a later, higher social location of the early Christians, somehow sees Christianity moving "upward" in society as one body.

Further, in this consensus there seems to be no need for a discussion of criteria for social level or of what constitutes a high or low position in society. It is enough to make common-sense (i.e., Western, early twentieth-century) suppositions that the low income level and low

---

[25] "Für das Verständnis der gesamten Grundrichtung des Christentums in ihrem Verhältnis zu den sozialen Problemen ist entscheidend die Erkenntnis, dass die Predigt Jesu und die Bildung der neuen Religionsgemeinde *keine Schöpfung einer sozialen Bewegung ist* [T.'s italics], das heisst nicht aus irgend einem Klassenkampf hervorgegangen oder auf ihn zugeschnitten ist und überhaupt nirgends direkt an die sozialen Umwälzungen der antiken Gesellschaft anknüpft." Ernst Troeltsch, *Die Soziallehren der christlichen Kirchen und Gruppen (in Gesammelte Schriften I*, Tübingen, 1912), 15 f.

[26] Ibid., 22-25.

[27] Of course this consensus could be more correctly characterized as a "near consensus," as does David C. Verner, *The Household of God: The Social World of the Pastoral Epistles*. Chico, 1983, 3, pointing to the work of Ernst von Dobschütz and Ernst Lohmeyer, who both held that the early church contained a small percentage of more highly placed members. Talking about "the old consensus" is justified, however, by the dominance of Deissmann's perspective during subsequent decades of New Testament research.

status of those occupied in manual work or slavery are signs of a low social level.

A modern variant of the old consensus
John G. Gager's pioneering work in sociological interpetation of the New Testament, *Kingdom and Community* (1975), contained the application of several different sociological theories. Here, however, we will only look at the way Gager finds information about one specific issue: the social level of the first Christians.

Basically, Gager's idea is that a correct sociological classification of the early Christians will provide information about their social location. First, in his second chapter,[28] he applies to early Christianity the model of "the millenarian movement" created by anthropologists. He describes some basic traits of such movements, and then adds: "Without further argument at this point, we will take it as given that earliest Christianity meets these criteria and thus deserves to be designated a millenarian movement."[29]

From this starting point Gager goes on to discuss the recruitment to the early Christian millenarian movement, the role of its prophet (Jesus), and its specific ethics and community atmosphere. Among the characteristics of such movements has been noted that "the millenarian movements that have been historically important . . . are movements of the disinherited."[30] One ought to find indications, then, that the first Christians were a community of the disinherited, alienated from political power, wealth, and social status. The political situation in contemporary Palestine can be described as evidencing "a premillenarian mood of political alienation and active resistance."[31] Although Jesus cannot be confidently placed in any of these movements, he was probably seen as being a politically dangerous person. Even if millenarian movements are not expressly political or organized as such, they do represent a political problem. Gager further points to several gospel sayings against wealth, which "reflect the fact that early believers came primarily from disadvantaged groups and that in return they were rewarded with the promise that poverty, not

---

[28] Gager, *Kingdom*, "Earliest Christianity as a Millenarian Movement," 20-37.
[29] Ibid., 21. David Bartlett ("John G. Gager's 'Kingdom and Community': A Summary and Response" in *Zygon. Journal of Religion and Science* 13, 1978, 109-122) rightly characterizes this procedure: "Having thus conceded the first point to himself by default, Gager . . .," 111.
[30] Peter Worsley, *The Trumpet Shall Sound. A Study of "Cargo" Cults in Melanesia.* New York, 1968, xlii; quoted from Gager, *Kingdom*, 22.
[31] Gager, *Kingdom*, 23.

wealth, was the key to the kingdom."[32] In this ethic of poverty the symbolic value of money is inverted, and all wealth treated as belonging to the evil side in a highly polarized view of society, marked by sharp binary oppositions: poor/rich, good/evil, pious/hypocrite, elect/damned.

In considering the question which groups in Jewish Palestine would have been most attracted to such a millenarian movement, Gager points to the fact that there were no Pharisees, or high priests, or Essenes, and generally no people from established sectors of Jewish society among the early followers of Jesus. He concludes from this and the many recorded conflicts between Jesus and the Pharisees that Jesus and his disciples must have been considered to belong among the *am ha'ares*, the impure outsiders, who did not observe the Law and therefore had a low social status. Naturally, the new movement tried to invert this value-scale ("Many that are the first will be last, and the last first").

Gager modifies his picture, however. The *am ha'ares* were not limited to the poor and ignorant, and it would be wrong simply to equate an outsider status in Jewish Palestine with belonging to the lowest social and economic strata. A decrease of social status or an experience of downward social mobility can appear at several levels of society and create a sense of alienation and repression, which anthropologists and sociologists term *relative deprivation*, an "uneven relation between expectation and the means of satisfaction."[33] This feeling of being the victim of deprivation is fertile ground for a new religious movement, in which it is often exaggerated and ideologized. Gager points to Jewish apocalypticism generally as evidence of this. The millenarian movement of the early Christian believers was recruited from Jews experiencing such a relative deprivation.

In his fourth chapter Gager turns back to the question of the social level of the first Christians.[34] He begins by drawing a general conclusion from the evidence of Christian authors and opponents[35] that

---

[32] Ibid., 24.

[33] Yonina Talmon, "Pursuit of the Millenium: The Relation between Religious and Social Change," *Archives Européennes de Sociologie* 3, 1962, 137; quoted from Gager, *Kingdom*, 27.

[34] Gager, *Kingdom*, 93-113, "Religion and Society in the Early Roman Empire," in which chapter Gager essentially resumes his essay on "Religion and Social Class in the Early Roman Empire" in S. Benko and J. J. O'Rourke (eds.), *The Catacombs and the Colosseum: The Roman Empire as the Setting of Primitive Christianity*. Valley Forge, 1971, 99-119. Gager understands his description of the social order in Rome (96-106) as indicative of conditions in the empire generally, idem., 108 note 3. This generalization is criticized by

Christian communities of the first several centuries derived their adherents from the disinherited of the Roman empire—slaves, freedmen,
freeborn Roman citizens of low rank, and non-Romans (*peregrini*) of
various nationalities.[36]

He even finds "something approaching a consensus" among classi-
cists like A. D. Nock, A. H. M. Jones, and E. R. Dodds on two aspects
of the social question:

> first, that for more than two hundred years Christianity was essentially
> a movement among disprivileged groups in the Empire; and second,
> that its appeal among these groups depended on social as much as
> ideological considerations.[37]

Gager is well aware of the looseness of the term "disprivileged,"
and careful to point out that dissatisfaction or a feeling of deprivation
is not simply dependent on lack of wealth. Relative deprivation can
just as well concern lack of social status. This broader conception of
deprivation should destroy "the romantic image of early Christians
as nothing but a collection of country yokels and impoverished
slaves,"[38] and makes it possible to reconcile the seemingly contradictory statements that Christianity was a religion of the disprivileged
and Pliny's comment that the churches in northern Asia Minor at the
beginning of the second century had attracted persons "of every social
rank (*omnis ordinis*)."[39] There were Christians who were neither poor
nor ignorant, although they felt deprived relative to other persons or
strata in their society.

What really interests Gager in this chapter, however, is a more wide-
ranging sociological question concerning a possible correlation between religion and social class or status. He therefore combines his

---

Abraham J. Malherbe, *Social Aspects of Early Christianity*. Baton Rouge and London,
1977, 85, where he sides with Judge in considering the Roman system of *ordo* as
concerning only the metropolitan aristocracy, being largely irrelevant in the provinces.
Cf. Edwin A. Judge, "Social Identity of the First Christians" (*Journal of Religious History*
11, 1980, 201-217), 207.

[35] Like Celsus, "they want and are able to convince only the foolish, dishonourable,
and stupid, and only slaves, women and little children"; quoted from Gager, *Kingdom*,
94.

[36] Ibid.

[37] Ibid., 96.

[38] This is, however, exactly the image that Celsus gives of the first Christians, and it
is accepted as evidence by Gager, although he concedes that the tone of Celsus' remarks
is exaggerated, 94.

[39] Ibid., 96.

previous conclusions from the millenarian character of the earliest Christianity with a slightly modified version of Max Weber's hypothesis of "elective affinity." This hypothesis states that different social strata in a society tend to choose different types of religion. The religions of nonprivileged strata belonging to the middle and lower-middle classes tend to exhibit three main characteristics: they have a congregational, community-focused structure, they are future-oriented with respect to promises of reward, and they are supported by a system of rational ethics, which is exactly what we find in the Christianity of the first three centuries.[40]

After devoting the best part of this chapter to a description of the rigid and well-defined Roman class system, Gager indicates how the middle and upper classes of the Roman Empire came to accept and embrace Christianity with its repelling ideology of poverty only after considerable internal reinterpretation of it. He also points out that the opposition between the church and the emergent Gnosticism in Rome was caused by social as well as by doctrinal differences. The Gnostics belonged to more wealthy and highly educated strata (evidenced by Marcion, Valentinus, Ptolemy, and Heracleon). This corroborates other evidence that Christianity in this period had a "fundamentally nonintellectual, nonaristocratic character."[41] Thus, the early Christians can be understood as deprived relative to other groups or strata in Roman society, and the Weberian hypothesis of correlation between type of religion and social location receives a substantiation.[42]

If we summarize Gager's position: the first Christians did not belong at the absolute bottom end of society, but they did not come from higher strata than the middle classes. Within these strata the early believers belonged to those who felt deprived relative to their expectations.

Gager's work represents several new approaches, also regarding the issue under discussion in this chapter. First, it is notable that his method is deductive throughout: he starts with two general theories from the social sciences, one on the emergence of millenarian movements, the other on correlations between a group's social level and its type of religion, and then proceeds to find some evidence that fits early Christianity into these patterns. Because it exhibited typically

---

[40] Ibid., 107.
[41] Ibid.
[42] Ibid., 95, 106-108. Cf. on 131 ". . . as late as the fourth century, Christianity was still found primarily in urban areas and that its adherents there were drawn largely, though not exclusively, from the lower-middle and middle classes."

millenaristic characteristics, early Christianity *had* to be made up of people experiencing distress and deprivation, and because it can be classified as a religion typical of nonprivileged urban classes, early Christianity had to be made up of people from disprivileged urban strata. Gager mentions a few counter-instances, but brushes them aside as atypical and insignificant. Early Christianity is made so homogeneous that one suspects that we have not been allowed to see the complete evidence. Were there no differences in social level or even in experienced deprivation between, for example, Christians in the Palestinian countryside and Christians owning large houses in the great cities of the empire? One is left with the impression that Gager's selection of data is too homogenized, made to fit a theoretical "cargo cult model."[43]

Throughout his work Gager uses terms like "disinherited, deprived, disadvantaged, outsiders, disprivileged, dispossessed," as if they were all exchangeable terms. But they are not: being an "outsider" and being "dispossessed" refers to two different kinds of alienation, one social and the other economic! Through this lack of precision in his analytical language Gager is able to mix two sets of concepts when describing the first Christians, although they need not have anything to do with each other. One refers to economic level ("class," "dispossessed"), the other refers to interior feelings of alienation from established society. He aligns himself with and quotes from scholars who have only the first set of criteria in mind, but guards himself by constant reference to a "relative deprivation," which is experienced especially by people of some means. Relative deprivation can actually be experienced by any person, at whatever level of society. Consequently it is useless as a criterion for indicating any social level.

Gager's unsharp terminology seems to reflect an oscillation between two different social scientific perspectives: (1) the first Christians were poor and therefore revolutionary millenarian, ready to break out of conventional society into a new sect, and (2) the first Christians were economically much like the rest of the population, but had more intense feelings of relative deprivation. The first perspective is a variant of the old consensus, while the second one focuses on shifts in individual or group consciousness, which are not necessarily related to the question of social level at all.

---

[43] G. S. R. Thomas has claimed that Gager had let his (millenarian) paradigm influence the selection of evidence, so that, e.g., the situation of Paul, a "very privileged" person, is ignored (information from Judge, "Social Identity of the First Christians," 206).

The "new consensus": The first Christians were on a higher social level

In 1977 Abraham Malherbe published *Social Aspects of Early Christianity*.[44] The importance of this work, besides adding a good discussion of the relation between social level and literary culture, and of the role of housechurches in early Christianity, lay in the fact that Malherbe introduced and discussed much of the previous sociological work done on the New Testament. On the issue under discussion in this chapter he concluded:

> It appears from the recent concern of scholars with the social level of early Christians, that a new consensus may be emerging. This consensus, if it is not premature to speak of one, is quite different from the one represented by Adolf Deissmann, which has held sway since the beginning of the century. The more recent scholarship has shown that the social status of early Christianity may be higher than Deissmann had supposed.[45]

In the next section I aim at following up Malherbe's conclusion concerning the "new consensus" by looking closely at the discussion about the social level of the first Christians, concentrating on the methodological aspect of this discussion. By studying the methods by which scholars have arrived at this new consensus, and by judging the merits of the criticisms that have been made against it, I hope to arrive at a well-founded answer to the question whether the new consensus really stands up to the pressure of critical scrutiny.

A challenge to the old consensus: Edwin A. Judge

The Australian classical historian Edwin A. Judge began challenging the old consensus in 1960 in his short book *The Social Pattern of the Christian Groups in the First Century*.[46] Judge underlines the fact that, although Christianity originated in an Aramaic-speaking, mainly rural milieu in Palestine, it flourished and its writings circulated among Jewish and Gentile Christians living under the urban Hellenistic social

---

[44] Abraham J. Malherbe, *Social Aspects of Early Christianity*, Baton Rouge and London, 1977. In the second edition (Philadelphia: Fortress Press, 1983) was added an essay on "The Inhospitality of Diotrephes," and an "Epilogue," discussing some of the literature and subjects that had appeared since the first edition.

[45] Ibid., 31.

[46] With the subtitle "Some Prolegomena to the Study of New Testament Ideas of Social Obligation"; published by Tyndale Press in London.

institutions. After surveying these political institutions (republican-ism, Caesarism, ruler cult, the role of citizenship), ancient household community with the *clientela*, and the unofficial or unincorporated associations, Judge devotes a chapter to the question concerning the social constituency of Christian groups.

He begins by pointing out how difficult it is to say anything detailed and definite about this, as the statistical material is inadequate, and what we have, i.e., information about prominent persons, does not represent the normal, typical Christian. One can draw some safer conclusions from matters like the type of social organization of the Christian groups, their social and charitable activities, the educational standard of their surviving writings, and their relations with the gen-eral public and the government, but this type of information is very general. What Judge wants to do anyway is to show that the few data we have can be interpreted in a different way from the one here named "the old consensus."

The scarce points of contact between the first-century Christians and the Roman aristocracy ("which amounted to an infinitesimally small fraction of the total population"[47]) does not constitute evidence of any low social position. Only information about their affiliations within their own communities is relevant.

If one looks at the first Christians in Jerusalem, one notices (a) that this mainly Galilean group had support from a number of influential persons in the capital, and (b) that a large part of the congregation was made up by Jews from abroad, who generally were people of means, and seem to have been the main contributors to the church funds. The latter group, the "Hellenists," were expelled from Jeru-salem, which made the church in Jerusalem notably poorer. It also moved the missionary energy of the Hellenists into the diaspora. One result of this was the vigorous propagation of the gospel among non-Jews, another was the creation of the writings we call the New Tes-tament. "Christianity in its canonical form, then, is not so much the work of Galileans, as of a very cultivated section of international Jewry; they were at any rate its principal sponsors."[48] The large amount of traveling and hospitality provided as a matter of course points to a fairly high level of affluence among this leading group.

Paul himself and his career tell the same story: highly esteemed in Jerusalem, as well as belonging to the privileged group of Hellenistic families that had also been accorded Roman citizenship, he moved

---

[47] Judge, *Pattern*, 52.
[48] Ibid., 57.

with ease in the best circles in the society of the eastern Mediterranean world. The connections and friendships he used in Athens, Corinth, Ephesus, and Malta confirm this. This feature does not apply only to the apostle himself, but in some degree also to his churches. In Corinth, we are told, the church contained some intellectuals, politicians, and persons of gentle birth, and their conflicts and habits seem to have dominated that church, just as a discussion of their affairs and positions take a large part of 1 Corinthians. From information in Paul's letters and the Acts of the Apostles one can gather that the first converts in several diaspora churches were wealthy or prominent persons, who were baptized together with their households, and that these "houses" remained the social basis for all congregational life in the newfounded churches.[49] Judge summarizes his interpretation:

> Far from being a socially depressed group, then, if the Corinthians are at all typical, the Christians were dominated by a socially pretentious section of the population of the big cities. Beyond that they seem to have drawn on a broad constituency, probably representing the household dependents of the leading members. . . . The dependent members of city households were by no means the most debased section of society. If lacking freedom, they still enjoyed security, and a moderate prosperity. The peasantry and persons in slavery on the land were the most underprivileged classes. Christianity left them largely untouched. . . . Except for Palestinians, then, there is nothing to suggest that Christianity penetrated beyond the civilized Greek-speaking classes.[50]

In another essay the same year ("The Early Christians as a Scholastic Community"),[51] Judge specifically addressed the methodological question concerning a social description and placing of the first Christians. Statistic material is scarce, and both our social models ("social classes," "church and state") and the ancient ones (*polis*, "democracy–oligarchy") are anachronistic and distortive as explanations. To his thesis in the earlier essay Judge now added an analysis of the activities of the first Christians as seen by outsiders. One could describe these as cultic activities, or focus on these groups' function as welfare organizations. But the fact that the early Christian church can be understood as a scholastic community is of special importance in forming a judgment on its social constituency.

---

[49] Ibid., 35 f, 58, 60.

[50] Ibid., 60. This resembles the statement by Floyd V. Filson in an important but disregarded article ("The Significance of the Early House Churches," *Journal of Biblical Literature* 58, 1939, 105-112): "The apostolic church was more nearly a cross section of society than we have sometimes thought." Quotation from page 111.

[51] In the Australian *Journal of Religious History* 1, 1960/61, 4-15, 125-137.

After some discussion of Jesus as a rabbi, and of his followers as an ascetic sect within Judaism, Judge focuses on Paul. The apostle changed style from his "second journey" on, and took up the role of a professional "sophist." Among the characteristics that unite Paul with other "sophists" (like Aelius Aristides, Dio Chrysostomus, Epictetus, and Apollonius from Tyana) are: traveling from place to place, being dependent on the hospitality of admirers, being a trained speaker and persuader, endowed by a sense of philosophical-religious "mission." A further, prosopographical survey of Acts and the Pauline letters shows that Paul the apostle had a large support organization, located among higher strata of society in central cities of the Hellenistic world, and a fairly large group of personal followers and co-workers, all bound to his person. As regards Paul's position and the position of the Pauline churches generally in society, this meant a definite move upward compared to Deissmann's picture.

Judge's work did not simply represent a different opinion or another interpretation of the data, but also methodological improvements. Firstly, he differentiated between separate times and milieus of early Christianity. The Aramaic-speaking, rural movement around Jesus is not simply the same thing as Jewish Christianity in Jerusalem, not to mention the groups we encounter ten years later in Syria or twenty-five years later in Corinth or Rome. Secondly, Judge relates the data concerning social level to social structures of the surrounding society, Palestinian, Greek, and Roman (class system, patrons, and their *clientela*). He also evidences a clearer grasp of the complexity of the issue as such: data are generally scarce, there exists no statistic material, and some of our information only permits of indirect, vague conclusions. Furthermore, he points out that the data that are more directly relevant, namely prosopographical information, may not have any high degree of representativity. Nonetheless, by introducing prosopographical analysis on a broader scale, Judge elicits important historical information from the sources.[52]

---

[52] Prosopography (literally "description of faces/persons") is the collection of available data (on origin, status, profession, wealth, etc.) of all individuals of a certain group, as contrasted with survey analysis and the sampling necessary in order to analyse large groups; Peter Burke, *Sociology and History*, London, 1980, 37 f. In his three-part division of methods to elicit sociologically relevant information, Gerd Theissen places prosopography and sociography (the description of whole groups) in his first category: constructive conclusions from direct information. Gerd Theissen, "Die soziologische Auswertung religiöser Überlieferungen: Ihre methodologischen Probleme am Beispiel des Urchristentums" (*Kairos* 17, 1975, 284-299), now in *Studien*, 35-54). Also published in idem, *The Social Setting of Pauline Christianity: Essays on Corinth*. Philadelphia: Fortress Press, 1982.

The impact of Judge's reinterpretation

Judge's approach seems to have been hardly noticed among New Testament scholars at first, although his book was published in Germany as well in 1964.[53] His conclusions about the socially mixed character of the early Christian communities received some support, though, from the work of a number of other scholars, like Heinz Kreissig, Clarence L. Lee, and Martin Hengel.[54] Kreissig noted that, once we leave the Palestinian church aside, we confront no small farmer or rural dayworker among Christians in New Testament texts. We find a few artisans, tentmakers, a physician, a trader in purple, a few officials, and mention of slave-owners and people with houses. The slaves and other socially lowly placed people may have been a majority, but did not form the influential or leading part of the early Christian churches.[55] Lee pointed out that the early period of the Roman Empire was generally a period of social stability, although much dissatisfaction existed, especially among the upper classes and marginal groups of downward mobility. But to the aristocrats Christianity was the worst example of all of the "vulgarisation" that had befallen society, and to those urban strata who felt alienated from the privileges of citizenship, a conversion to the new Christian sect would only have served to alienate them further from the participation in society they longed for. There is no sign of any revolutionary atmosphere among the lower classes, especially not among the slaves, which allegedly could have been used by the church in attracting converts.[56]

---

[53] Edwin A. Judge, *Christliche Gruppen in nichtchristlicher Gesellschaft: Die Sozialstruktur christlicher Gruppen im ersten Jahrhundert*. Wuppertal, 1964.

[54] Martin Hengel, *Eigentum und Reichtum in der frühen Kirche. Aspekte einer frühchristlichen Sozialgeschichte*. Stuttgart, 1973. Published as *Property and Riches in the Early Church: Aspects of a Social History of Early Christianity*. London, 1974; cf. on page 37: "The majority of early Christians will have belonged to the 'middle class' of antiquity from which the 'godfearers' of the Jewish mission were recruited."

[55] Kreissig, "Zusammensetzung," 96-99. Malherbe rightly found the prosopographical analysis of Kreissig "somewhat less significant," as it is to a large extent based on the Acts, the Pastoral Epistles, and even later writings, which all have "a recognized tendency to describe Christianity as 'middle class' ," *Social Aspects*, 1977, 30 f. On the other hand, tendency in sources is a well-known problem of historical research, which must be handled by critical analysis and judgment, not by completely disqualifying the information they give.

[56] Clarence E. Lee, "Soziale Unruhe und Urchristentum," in Wayne A. Meeks (ed.), *Zur Soziologie des Urchristentums*. München, 1979, 67-87. [Orig. "Social Unrest and Primitive Christianity," in S. Benko and J.J. O'Rourke, The *Catacombs and the Colosseum*. Valley Forge, Pa., 1971].

Henneke Gülzow expressly confirmed the picture of Judge, both in his dissertation on the early church and slavery,[57] and in a later essay on the social conditions of the early Christian mission.[58] Gülzow claimed that Christianity in the first century did not spread so much through slaves (this was a romantic idea of the nineteenth century),[59] as through members of the more highly placed group of "godfearers," especially women. A few Christian slaves lived in pagan households, but most of them appear to have become Christians together with their masters.[60] One of the remarkable facts of the early Christian church is that its social base to a high degree consisted of private homes of the wealthy, the only houses large enough to receive guests and regular congregational meetings and meals, and Gülzow states: "In its beginnings Christianity was a socially well-placed movement in large Hellenistic cities."[61]

The social heterogeneity of the Christian movement and the successful unification of strongly separate social interests in a common life was in fact uniquely characteristic of the church. If any part of the social spectrum was missing, it would have been the middle stratum.[62] This heterogeneity is specifically mentioned in the famous letter of Pliny to the Emperor Trajan, where he notes that the Christians have attracted a great number of people of all estates *(multi enim . . . omnis ordinis . . . vocantur).* The impression given by a critic like Celsus that Christians belonged only to the lower and uneducated strata of society should not be accepted at its face value. It is part of his anti-Christian propaganda that was aimed at the socially higher

---

[57] Henneke Gülzow, *Christentum und Sklaverei in den ersten drei Jahrhunderten* (Diss. Kiel, 1966). Bonn, 1969, 28: "Die christlichen Gemeinden zeichneten sich gleich von Anfang an dadurch aus, dass in ihnen alle möglichen Stände vertreten waren" (with reference to the work of Judge and R. Schumacher).

[58] Henneke Gülzow, "Soziale Gegebenheiten der altkirchlichen Mission" (in Heinzgünter Frohnes und Uwe W. Knorr (eds.), *Kirchengeschichte als Missionsgeschichte. Band 1. Die alte Kirche.* München, 1974, 189-226, esp. 220 ff).

[59] Gülzow, *Sklaverei* (1969), 26 note 3; 174. F. Bömer has shown, contrary to ancient and scholarly opinion, that slaves from the East did not play an important role in spreading the Oriental religions in Roman society; idem, 50 note 6.

[60] Ibid., 42 ff; 52 note 1.

[61] "Das Christentum war in seinen Anfängen eine sozial gutsituierte Bewegung der grossen hellenistischen Städte," "Soziale Gegebenheiten," 220.

[62] On Corinth: "Dagegen vermisst man diejenigen, die auf Grund ihres mittleren Standes die sozialen Gegensätze innerhalb der Gemeinde ausgleichen und mildern könnten," Gülzow, *Sklaverei*, 41. Even if such a middle stratum existed in society, one wonders whether it functioned as a moderating factor between other social strata. Social relations in antiquity were not "horizontally" oriented (i.e., mainly with persons of the same income and status level), but rather "vertically," through loyalty to one's patron.

placed people, who were attracted by this new religion from the East. Celsus wanted to remind his educated readers from noble families of the chasm that normally (and in his opinion, rightly) separated them from the majority of insignificant and lowly people, who did not care about higher matters like the welfare of the whole society. He thus appealed to feelings of "upper-class" superiority, which this new Christian movement had to some degree overcome. There are, however, numerous conflicts between Christians of different social standing in the first few centuries, which bear witness to the fact that this chasm was a social reality that affected the interior life of the church as well.[63]

Judge's perspective has not gone unchallenged, however. One specific point of disagreement is Judge's interpretation of the data concerning the apostle Paul, and what conclusions could be drawn from them. Stanley Kent Stowers has questioned Judge's category of the professional "sophist," who belongs to "the class of touring lecturers," and finds this broad, heterogeneous category as unhistorical as the "divine man."[64] Furthermore, Paul, who was a leatherworker, would have been immediately categorized as a person of low public status, and would not have been invited by community leaders to give a public speech. His alternatives in acquiring an audience for his message after he had been expelled from the synagogue were two: either act as a Cynic street philosopher and grab hold of someone in the marketplace and accost him in a way interesting enough for others to stop and listen,[65] or be invited to speak in a private house before guests invited by the host, not an uncommon method of teaching philosophy. Both from Acts and the Pauline letters we see that Paul also had connections with houseowners.

But, as Ronald Hock has tried to show, Paul seems to have made a conscious effort not to become a typical house-philosopher, dependent on rich sponsors.[66] According to Hock, Paul himself originally had a fairly high social status, as can be seen from three circumstances.

---

[63] Gülzow, "Soziale Gegebenheiten" (1974), 222-224.

[64] Stanley Kent Stowers, "Social Status, Public Speaking and Private Teaching: The Circumstances of Paul's Preaching Activity" (*Novum Testamentum* 26, 1984, 59-82).

[65] Stowers points out that, although there are some similarities between a Cynic outlook on teaching and that of Paul, the Cynic marketplace approach was not well suited to someone who wanted to build a permanent community, op. cit., 80.

[66] Ronald F. Hock, "Paul's Tentmaking and the Problem of His Social Class" (*Journal of Biblical Literature* 97, 1978, 555-564). This perspective is given its fullest exposition in Hock's dissertation, *The Social Context of Paul's Ministry: Tentmaking and Apostleship*. Philadelphia, 1980.

The high linguistic and literary level of his writings witnesses to a prolonged, expensive education, such as could be afforded only by a wealthy family. His being a Roman citizen by birth points to the same type of background.[67] Thirdly, the attitude to the tentmaking he made his living from: Paul refers to his manual work[68] in a way typical of ancient upper class people: as slave's work, a humiliating, albeit sacrificial way of life undertaken on behalf of the gospel and as a specific calling by Christ.[69] Nonetheless, Paul chose to move socially downward, and take up a slightly degrading way of life, which made it possible for him to remain independent of his "patrons," or hosts. There are parallels to this life as a workshop philosopher in some Cynical philosophers.[70]

More generally, Abraham Malherbe found Judge's picture of Pauline Christianity as a rather academic type of school of popular philosophy overstating the case and in need of nuancing. Probably "academic" belief and religious practice were not so strongly differentiated within the Christian groups as Judge made them, even if Jewish and Christian groups with their intellectual tradition and moral emphasis would have appeared rather philosophical or "school-like" to outsiders.[71] Meeks has reviewed what is known of the Pythagorean and Epicurean schools, noted some similarities with Pauline Christianity, especially

---

[67] The apostle's Roman citizenship would have "placed Paul amid the aristocracy of any provincial town," as W. M. Ramsay put it in his *St. Paul the Traveller and the Roman Citizen*. New York, 1896; quoted from Hock (1978), 557. Paul's Roman citizenship has been contested by Wolfgang Stegemann as a Lucan fiction or misunderstanding, in "War der Apostel Paulus ein römischer Bürger?" (*Zeitschrift für neutestamentliche Wissenschaft 78*, 1987, 200-229), and defended by Gerd Lüdemann in the excursus "Zum römischen Bürgerrecht des Paulus" in idem, *Das frühe Christentum nach den Traditionen der Apostelgeschichte: Ein Kommentar.* Göttingen, 1987, 249-250, and also by Gillian Clark, "The Social Status of Paul," *Expository Times 96*, 1984-85, 110-111.

[68] The stigma of manual work has often been explained away as a characteristic habit of rabbinical teachers, who combined the study of Tora with learning a trade—a habit that is not established before the mid-second century. Hock, "Tentmaking," 557. Already Chrysostom and other church fathers of the early centuries concluded from the statement in Acts 18:3 on Paul's occupation as a "tentmaker," that he could not have been from a distinguished family, but rather was "a common man"; idem, 556 note 11.

[69] Contested by Stegemann, "Paulus ein römischer Bürger?," 227 f. Luke's notice about Paul's manual work as a tentmaker in Acts 18:1-3 does not evidence any contemptuous attitude; in this Luke is typical of the tradition of "scientific" writers of the period, Loveday Alexander, "Luke's Preface in the Context of Greek Preface-Writing" (*Novum Testamentum 18*, 1986, 70).

[70] Ronald F. Hock, "The Workshop as a Social Setting for Paul's Missionary Preaching" (*Catholic Biblical Quarterly 41*, 1979, 439-450).

[71] Malherbe 1977, 45-59.

in the character of functioning as modified households or voluntary associations, but concluded that these elements are ancillary and not constitutive. And Judge prematurely rejected other analogies, such as the cultic community.[72]

None of these modifications fundamentally invalidate the picture given by Judge. Adolf Deissmann himself found both "higher" and "lower" traits in Paul, also in the apostle's language that is neither literary nor vulgar, but then concluded:

> If we finally ask in which direction the apostle, who thus stands in the middle, is leaning, the answer must be: according to his whole development and sympathies and living conditions he belongs much more to the middle and lower strata than to the upper stratum. He is no upstart who has lost his roots. As a missionary working primarily among the unliterary masses of the large cities, Paul is not a man who benignly has stepped down into a world unknown to him; he has remained in his own social world.[73]

The important difference between this position and that of Judge does not concern the judgment about Paul's personal social level (here Judge, modified by Stowers and Hock,[74] may not be too far from Deissmann), but the conclusions drawn from this and other data about the social level of Pauline Christianity as a whole. And this is where one has to state that Judge's interpretation of the prosopographical information available in the texts is more down-to-earth and plausible than the generalizations of Deissmann on "the unliterary masses."

Corinthian prosopography: Gerd Theissen
The most decisive contribution to the new consensus was made by Gerd Theissen in a series of articles published in 1974 and 1975, in which he analysed the social constituency of the church in Corinth.[75]

---

[72] Wayne A. Meeks, *The First Urban Christians: The Social World of the Apostle Paul.* New Haven and London, 1983, 82-84.

[73] "Wenn man dann schliesslich fragt, nach welcher Seite der so in der Mitte stehende Apostel mehr neigt, so muss die Antwort lauten: er gehört seinem ganzen Wuchse nach, seinen Sympathien und Lebensbedingungen nach viel mehr zu den mittleren und unteren Schichten, als zur Oberschicht. Er ist kein wurzellos gewordener Emporkömmling. Als Missionar hauptsächlich in der unliterarischen Masse der Grossstädte wirkend, ist Paulus aber auch nicht gönnerhaft herabgestiegen in eine ihm fremde Welt; er ist in seiner eigenen sozialen Welt geblieben." Adolf Deissmann, *Paulus: Eine kultur- und religionsgeschichtliche Skizze,* 2. Aufl., Tübingen, 1925, 43.

[74] Judge seems to accept Hock's work, in his essay "The Social Identity of the First Christians," 213 f.

[75] Gerd Theissen, "Legitimation und Lebensunterhalt: Ein Beitrag zur Soziologie ur-

Starting from the information in 1 Cor 1: 26-29 that the church in Corinth had some members with education, power, and of noble birth, Theissen set out to find and if possible identify them. He used four criteria indicating high social status: (1) to have a civil or religious office in the city,[76] (2) to have a "house," (3) to have been of service to the church or Paul, (4) to travel (for the church). The last two criteria are not sufficient in themselves to indicate high status. The prosopographical analysis shows that a large part of the most active and influential members of this church—which Theissen for structural reasons considered to be typical of the Hellenistic churches in general—probably belonged to the small group of Christians with high social status. A further analysis of the conflict about the Lord's supper (1 Corinthians 11) and generally of the relations between the "strong"and the "weak" fills out the picture: the church was not homogeneous, but contained a fairly wealthy and highly placed minority and a poorer majority. The wealthy and cultured members of the congregation were generally the leaders, taking responsibility (not always wisely) for the common life of the church in Corinth, acting as hosts for their fellow believers, and as heads of the different factions within the church—they were clearly a dominant minority.

In a recent article, Theissen has summarized his views on the social level of the first Christians in Hellenistic urban societies (Corinth, Rome, and Carthage). He concludes that these communities were deeply rooted in the lower classes, had no contacts with the imperial upper class, but penetrated a little into the marginal strata of the local

---

christlicher Missionare" *(New Testament Studies* 21, 1974/75, 192-221; now in *Studien zur Soziologie des Urchristentums*, Tübingen, ²1983, 201-230). "Soziale Schichtung in der korinthischen Gemeinde. Ein Beitrag zur Soziologie des hellenistischen Urchristentums" *(Zeitschrift für neutestamentliche Wissenschaft* 65, 1974, 232-273; now in *Studien*, 231-271); idem, "Soziale Integration und sakramentales Handeln: Eine Analyse von 1 Cor. XI 17-34" *(Novum Testamentum* 16, 1974, 179-206; now in *Studien*, 290-317); idem, "Die Starken und Schwachen in Korinth: Soziologische Analyse eines theologischen Streites" *(Evangelische Theologie* 35, 1975, 155-172; now in *Studien*, 272-289). These articles have also been published in an American (smaller) collection of his essays, *The Social Setting of Pauline Christianity: Essays on Corinth*. Ed. by John H. Schütz. Philadelphia, 1982.

[76] Already Gülzow pointed out that the letters of Paul show us a congregation, in which several members participate in the public and social life of Corinth, and came into contact with non-Christian courts, cults, and banquets. Some mixed marriages could also be found there—an impossible thing even in the most liberal synagogue; Gülzow, *Sklaverei*, 41 f. A somewhat different analysis of roles and status positions in the Corinthian congregation is offered by Aloys Funk, *Status und Rollen in den Paulusbriefen. Eine inhaltsanalytische Untersuchung zur Religionssoziologie.* Innsbruck, 1981.

governing stratum in provincial cities. This situation is explained by the hypothesis that early Christianity spread especially in those sectors where the larger society reached the limit of its power to integrate people. There Christianity could offer alternatives to the three main integrative factors: a supra-regional loyalty (to the Lord Jesus instead of the Lord Caesar), a supra-regional, "oecumenical" culture and fellowship (characterized as a "Judaism for non-Jews"), and a local *polis*-based culture of equal citizenship (equality as Christian siblings, tempered by realities to what Theissen has termed "love-patriarchalism").[77]

Theissen dearly continued the work of Judge, only with better methods. He presents a wealth of ancient background material, especially on social life in Corinth, he applies clearer criteria of what identifies a higher social level, and exhibits a more nuanced use of the sources. Because of this and because he concentrates on Corinth only, Theissen is able to reach past a suggestive sketch to a historically plausible picture of the social constituency and social structure of the church in Corinth, and the Pauline church generally.

Theissen on early Palestinian Christianity
When attempting to reconstruct the life of the earliest Palestinian Christianity, including the question concerning the social level of the first Jewish Christians, Theissen parted ways completely with Judge.[78]

---

[77] "Vers une théorie de l'histoire sociale du christianisme primitif" (*Études Théologiques et Religieuses* 63, 1988, 199-225), 209-217. For a critique of Theissen's understanding of "love patriarchalism" as a compromise between ideal and social reality, see Troels Engberg-Pedersen, "The Gospel and Social Practice According to 1 Corinthians" (*New Testament Studies* 33, 1987, 557-584).

[78] This perspective was worked out in a number of essays published by Gerd Theissen between 1973 and 1977: "Wanderradikalismus. Literatursoziologische Aspekte der Überlieferung von Worten Jesu im Urchristentum" (*Zeitschrift für Theologie und Kirche* 70, 1973, 245-271; now in *Studien*, 79-105), continued in idem, "Legitimation und Lebensunterhalt: Ein Beitrag zur Soziologie urchristlicher Missionare" (*New Testament Studies* 21, 1974/75, 192-221; reprinted in *Studien*, 201-230; esp. 202-209, the remainder is on Paul), idem, "Die Tempelweissagung Jesu: Prophetie im Spannungsfeld von Stadt und Land" (*Theologische Zeitschrift* 32, 1976, 144-158; reprinted in *Studien*, 142-159), and idem, " 'Wir haben alles verlassen' (Mc. X, 28). Nachfolge und soziale Entwurzelung in der jüdisch-palästinischen Gesellschaft des 1. Jahrhunderts n. Chr." (*Novum Testamentum* 19, 1977, 161-196; reprinted in *Studien*, 106-141). One part of this work appeared as a section in Theissen's book, *Urchristliche Wundergeschichten: Ein Beitrag zur formgeschichtlichen Erforschung der synoptischen Evangelien* (Studien zum Neuen Testament 8). Gütersloh 1974, 229-261: "Die soziale Funktion urchristlicher Wundergeschichten." This whole perspective was summarized in the deceptively slender book *Soziologie der Jesusbewegung: Ein Beitrag zur Entstehungsgeschichte des Urchristentums*. München, 1977,

Like most exegetes since the inception of the form critical method, Theissen does not view the Gospels or the Acts as anywhere near the type of firsthand sources we find in the letters of Paul. If one wants to do a historical reconstruction of the life of Jesus and of the earliest "Jesus movement" in Palestine, one must realize that the road through the Gospels to historically ascertainable data is thorny and complex.

Following the form critical approach to the social reality behind the Synoptic Gospels, Theissen concluded from the strong ethical radicalism characteristic of the gospel tradition to the existence of a group of tradition carriers, whose life was characterized by homelessness, an afamiliar ethos, and disapproval of wealth and ownership: the wandering, charismatic "prophets" or "apostles," who lived in a voluntary poverty like their Master had done. We have direct evidence about this group in the synoptic commissioning of the Twelve (Mt 10 et par) and in Didache, and the Cynic wandering philosophers offer a contemporary analogy to their way of life.[79] These wandering charismatics lived by way of a "higher" type of begging.[80] They were prohibited from any kind of planned work or earning of a livelihood, but had to rely on being fed by the mercy of God, day by day, as they roamed from one place to another. A "disciple" could not count on being received as anything else than an outcast or a despicable beggar, too lazy to work for his living. These wandering charismatics were real outsiders, and lived by offering blessings, healings, and eschatological protection in exchange for support from local people, who adhered to the teachings of Jesus but themselves continued their work and ordinary way of life. Probably these supporters were also marginal people, poor, hungry, and ready to hear and believe the words of one who had pronounced the poor blessed.[81]

These marginal groups seem to have been situated in the Palestinian countryside, a rural, conservative, and rather particularistic context, not much open toward the non-Jewish world or the higher strata of society, which were situated in the cities.[82] When the followers of

---

which was published in 1978 as *The First Followers of Jesus* by SCM, London, and in the same year by Fortress Press, Philadelphia, as *Sociology of Early Palestinian Christianity*, and in 1979 as *Jesusoverleveringen og dens sociale baggrund. Et sociologisk bidrag till den tidligste kristendoms historie*, by Reitzel in Copenhagen. In his book Theissen is somewhat more one-sided in his selection and evaluation of the evidence than in his essays, which may help explain why some have criticized him for exaggerating the poverty of the earliest Christians.

[79] Theissen, "Wanderradikalismus" (1973), *Studien*, 86-90.
[80] Ibid., 92-102.
[81] Cf. ibid., *Jesusbewegung*, 14-26, and "Legitimation," *Studien*, 202-209.
[82] See Theissen's essay on "Tempelweissagung" (1976), mentioned above.

Jesus did settle in Jerusalem, after his death and resurrection, the Christian community was made up of two marginal groups, which both were outsiders in regard to the majority of the inhabitants of the holy city: on the one hand there were poor Galileans, who had become even poorer by giving up their work and familial support back home, and on the other hand wealthier Greek-speaking Jews from the diaspora, the "Hellenists."[83] The socioeconomic difference between these two groups is part of the explanation why there arose conflicts between them, but also why the Hellenists, when they later had to leave Jerusalem, continued to support "the poor" in Jerusalem.[84]

Theissen was careful to point out that Jesus' followers were not coming from the lowest strata of Jewish society (tenant farmers, day labourers, servants, and slaves), but rather from a middle stratum, consisting of artisans, fishermen, tax collectors, and landowning peasants with small holdings.[85] The really poor and destitute are objects of help and healing, but are not called to become disciples (the blind Bartimaeus is an exception). The term "middle stratum" should not be understood as signifying anything like a middle class existence in our times. Fishermen like Simon and Andrew probably lived in small circumstances and, like most working people in the unaffluent Palestinian economy, were victims of economic pressure. But they had something they could leave, an economic security to give up, and that is why their step into discipleship must be considered a premeditated, voluntary relinquishing of property, family ties, and a socially secure position.

Theissen envisages the phenomenon of homelessness and uprootedness as quite common in contemporary Palestine, being the result of a widespread economic and political crisis.[86] An increasingly heavy taxation, concentration of property to fewer owners, coupled with ecological crises like famines had hit the middle and lower strata hardest and caused a generally anomic situation. It has to be remembered, though, that several strata, high, middle, and low, can experience strong feelings of insecurity concerning norms, beliefs, and

---

[83] Cf. Judge, *Pattern*, 54 f. Naom G. Cohen, "The Greek and Latin Transliterations Mariam and Maria: Their Sociological Significance" (*Lesh* 38, 1974, 170-180; from the abstract in *Internationale Zeitschriftenschau für Bibelwissenschaft und Grenzgebieten* 22, No. 2341) has proposed that the names of John Mark and his mother Maria, which suggest closer than usual relations to the Romans, and the fact that this family owned a house in Jerusalem, big enough to serve as a meeting place for the first Christians, indicate a somewhat higher social standing.

[84] Cf. also the summary in Theissen, *Jesusbewegung*, 47-56.

[85] Theissen, " 'Wir haben alles verlassen' " (1977), *Studien*, 110-112.

[86] Ibid., 133-141. Idem, *Jesusbewegung*, 34-46.

behaviour patterns in such a situation of crisis and rapid change. The decisive factor is social mobility as such, not the level at which one is situated. Therefore the members of renewal movements typically come from groups who have begun to experience losses, not from those who were at the poor end of society to begin with. People like this could be described as victims of "relative deprivation," which means that they felt deprived in relation to other groups, although they were not so poor as many others. So when the disciples of Jesus took up the deviant pattern of wandering around begging, this was a combination of outside socioeconomic factors and a deliberate stepping down in society, made for religious reasons connected with their teacher and his preaching.[87] According to Theissen the social level of Jewish Christianity was considerably lower than the social level of Hellenistic and Pauline Christianity. And the social constituency of Jewish Christianity was homogeneously low; the short period when more affluent Hellenistic Jews were members of the church in Jerusalem can only be seen as the exception that proves this rule.[88]

Methodologically, Theissen introduced something new in his analysis of source material pertaining to the earliest Palestinian Christianity (esp. the Synoptic Gospels). In order to elicit data for social description and sociological interpretation, he used three different types of inferential procedures: the constructive or more direct, the analytical and indirect, and the comparative, drawing conclusions from analogous phenomena.[89] In his summarizing book *Soziologie der Jesusbewegung* (1977), he exhibits clearly the role of each one of these procedures. This book also makes it clear that in treating gospel material Theissen leaves socio- and prosopographical analyses aside, and relies much more on inferences concerning the probable behaviour of an alleged group of tradition carriers, and on a frequent use of analogies from contemporary Palestinian social, political, and cultural history.

In relying so heavily on the most tenuous type of inferential procedure (the conclusion from an analysis of normative and symbolical material), Theissen seems to disregard his own warnings and strictures against this type of fact-finding.[90] Probably he felt constrained

---

[87] *Jesusbewegung*, 40 f, 46.

[88] See *Jesusbewegung*, 104-111.

[89] Theissen had presented and discussed these procedures in his 1975 essay "Die soziologische Auswertung religiöser Überlieferungen" (*Studien*, 35-54).

[90] Theissen, "Auswertung," in *Studien*, 40-51; esp. on the analysis of norms contained in material not explicitly paraenetic. A discussion of these problems will be given in chapter 4.

to this methodological shift because of the difficult source material, but the result lacks the sharp details and concrete character of his Corinthian analysis. In Theissen's investigations early Jewish Christianity remains a fairly nebulous, yet somehow homogeneous entity, loosely occupying a period between c. A.D. 30 and 70, and the vast territory of Palestine and Syria.[91]

Questions on Theissen's picture of the "Jesus movement"
There has been a lively discussion of Gerd Theissen's work on Palestinian Christianity, but here I will illustrate only from that part of the discussion that concerns the question of the social level of these Christians.

The position of Theissen concerning the social level of the first Palestinian Christians has received support by investigations of other scholars, among which can be mentioned Bernhard Grimm,[92] Theodor Schleich,[93] and Sean Freyne.[94] But Theissen's description of the social situation of Palestine as a whole has not gone unchallenged. For example, A. E. Harvey pointed out in his review of Theissen's *The First Followers of Jesus*[95] that there is no evidence for serious political unrest in Palestine during the first half of the first century A.D. Rather,

---

[91] Cf. the definition given in the opening paragraph of Theissen's *Jesusbewegung*, 9.

[92] According to Kümmel's survey "Das Urchristentum. II.b. Zur Sozialgeschichte und Soziologie der Urkirche" (*Theologische Rundschau* 50, 1985, 327-363, here 339 f) Bernhard Grimm (in *Untersuchungen zur sozialen Stellung der frühen Christen in der römischen Gesellschaft*. Diss.phil. München, 1975 [not available to me]) states that Jesus cannot be seen as especially linked with lower strata, although he had pronounced sympathy toward them.

[93] Theodor Schleich, "Missionsgeschichte und Sozialstruktur des vorkonstantinischen Christentums" (*GWU* 33, 1982, 269-296 [not available to me]). This essay, which is summarized by Kümmel, op. cit., 353 f, supports Theissen's position in almost every respect: Christianity up to the time of Constantine was never dominantly a religion of the lower strata. Jesus did not call any really poor as disciples. Even if Jesus solidarizes himself with the poor and declassed, the social location of his disciples is rather a marginal middle stratum. In the earliest period there were charismatic wandering missionaries, but as Christianity increasingly became a religion of the urban middle strata, this type was eventually substituted by the self-supporting missionary.

[94] Sean Freyne, *Galilee from Alexander the Great to Hadrian, 332 B.C.E. to 135 C.E.: A Study of Second Temple Judaism*. Wilmington and Notre Dame, 1980. According to Carolyn Osiek RSCJ, *What Are They Saying about the Social Setting of the New Testament?* Ramsey 1984, 44, Freyne "has more carefully documented the literary, historical, archeological, and inscriptional evidence [sc. on this region], tried some of Theissen's analyses, and found them to fit."

[95] In *Journal of Theological Studies* 30, Oxford, 1979, 279-282.

the period was marked by a certain peaceful prosperity and com-
mercial expansion.[96] This undermines the plausibility of Theissen's
"factor analysis," where he describes the social situation instrumental
in forming the movement of the first Palestinian Jewish Christians.
There are also different opinions among scholars concerning the social
position of fishermen of Palestine at this time. Several scholars seem
to place this group at a higher social level than Theissen. S. W. Baron
considers fishermen to have had a "reputable, if not high social standing."[97] Bo Reicke mentions the fishing industry as an example of
prosperity in Galilee:

> A typical example of the relative prosperity was the fishing industry
> on the Sea of Galilee, mentioned in the New Testament. Commercial
> firms shipped the dried or salt fish even to foreign countries. One such
> center of the fishing industry was Magdala or Tarichea (Greek *taricheuo*,
> 'to salt') on the western shore of the Sea of Galilee, which is known to
> have been a home of men working in this industry at least since 53 B.C.
> (Josephus Ant. xiv. 120). The fishermen of Galilee formed partnerships
> (Luke 5:10) and were able to acquire comparatively expensive equipment
> (Matt. 13:47-50); they should not be thought of as primitive. . . . Thus
> we may reckon in the New Testament period with an increase in Jewish
> income that was due in part to the achievements of Herod.[98]

These different evaluations alert us to the fact that judgments concerning social level are not data in themselves, but necessarily interpretations of them. The precariousness or falsifiability of such
interpretations is of course increased when the data are few and lend
themselves to more than one interpretation.

Wolfgang Stegemann has subjected Theissen's hypothesis of a voluntary "Wanderkarismatikertum" to strong criticism. His main contention is that it cannot stand when analysed source-critically. The
idea of a voluntary renunciation of property, work, and family life as
necessary for a true disciple of Jesus is a literary fiction, a Lucan
idealization of the original times made by the evangelist in order to

---

[96] Cf. Reicke's opinion: "Financially, Herod's regime benefited the land; his buildings
provided the clearest evidence of this. Newly established contacts promoted trade with
other parts of the Roman commonwealth," Bo Reicke, *The New Testament Era: The World
of the Bible from 500 B.C. to A.D. 100*. London, 1974, 102-103.
[97] S. W. Baron, *A Social and Religious History of the Jews, I*. New York, 1952, 254; quoted
from Theissen, "Verlassen" (1977), *Studien*, 111 note 15.
[98] Reicke, op. cit., 102-103. Cf also the remarks of Daniel J. Harrington, "Sociological
Concepts and the Early Church: A Decade of Research" (*Theological Studies* 41, 1980,
181-190; here 185 f).

criticize the rich Christians of his own day and spur them to active generosity toward the poor. Once we subtract these secondary layers, we are left with very little evidence concerning a group of wandering charismatics. The homeless, wandering life of Jesus and his first followers (esp. the prophets behind the source Q) was rather the nonvoluntary flight and liberation of oppressed people from a heavily debt-laden and distressed situation. They belonged to the genuinely poor, whose day-to-day problem was how to find something to eat. What Jesus and the prophets behind the Q material wanted to instill in their hearers was a strong trust in God instead of anxious fretting for their livelihood.[99]

Stegemann is most convincing in his criticism of the idea that the wandering charismatic prophets were the leaders of Palestinian Jewish Christianity all through the first century into the second; the sources do not bear this out. But one cannot decide the question concerning the social standing of the first disciples simply by making the criticism against Theissen that his interpretation depends too much on seeing things through the glasses of affluent people, who cannot think of poverty as necessary. Of course, one should beware of unconsciously projecting a modern understanding of "middle class" onto the "middle strata" to which Jesus and his closest disciples belonged, or of losing oneself in nostalgic fantasies about the idyllic life of poor people. But what decides any historical question is the evidence.[100] And the evidence shows that Stegemann's contention that only Luke or Q picture Jesus as calling people who are affluent enough to have something to leave or sell is not correct: it goes for Mark, Matthew, and Didache as well.[101] The disciples of Jesus could have been genuinely poor in

---

[99] Wolfgang Stegemann, "Nachfolge Jesu als solidarische Gemeinschaft der reichen und angesehenen Christen mit den bedürftigen und verachteten Christen. Das Lukasevangelium" (= ch. 3 in Luise Schottroff—Wolfgang Stegemann, Jesus von Nazareth— Hoffnung der Armen. Stuttgart, 1978, 89-153), 106, and esp. idem, "Wanderradikalismus im Urchristentum? Historische und theologische Auseinandersetzung mit einer interessanten These" (in Schottroff-Stegemann (eds.), Der Gott der kleinen Leute. Sozialgeschichtliche Bibelauslegungen. Bd 2. Neues Testament. München-Gelnhausen, 1979, 94-120).

[100] Theissen, "Forschung," Studien, 28 note 71.

[101] Theissen points to Mk 10:29 where the giving up of fields and houses is mentioned, Mk 1:20 where the sons of Zebedee leave a fishing firm with hired servants, Mk 10: 21 where the young man is called to leave a large wealth, Mk 2:15 where Levi seems to have invited several guests beside Jesus and his disciples to a meal in his own house. In Mt one could point to 10:23 and 10:40 f, in Didache to 10:7 and 11:4 ff. And one should not overlook that Luke, beside his idealizing of poverty, also criticizes wandering charismatics in Lk 22:35 ff, 10:9 and 21:8. Theissen, "Gewaltverzicht," Studien, 187 f note 62.

some cases, but in the main the Synoptic Gospels accurately picture the life of charismatic poverty of the followers of Jesus as a voluntary relinquishing of property, work, and income.[102]

Günther Baumbach has raised some questions on Theissen's picture of the first Christians.[103] His first objection concerns the wandering life-style of the early Christian leaders. Paul's information in Gal 1: 18 that he met only Cephas and James in Jerusalem need not be understood to mean that the others were out walking, as it is rather a demonstration of Paul's lack of interest in establishing contact with all the original apostles. It is also much more in keeping with their centripetal mission idea that all peoples will be drawn up to the holy city, that these Galilean apostles remained in Jerusualem, which was soon to be the eschatological Zion. Baumbach adds that it was probably the theological differences between the Galileans and the Hellenists that led to the eventual expulsion of the latter and to their consequent "wandering" type of mission work throughout Palestine and outside. Thus, wandering missionaries did not arise as a result of a continuity with or conscious emulation of Jesus' own example, but as a result of the specific political, social, and cultural situation in Judaea and its capital during the first years of the Christian movement, which forced the Hellenists out into this new and unexpected behaviour.

The transition from a lowly placed, sectarian Jewish Christianity to a predominantly urban, socially better situated Hellenistic Christianity is to Theissen also a transition from the social pattern of "communism of love" to that of "patriarchalism of love" (Troeltsch's terms). Baumbach thinks this generalization and typification much too sweeping, and takes exception both with Theissen's statement that there was much less social tension in Hellenistic societies and churches, and with the way he presses the social form of "institutional church" ("Anstaltskirche," a form Troeltsch saw fully developed first in the Middle Ages) upon the Pauline Hellenistic churches. One might add that the facile separation of early Christianity into two strongly divergent parts, one "Jewish" and the other "Hellenistic," also seems to be a throwback to earlier and outmoded historical perspectives.

One basic criticism of Theissen's method of fact-finding concerns the fundamental postulates of form criticism as such. Klaus Haacker has pointed out that form criticism (at least as handled by Dibelius)

---

[102] "Zur forschungsgeschichtlichen Einordnung der soziologischen Fragestellung," in, *Studien*, 3-34, esp. 27 f.
[103] Günter Baumbach, "Die Anfänge der Kirchwerdung im Urchristentum" (*Kairos* 24, Salzburg 1982, 17-30, esp. 22-27).

generally operates with a specific model of the social location of the early Christians. They were "unliterary people," not well educated and not capable of producing or wanting literary texts, but only simple, straightforward folk tales. This axiom tends to bias any form critical reconstruction of the social reality behind the gospel tradition in the direction of putting the social level of the tradition carriers rather low. Against such a presumption stands the fact that all Christian congregations we know of from the New Testament were urban communities, and that their leading persons as far as known were neither slaves nor peasants, i.e., did not belong to the lowest stratum of education. Furthermore, the Greek gospels themselves witness to a situation, where the early Christians stood before and tried to communicate their message to an urban audience, which demanded some intellectual and literary effort.[104] This would speak against construing the earliest Jewish Christianity as necessarily very rural and poverty-stricken.[105]

Literary level as a criterion of social level
Malherbe's own contribution to the new consensus was a critique of the presuppositions of Deissmann, especially his belief in a correlation between social class and literary culture.[106] First, one has to recognize the diversity as regards literary level of New Testament Greek, and the fact that even at its crudest level it is not so vulgar as the majority of nonliterary papyri on which Deissmann rested his case.[107] Second and generally, the relationship between the literary level of a document

---

[104] Klaus Haacker, "Dibelius und Cornelius. Ein Beispiel formgeschichtlicher Überlieferungskritik" *(Biblische Zeitschrift N. F.* 24, 1980, 234-251), 248 f. The community behind the Gospel of Matthew does not fit into the charismatic poverty perspective of Theissen (and Gager and Kee), as they appear to have been urban, well-to-do, educated, and somewhat anti-charismatic. R. H. Smith, "Were the Early Christians Middle-Class? A Sociological Analysis of the New Testament" *(Currents in Theology and Mission* 7, St. Louis, 1980, 260-276).

[105] Two further realities point in the same direction: (1) The tension between early Jewish Christianity and the surrounding Jewish society seems to have occurred primarily in relation to the Pharisees, who were clearly an urban movement, so probably the Jesus movement must have been to some degree urban; (2) The affluent women who are reported to have followed and supported Jesus in Lk 8: 3 also point to a more sophisticated social context. John E. Stambaugh and David L. Balch, *The New Testament in Its Social Environment.* Philadelphia, 1986, 103 f.

[106] Malherbe, *Social Aspects,* 29-59, "Social Level and Literary Culture."

[107] The vulgarity of New Testament Greek was much exaggerated by Deissmann, as has been shown especially by Albert Wifstrand and his student Lars Rydbeck in *Fachprosa, vermeintliche Volkssprache und Neues Testament,* Uppsala, 1967.

and the social level of its author (not to speak of its readers) is not straightforward and direct.[108] As a high educational level in antiquity is somehow correlated with affluence and social position (cf. however Epictetus and other cultured slaves), one could surmise that a high literary level of a document is indirect evidence of a higher social position of the community in which it belonged.[109] But against this assumption must be held an awareness of how many different relationships there may exist between literature and the community to which it was addressed.

> We must, for instance, resist the temptation to see so much of early Christian literature either as a community product or as reflecting the actual circumstances of the communities with which the writings are associated. We too frequently read of communities that virtually produced one or another of the Gospels or for which they were produced. It is at least possible that some documents were rescued from obscurity, not because they represented the viewpoints of communities, but precisely because they challenged them.[110]

Having delivered this warning of using literary level as a criterion of social level of the receiving part, Malherbe ends by stating that Paul's style indicates a personal educational level higher than the one accorded him by Deissmann.[111]

---

[108] Cf. the remarks of Malherbe 1977, 56. Peter Lampe states: "Even if a higher social provenance generally increases the chances of education for the individual, education can in principle be connected with *any* kind of social origin. (Auch wenn eine höhere soziale Herkunft in allgemeinen die Bildungschancen des einzelnen erhöht, kann grundsätzlich Bildung mit *jedem* sozialen Herkommen verkoppelt sein)." Idem, *Die stadtrömischen Christen in den ersten beiden Jahrhunderten: Untersuchungen zur Sozialgeschichte* (WUNT Reihe 2, 18). 2. Aufl. Tübingen, 1989, 299. For an instructive discussion of these issues, see Edwin A. Judge, "St. Paul and Classical Society" (*Jahrbuch für Antike und Christentum* 15, 1972, 19-36), 29 ff.

[109] Cf. Loveday Alexander, "Luke's Preface in the Context of Greek Preface-Writing" (*Novum Testamentum* 18, 1986, 48-74), 51: ". . . literary analysis (of style, vocabulary and composition . . .) must lead inevitably to certain conclusions about audience and social setting;" Luke's preface to his Gospel seems to evidence his familiarity with scientific-technical manuals, which indicates a belonging in the world of crafts and professions of the Greek East in general (66). Teachers and practitioners of the Greek scientific tradition themselves often were educated slaves or freedmen in great households (70).

[110] Malherbe (1977),13.

[111] Ibid., 59.

Summarizing the new consensus: Wayne A. Meeks

The most detailed and sophisticated treatment so far of the issue concerning the social level of the first Christians is to be found in Wayne A. Meeks' *The First Urban Christians* (1983), who in his second chapter ("The Social Level of Pauline Christians") summarized the whole previous discussion and added some interesting points of his own.[112]

After reviewing scholarly efforts in the field, Meeks starts by discussing how social stratification in antiquity can be measured at all. In ancient society one could (following Max Weber and Moses 1. Finley) distinguish three different kinds of ranking: class, *ordo*, and status. As class categories are defined and used in sociology, "class" is an anachronistic concept that lumps "together groups who clearly were regarded in antiquity as different."[113] Looking at the *ordines* or "estates" of imperial Roman society is equally unhelpful in an investigation of the social level of the first Christians, since the three uppermost divisions of this system comprise less than even the topmost percent of the population, where probably no Christian of the first century was located. To add the remaining two: the *plebs*, or free citizens of Rome, and *ordo libertinorum*, the freedmen, is almost equivalent to saying "and everybody else."[114]

This lack of "discriminating power" of the two first-mentioned categories leaves us with status as the only useful concept in measuring social stratification in ancient society and Christian groups within it. The first scholar to enter "status" into the discussion was John Gager, when he started talking of "relative deprivation" as a fact among higher strata, referring to a discrepancy between achieved and attributed status (or the status you think you have and the status you are given by society). Meeks considers Gager to have been on the right track, although his argument needs more precision.[115]

Meeks carefully points out that status cannot be measured along a single scale, as stratification is nowadays seen as a multidimensional phenomenon. You have to locate a person's status along several different variables, like power, wealth, occupation, ethnic background, education, family connections. The *generalized status* of a person is a

---

[112] Meeks, *Urban*, 51-73.

[113] Ibid., 53.

[114] Meeks, *Urban*, 54. As Meeks points out in note 20 (page 215) this considerably lessens the value of the survey given by Gager, *Kingdom* (93-113), where he discusses the social level of Christians as related mainly to the Roman *ordines*. (We have met this observation and objection in the writings of Judge and Malherbe).

[115] Ibid., 215 note 20.

composite of his or her ranks in all the relevant dimensions. But there are complications here: not all dimensions have the same weight, and they can have different weight in different contexts.[116] Perhaps the most important dimension of status is the degree of correlation among one's various rankings. If you are ranked much higher on some variables than on others, you would, in sociological parlance, have a low status crystallization (or *status consistency* or status congruence). This means that we should beware of assigning Christian individuals and groups of the early church to one general level. As status is a multidimensional phenomenon we would have to look at their ranking from several different aspects, like ethnic origins, wealth, personal liberty, office in the city or voluntary associations, occupation, and sex in order to say something about their status.

Meeks then marshals two kinds of evidence, first prosopographic and then indirect evidence of social level. In the first part he follows Theissen's procedure in establishing which persons around Paul we know and what we know about their social position. Meeks includes evidence from outside the Corinthian correspondence. The survey shows that a significant number of Pauline co-workers and local Christians belong to a fairly well-to-do level of society.[117] This is coupled with indirect evidence, such as the mention in Phil 4:22 that there were Christians in "the household of Caesar" (a group with great opportunities for upward social mobility), that there were both slaves and slave-owners in the Pauline congregations, that exhortation seems directed to "free artisans or craftsmen,"[118] that the instructions concerning Paul's collection for Jerusalem are geared to the economy of people with small but regular income, and that conflicts between Christians (such as the lawsuits in 1 Cor 6: 1-11, and the divisions

---

[116] "For example, to be a freedman in the early years in Roman Corinth, a colony whose settlers were mostly freedmen, would surely have been less of a social disability than it would have been in Rome or Antioch," Meeks, *Urban*, 55. One could also compare the different evaluation accorded to sheer wealth in ancient Rome and in modern Western societies.

[117] Peter Lampe's painstaking prosopographical analysis of Romans 16 shows that a majority of the Roman Christians mentioned in this list of farewell greetings seem to belong in lower social strata, although a few probably have a somewhat higher standing. Idem, *Die stadtrömischen Christen in den ersten beiden Jahrhunderten: Untersuchungen zur Sozialgeschichte* (WUNT Reihe 2, 18). 2. Aufl. Tübingen, 1989, 124-153 (English trans. forthcoming from Fortress Press). Cf. ibid., 112: this should be taken together with the fact that Paul in Rom 12: 13 and 8 expects some Christians to be wealthy enough to support poorer members of the church, p. 63. Cf. also the description of the earliest Roman church in Gülzow, *Sklaverei*, 46-56.

[118] Meeks, *Urban*, 64.

surfacing in the celebration of the Lord's Supper, 1 Cor 11: 17-34) point to the existence of several strata of wealth and social position among the Corinthian Christians.[119] Meeks' only criticism of Theissen, whom he closely follows, is that he has ascribed both high economic status and a high degree of social integration to "the strong" in Corinth, which is historically unlikely. This is probably because Theissen understood social status as a one-dimensional phenomenon, and has not taken into account the possibility and the probability of a discrepancy between different dimensions of rank.[120]

Although the evidence surveyed is fragmentary, random, and often unclear and does not provide the basis of a full description of the social level of even a single Pauline Christian, Meeks considers that the resultant picture allows of some confident generalizations about the social level of Pauline Christians. Only the extreme top and bottom of the Greco-Roman social scale are missing from the picture. "The 'emerging consensus' that Malherbe reports seems to be valid: a Pauline congregation generally reflected a fair cross-section of urban society."[121]

As Meeks has noted, however, the new consensus can have different accents. Judge (and Robert Grant) focus on the higher strata, considering the others to be their social dependents. The early churches thus reflect and conform to the social structure of the surrounding society. Meeks and Theissen, on the other hand, acknowledge the presence of members from these higher groups, but consider the remarkable fact to be the variety of social strata integrated within one community, which rather manifests a *conflict* between the values of the Christian group and those of the surrounding society.[122]

---

[119] In his book *The Thessalonian Correspondence: Pauline Rhetoric and Millenarian Piety* (Philadelphia, 1986, 118-123), Robert Jewett concludes to "a somewhat narrower range of social levels in the Thessalonian church than in other Pauline congregations." Probably it consisted mainly of what Meeks called "typical" Christians, i.e., free artisans and small traders, coming from a stratum of the population that had to witness the economic advancement of others, but participating in it only marginally, thus suffering from a degree of relative deprivation. Ronald Russell differs from Jewett in finding a more "Corinthian" social makeup in this church. The instruction to avoid idleness and work with one's hands seems directed, not to members of a leisured upper class (Malherbe and Hock lean in this direction), but to urban poor, who exploited the generosity of the Christian community, and especially its few wealthier members. Ronald Russell, "The Idle in 2 Thess 3:6-12: An Eschatological or A Social Problem?" *(New Testament Studies* 34, 1988, 105-119).

[120] Meeks, *Urban*, 70.

[121] Malherbe on the "new consensus," *Social Aspects,* 31. Meeks, *Urban,* 73.

[122] Wayne A. Meeks, "The Social Context of Pauline Theology" *(Interpretation* 36, 1982,

What Meeks added methodologically to the scholarly debate on the social level of the first Christians, in addition to expanding the prosopographical analysis of Theissen a little and decisively removing the Roman aristocratic *ordines* from the discussion, lies in his use of the category of status. The introduction of this modern sociological concept and Meeks' perceptive discussion of it has resulted in the breaking up of "social level" into a composite and quite complex phenomenon. We are made aware that a person cannot simply be placed at one level along a scale of social status, and not even on an average level of his or her status-ranking along all the scales (generalized status), or of an average of achieved and attributed status. The tension between the latter two types of status (his foremost example of status inconsistency) makes Meeks introduce a dynamic element into the understanding of social level. Persons who are high in some status dimensions and low in others must somehow be considered to be at more than one social level simultaneously.[123]

The main part of scholarly work in the social description of the first Christians has been directed toward an analysis of the Pauline material. These sources are fairly early, and contain information that is both firsthand and somewhat richer than material from other parts of first-century Christianity. But there are several investigations on other New Testament texts, of which I will just mention three:

David C. Verner has analyzed the social world of the Pastoral letters against the background of our knowledge about the household in the Hellenistic-Roman world.[124] Among much information of sociographical importance is the estimation that only one fourth of the free families were wealthy enough to own even one slave.[125] The fact that slave-owners are admonished in the deutero-Pauline literature (and in the undoubtedly genuine letter to Philemon!) thus tells something of the socioeconomic range of the receiving congregations.[126] In Verner's work

---

266-277), 267. This difference within the new consensus is underlined also by Theissen, "Vers une théorie de l'histoire sociale du christianisme primitif" (*Études Théologiques et Religieuses* 63, 1988, 199-225), 206 note 10, cf. 215. Theissen's emphasis on the unique integrative power of the early Christian church is shared by Gülzow, as was stated above.

[123] Meeks' hypothesis that such people are consequently more change-oriented and conversion-prone than people who have a more unambiguous and well-crystallized social status will be discussed in chapter 4.

[124] David C. Verner, *The Household of God: The Social World of the Pastoral Epistles,* Chico, 1983.

[125] Ibid., 60 f.

[126] Cf. Norman R. Petersen, *Rediscovering Paul: Philemon and the Sociology of Paul's Narrative World.* Philadelphia, 1985, 93-102.

the church of the Pastorals emerges as a social entity of considerable size and diversity, and as a community with substantial personal and financial resources. The church membership covered a wide spectrum of urban social strata, and the leaders of the church were a group that consisted in large part of prosperous householders.[127]

The social constituency of the Lucan community has been investigated by several scholars, among which I would point especially to Philip Francis Esler, as he systematically discusses the relation between Lucan theology and the social reality behind it.[128] It is clear that this community had both wealthy and poor members, and that the former are strongly enjoined to help and support the latter. According to Esler, Luke had a radical "theology of poverty," which included a demand directed at the rich Christians for this worldly redemption of the poor, in addition to the certain eschatological, eternal bliss.[129]

John H. Elliott has made a "sociological exegesis" of 1 Peter, part of which is an attempt to determine the actual social circumstances of the letter receivers in northern Asia Minor. He considers these Christians to have belonged to the predominantly rural population in the inner parts of Asia Minor, and "the vast majority . . . were from the working proletariat of the urban and rural areas," tenant farmers, slaves, and local artisans, thereby differing from what we find in the Pauline churches.[130]

Criticism of the new consensus

Gager's response to the new consensus
John Gager's work on the social constituency of the early Christian movement was done before the closer prosopographical study of Pauline Christianity undertaken by Theissen and the emerging new consensus. Gager reacted to the "new consensus" in one article from 1979, where he reviewed the work of Robert Grant, Abraham Malherbe, and Gerd Theissen,[131] and in another article from 1982, where

---

[127] Verner, *The Household,* 180 f.

[128] Esler, *Community and Gospel,* ch. 7, "The poor and the rich," 164-200.

[129] For further literature, see Russell, "The Idle," 111 note 57.

[130] John H. Elliott, *A Home for the Homeless: A Sociological Exegesis of 1 Peter, Its Situation and Strategy,* Philadelphia, 1981, esp. ch. 2, pages 59-100; quotation from 70.

[131] John G. Gager, "Social Description and Sociological Explanation" (*Religious Study Review* 5, 1979, 174-180; reprinted in Norman K. Gottwald (ed.), *Bible and Liberation: Political and Social Hermeneutics.* Maryknoll, 1983, 428-440); in the following: "Social Description."

he surveyed sociological research on the New Testament.[132] As the differences between them on the issue under discussion are slight, I will use them together.

To begin with, Gager objected that the picture drawn by Malherbe really focused on the letters and the person of Paul only, and that no weighty conclusions could be drawn from this to the social constituency of early Christianity as a whole. This comment on the degree of representativity of the new consensus is, of course, true—first-century Christianity consisted of more than the Pauline churches. On the other hand, Gager did distance himself somewhat from the old consensus, as consisting in "presentations of early Christianity as exclusively proletarian, a movement of slaves, labourers, and outcasts of various sorts . . . it may be seriously doubted that such a view ever existed apart from a few romantics and early Marxists. . . ."[133] In his 1982 article, however, Gager seems to draw nearer to his original position again. The early Christians may not have been poverty-stricken slaves, but they were among the disinherited of the Roman social order.

> Recent times have seen a rather lively debate about the social status of the early Christians and about what it meant to be among the disinherited in the Roman world. One side of the debate, represented by Theissen and myself, holds that most of the members of Christian communities came from the lower classes. The other side, represented by E. A. Judge, Abraham Malherbe, Robert Grant, holds that 'the triumph of Christianity took place from the top down.'[134]

This description of the discussion is not very precise, as it overlooks the considerable difference between Theissen's and Gager's positions.

---

[132] John G. Gager, "Shall We Marry Our Enemies? Sociology and the New Testament," *Interpretation* 36, 1982, 256-265; in the following "Marry."

[133] Gager, "Social Description," 438. As Judge points out (1980, 207 note 18), this is a retreat from Gager's original position in *Kingdom* (1975 = 1971).

[134] Gager, "Marry," 261 f. The final quotation is ascribed to Malherbe, but comes from Grant, in a context where he discusses the effects of Constantine's conversion on the Christianization of the Roman world. Malherbe criticizes this misrepresentation of his views in the second edition of his *Social Aspects of Early Christianity* (1983, 118-121), and concludes by pointing out that he acknowledges that the majority of Christians belonged to the lower strata. The important point, however, is the one demonstrated by Theissen (and others) that the minority of high-status leaders dominated the situation, and probably not only in Corinth.

Theissen does not think early Christianity to have been socially homogeneous (as Gager), and his study of the social constituency of the Corinthian church is one of the main supports of the new consensus.

Gager added: (a) The constant factor that needs explaining in early Christianity is its "revolutionary" character. Formerly this was explained by using the postulate that revolutions arise from the downtrodden mass of the lowest social classes, but today by pointing to the fact that the social roots of revolution are to be found in groups of people who have begun to move downward socially from an upper- or middle-class position. The relative deprivation hypothesis thus replaced the proletariat hypothesis, their common element being that social dissatisfaction is assumed to be the driving force behind early Christianity.[135]

Even if one conceded this new hypothesis to Gager, and agreed that this placing of early Christianity in higher social strata of society follows from its revolutionary character, one would have to conclude that it speaks against Gager's previous position and rather strengthens the "new consensus." Gager's first comment is thus no objection at all to the "new consensus." Perhaps it should also be pointed out that the issue of the social level of the first Christians is not necessarily part of any explanation of the "revolutionary" character of early Christianity.

(b) Gager's second comment was that one must make a distinction between social class and social status in ancient Roman society. Social class was clearly defined in the *ordines*, and "this system of classes or orders prevailed throughout the Roman Empire."[136] There were many persons whose wealth, education, and political influence, in short, whose social status exceeded that of persons in the higher classes, but nonetheless belonged to a low class. Gager thinks that this discrepancy even helps explain why some persons of relatively high social status were attracted to Christianity. Here, in a religion with revolutionary implications, they found an outlet or substitute for their frustrated social aspirations.[137]

---

[135] Judge considers the underlying basic assumption of revolution as a consequence of deprivation to be anachronistic, "Gesellschaft/ Gesellschaft und Christentum III. Neues Testament" (in *Theologische Realenzyklopädie*, vol. 12, New York, Berlin, 1984, 764-769), 766.

[136] Gager, "Social Description," 439. Already in 1977 Malherbe criticized Gager because he uncritically followed Gagé in transposing the Roman system of rank to the whole of the empire, Malherbe, *Social Aspects*, 85 note 49.

[137] "Those who were attracted to the Christian movement as a religion with unmistakably revolutionary implications were not those who stood at the very bottom of the social ladder, that is, the deprived in an absolute sense, but rather those with social aspirations who found their path blocked by the rigidity of the Roman class structure," Gager, "Marry," 263.

This hypothesis is doubly anachronistic. First it applies the concept of "class" to ancient Roman society. As noted above, class is a modern distinguishing criterion of low importance in first-century Mediterranean society. Important differences concerned hereditary status, and such differences may well have cut across separate levels of income. Secondly, as Judge comments on this last hypothesis, although the discord between formal rank (e.g., Roman citizenship) and social status based on wealth was a constant source of tension, "it is beyond historical plausibility that Greeks in the mid-first century could have seriously aspired to senatorial or equestrian enrolment"[138]—something that occurred only two centuries later, as Gager himself mentions. No Greeks were related to the *ordo*-system in the first century, and their reference group was not the aristocracy of the city of Rome, but rather their own peers in the provincial cities.[139] So the idea that the rich sponsors of Paul were frustrated because their locally high status was not honoured in the Roman class-system must be considered anachronistic and completely unproven.[140]

(c) Thirdly, Gager turned to another aspect of the representativity of the new consensus. The few members from higher and more revolutionary classes in early Christianity represent only a small percentage of the church, although 90 percent of our information concerns them. Most of the early Christians came from the lower classes. To Malherbe's (and Theissen's) point that this minority was a dominating minority,[141] Gager replied that "we need to distinguish properly between the issues of political leadership and social constituency," and added that "the methodological issue at stake here . . . concerns the relative weight to be assigned to followers and leaders in any definition and description of the social world of early Christianity."[142]

Having had to admit that early Christianity received members from higher social strata, Gager countered by pointing to their revolutionary character, which actually does qualify them as a dominating minority! But here Gager shifts ground again: now the question is said to concern the social background of the majority of members. But in ancient society the issues of leadership and social constituency fade into each

---

[138] Judge, "The Social Identity of the First Christians," 207 note 18.
[139] So also Meeks, *First Urban*, 215 note 20.
[140] "Dass aber die reichen Gönner des Paulus frustriert gewesen seien, weil ihr hoher Status in ihren Heimatstädten innerhalb des römischen Klassensystems nicht honoriert worden sei, dafür wäre viel mehr beweiskräftiges Material nötig." Judge, in *Theologische Realenzyklopädie* (1984), 766.
[141] Malherbe, *Social Aspects* (1977), 72.
[142] Gager, "Social Description," 436.

other. If the unheard majority in the early Christian house churches was attached to the leading stratum through patron-client relationships (as Judge and Malherbe have made plausible), social constituency was not simply a question of how much a person earned or what status he or she had as a unique individual. It was also a question of belonging to, being dependent on, and loyal to a certain "house" and its patron. Consequently, the leading stratum of wealthy, educated, and energetic Christians from higher social strata would have to be assigned a high relative weight in any description of the social status of the Christians groups.

It seems, then, that Gager somewhat reluctantly has had to concede a number of points to the new consensus:
—the early Christian movement was not proletarian, although its majority came from the lower classes,
—this majority was not a very revolutionary or innovative one, which makes it harder to believe that they engaged in religious renewal in compensation for any experienced deprivation,
—the dominant minority of this movement were members of the higher classes.
I think it fair to say that the new consensus has not really been shaken by the criticism from Gager.

How representative is the new consensus?
In his 1980 report on the state of research in the sociological interpretation of the New Testament, Robin Scroggs found it remarkable that the same data concerning social level as those used by the old consensus could now be made to support such different conclusions.[143] This must come from the specific emphasis that the proponents of the new consensus[144] put on some parts of the evidence while disregarding other parts, i.e., by emphasizing the Acts of the Apostles and their historical veracity, while de-emphasizing the synoptic material. Furthermore they determine the social location of the community as a whole from the position of a small, wealthy elite within it, and disregard other forms of social alienation than the economic, thus equating social level with economic level. To summarize: the new consensus does not represent all the evidence, but only the situation

---

[143] Robin Scroggs, "The Sociological Interpretation of the New Testament: The Present State of Research" (*New Testament Studies* 26, 1980, 164-179), 168-171.
[144] Scroggs here refers to Judge, Malherbe, Theissen, Hengel, Grant, Lee, Wuellner, and Buchanan.

in Pauline Christianity, and within this it focuses on a small, non-representative elite.

Edwin Judge has attempted an answer to Scroggs' critique.[145] He begins by pointing out the ambiguity inherent in the statement that the synoptics "speak for important segments of the first-century church." The assumption of Scroggs (and, one might add, of form criticism) is that the contents of the Gospels has been shaped in a direct, simple fashion by the interests of these communities. "Therefore if the gospels condemn wealth, this implies a community which does not enjoy it."[146] But that conclusion is not a necessary one. It is easy to imagine an evangelist who, like the author of the Epistle of James, is sharply critical of the use of wealth amongst those for whom he wrote, and uses the tradition to counter this.[147] The Synoptic Gospels can't then be used as evidence that contradicts the conclusions of the new consensus.

The historical trustworthiness of the Acts of the Apostles is a matter under discussion. Classical scholars and historians, and increasingly also the exegetes, put it fairly high, as Luke does not commit any anachronisms in that historical information that can be checked from other sources. But the new consensus does not stand or fall with this, as it is to a large extent argued from the first-hand evidence of the Pauline letters.

Scroggs contends like Gager that the majority of early Christians belonged to lower strata, and that the majority must determine our picture of the social location of the whole community. Judge's answer is that the movement of new ideas and beliefs being spread to broad strata is "the work of highly articulate people with social influence," or in other words, that the minority in question dominates the interior and exterior life of the Christian groups.

I would add that "the social location of the community as a whole" seems to be a question-begging formulation, as it presupposes a homogeneity of the first Christians, which in itself is unlikely and would first have to be proved. If it be granted that the community was in fact constituted by people from several social strata, how would the category "social location of the community as a whole" be understood, except as a statistical mean of some quantifiable factor like affluence?

---

[145] Judge 1980, 208 f.

[146] Ibid.

[147] This is actually how Philip F. Esler understands the Gospel of Luke in his *Community and Gospel* (1987), esp. ch. 2 and 7, and also—somewhat differently—Wolfgang Stegemann, "Nachfolge Jesu," 149-153.

As Scroggs wants to introduce relative deprivation as a factor, and Gager and others consider it important in explaining recruitment to the millenarian Christian movement, it should be remembered that this hypothetical concept, in spite of its attractiveness, is considered to be completely unusable as a sociological instrument by many sociologists. In the main it is an interior, subjective feeling, which may refer to real or fictive deprivation in all areas of life, and it may be conscious and verbalized or merely felt as a vague uneasiness, all of which means that a statement that a certain person or group is experiencing relative deprivation can hardly be falsified.[148] James Beckford has pointed out that it is very hard to decide objectively where it occurs, how strong it is, and how common within a specific group, and that there is as yet no way of disproving relative deprivation as a causal factor, which, of course, means that it does not explain anything either. He concludes: "Blanket explanations of this kind are an interesting exercise in metaphysics but hardly a convincing demonstration of scientific precision."[149] Roy Wallis has shown that often it is simply the ideological system of a movement that provides the material from which conclusions are made to a previous state of deprivation. As the reasoning goes, the movement emphatically offers the factor "x," therefore those who are recruited to the movement must have felt deprived of "x," regardless of whether this is actually verified by asking them.[150] And a methodological weakness of this theory is that one actually concludes from something known (the existence of a specific religious movement or sect) to something unknown, namely the real reason for the sect's origin and the reason why people join it. Then one turns around and considers the result of the first operation (some form of relative deprivation) to be the explanation of the known phenomenon one started with (the sect's existence)—a clear instance of a "post factum" interpretation.[151] Judge rightly states that the only observed basic source of alienation for

[148] Truly "a weasel term," as O. C. Edwards Jr. puts it in his review of Gager's work, *Anglican Theological Review* 65, 1983, 434.

[149] James Beckford,The *Trumpet of Prophecy: A Sociological Study of Jehovah's Witnesses.* Oxford, 1975, 154-158.

[150] Roy Wallis, "Relative Deprivation and Social Movements: A Cautionary Note" (*British Journal of Sociology* 26, 1975, 360-363).

[151] Bryan R. Wilson, *Magic and the Millennium*, London 1973, 289. Cf. also the remarks of Michael White on recent revision of the role and nature of deprivation as a factor in religious commitment in the work of Charles Glock and Rodney Stark, "Sociological Analysis of Early Christian Groups: A Social Historian's Response" (*Sociological Analysis* 47, 1986, 249-266), 260.

Christians in the ancient society was their refusal to participate in cultic ceremonies. And this is, of course, not a cause but a result of their becoming Christians.

Scroggs adds a fifth question concerning the sociology of knowledge of New Testament research: May not the new consensus be related to a wish of finding a more respectable, middle-class origin of the church, a wish typical of the more conventional, "post-revolutionary" 1970s? One could counter, as Scroggs himself does, with a question concerning the motives of those who want a church beginning in poverty. Interesting as the sociology of research is, it can obviously not decide an argument that must be resolved by reference to historical evidence. Besides, some scholars (e.g., Judge) did put forward their new perspective well before the change of mood Scroggs refers to.

Is New Testament social history possible?
Georg Schöllgen has delivered a sharp critique of the work of Meeks, which in some respects affects the whole tradition of social historical analysis stretching behind him to Theissen and Judge.[152] Schöllgen's basic contention is that we know too little about the social facts of the ancient cities and of the Christian congregations in them to draw any valid conclusions concerning the social structure of the latter. The ancient cities were not homogeneously "urban," to begin with. Most small towns in ancient times had a strong agrarian character,[153] and the small, backward towns of Galatia with their high proportion of autochthonous inhabitants were very dissimilar from a bustling, cosmopolitan city like Corinth, which started as a Roman colony and had a very mixed, international population. Meeks' picture of the inhabitants is anachronistic: all were not artisans or traders, many were simply farmers on the lands adjoining the town, and not a few were casual workers.

Turning to Meeks' picture of the Pauline churches, Schöllgen finds it very unlikely that they all had the same social stratification.[154] This would presuppose that Pauline mission in every place tried to reach some specific strata, or that it tried to reach people from all strata and succeeded uniformly in converting the same proportion of highly and lowly situated people. This is improbable, and the available evidence

---

[152] Georg Schöllgen, "Was missen wir über die Sozialstruktur der paulinischen Gemeinden?" (*New Testament Studies* 34, 1988, 71-82).
[153] Cf. Schöllgen, "Die Didache—ein frühes Zeugnis für Landgemeinden?" (*Zeitschrift für neutestamentliche Wissenschaft* 76, 1985, 140-143).
[154] In this he receives support from Peter Lampe, *Die stadtrömischen Christen*, 451.

indicates that there existed socioeconomic differences between Pauline churches, e.g., between the poor Macedonian Christians and the well-to-do Corinthians. In fact, Corinth is the only Pauline church we know enough about to draw any conclusions at all concerning its social constituency. Further, Schöllgen contends the validity of the direct and indirect indicators of higher social status used by Meeks (and before him Theissen): living in a "house" could mean having a small house or a rented apartment, travels can be made at the cost of other people, working with one's hands was not a characteristic of artisans only, there is no possibility of quantifying the social differences evidenced by the conflicts in Corinth. And, even granting the higher status of some individuals among the thirty or so persons scrutinized in prosopographical analysis, we cannot be sure that they are at all representative for Pauline Christianity generally. Finally, it would also be a methodological mistake to consider that several interpretations, which in themselves are just possible, when put together acquire a cumulative, convergent power, which lifts the thesis as a whole to a higher level of probability.

This critique leads Schöllgen on to a fundamental questioning of the New Testament social historical enterprise as such. To begin with, the ancient sources in general are so scarce and so meagre that very little can be concluded from them concerning social history, except for the higher classes, such as the Roman aristocracy. This difficulty is even more acute when we come to the Christian sources, which say very little about this dimension of reality. And, as the little information they give is of a doubtful representativity, he concludes:

> However exegetically and theologically justified the question concerning the social structure of the early Christian congregations may be, it seems to me necessary to admit that it cannot receive an adequate answer because of the lack of information of the source material in the present state of exegesis. This, by the way, applies to the whole pre-Constantinian period. Even the churches of Carthage, Rome and Alexandria in the first half of the third century, for which considerably richer sources are available, remain to a large extent in the dark, as far as their social stratification is concerned.[155]

This negative judgment on the possibility of New Testament social history as such results from the type of demands Schöllgen makes on it. In order to be a complete analysis, social history must be able

---

[155] Schöllgen, "Sozialstruktur" (1988), 78; my translation.

to make two things: (a) to show in which different social strata the members of a congregation are represented [which could be called "representation analysis"; my term], and (b) to show how many Christians belong to each stratum, and how they are related to each other quantitatively [correspondingly: "distribution analysis"]. And because one cannot presuppose any homogeneity of early Christianity, these two analyses have to be made on all different types of congregations of the early church. For a few churches, like Corinth or Carthage,[156] one could possibly make a fact-finding investigation sufficient for a representation analysis, while the material is everywhere insufficient for an analysis of quantitative distribution.

I think it is correct to state that a full analysis of social structure must provide a picture of the quantitative relations between different social strata, and that ancient Christian source material simply does not meet that requirement. But it seems reasonable to distinguish between degrees of knowledge concerning the social structure of a community, and between the corresponding levels of analysis. It is a step above zero to know which social strata are represented at all in early Christian groups. And such a "representation analysis" is what Judge, Theissen, and Meeks have made through their careful sifting of prosopographical evidence. Their results confirm that the early Christian movement in Asia Minor, Greece, and Italy in the middle of the first century was not exclusively a movement among the poorest strata of society. This is important information that has repercussions on our whole understanding of first-century Christianity, e.g., on the plausibility of hypotheses operating with the idea that Christianity was a phenomenon of millenarian compensation for the deprived, downtrodden masses.

And even if no one of these scholars has even aimed at completing his work with a "distribution analysis," the work of Theissen approaches in that direction. Through his close analysis of Corinthian social relations, showing what a dominant role Christians from the upper strata played there, Theissen has provided a deeper understanding of the functioning and experienced reality of the social structure in this church, which with some justification could be characterized as constituting a *qualitative* distribution analysis.

---

[156] Schöllgen has made a social historical analysis of the church in Carthage in his *Ecclesia sordida? Zur Frage der sozialen Schichtung frühchristlicher Gemeinden am Beispiel Karthagos zur Zeit Tertullians*, Münster, 1984.

Conceptual weaknesses in New Testament social description
Another type of general criticism is delivered by Richard Rohrbaugh, who finds a considerable conceptual confusion in the discussion among exegetes during the last twenty-five years of the question concerning the social level of the first Christians.[157] In his opinion, the main methodological weakness is the lack of a precise and clear definition of the concept "social class." Instead, many exegetes use the term in a popular, nontechnical way, usually presuming that level of income is the apposite criterion for determining social class.[158] John Gager started to shift the ground from income statistics to the psychology of alienation, and from a discussion of class to one about status, by introducing the term relative deprivation from Glock and Aberle, and characterizing early Christianity as a movement of the disprivileged. This approach has certain advantages, but leaves the concept of class untreated in the background. Both John Elliott and Wayne Meeks avoid "class" altogether as an anachronistic and too undistinct criterion, and the latter puts in its place a synthetic, multivariable, and gradational notion of social status, which has some problems of its own.

Rohrbaugh makes a careful analysis of social class theory, following the social scientists Stanislaw Ossowski, Rodolfo Stavenhagen, and Erik Olin Wright. He distinguishes between gradational and relational conceptions of class, where the first type is exemplified by the quantifiable gradation scheme offered by using the criterion of income level. Introducing a number of other variables, such as education, political position, heredity, creates what Ossowski termed a synthetic gradational approach, which quickly becomes very complex. The real weakness of this approach, however, is that the variables are not commensurable, wherefore their relative weight has to be left to the subjective judgment and predilections of the observer.[159]

---

[157] Richard L. Rohrbaugh, "Methodological Considerations in the Debate over the Social Class Status of Early Christians" (*Journal of the American Academy of Religion* 52, Chico 1984, 519-546). Rohrbaugh has some useful general remarks on the choices to make in the interest of clarity when investigating this issue: Which social universe do we refer to: Rome or also other cities? cities or countryside? which areas? Are we discussing individuals or social groups? A class is always part of a social system, which must be described analytically as a whole. Relations between class and status are difficult to describe—which is to be the frame of reference? And, finally, we have to decide which is our interest: hermeneutical (aiming at a comparison between early and our contemporary Christianity), or exegetical (what did these writings say to their own first readers?). Ibid., 521 f.

[158] Rohrbaugh mentions Hengel, Malherbe, and Theissen, "Social Class," 523-525.

[159] This is also a weakness of Meeks' synthetic approach, Rohrbaugh, "Social Class," 530.

Relational conceptions of class focus on qualitative position in relation to other actors. Being a father in relation to a son, or an owner, creditor, and master in relation to one who is a nonowner, debtor, and employee or slave points to a more decisive criterion of social position than simply the amount of money, or education, etc., that the two persons have at their command. Relational conceptions of class are analytical and not static, aiming at explaining both the source of inequality and its dynamic. In Marxist perspective the dominant class is made up of those who own the means of production, employ or control others, and do not produce anything themselves, and these three dichotomies may have some heuristical value in finding out about the social stratification of the first Christians.

Stavenhagen has shown that one must distinguish between class and status systems. The former concerns economic stratification as it is functioning, while the latter reflects a widely understood, fixed value system that originally mirrored the economic control system, which has since changed. That is why there exist discrepancies between status and class systems, so that persons who have a high social status actually may not be identical with those who control the economy. Status systems are often conservative, and the relative deprivation felt within them is individualistic and unrelated to any class conflict. Therefore, New Testament scholars ought to separate the question of status from the question concerning class.[160] "The individualistic character of status positions, for example, makes status analysis useful in estimating feelings of relative deprivation" and social aspirations in general, but not in making judgments about the politico-economic system. Rohrbaugh's conclusion is that "a variety of particular politico-economic relational oppositions might prove useful as heuristic tools" in finding an answer to questions concerning social level in early Christianity. This is more helpful than looking at status positions, or using gradational class conceptions, as these two approaches cannot avoid the subjectivity of synthetic judgments.[161]

Rohrbaugh indicates "that a broadly defined understanding of social class as a politico-economic power group will best serve the needs of the New Testament scholar," and points out that the important ranking factor in antiquity was to have political power, because there wealth tended to follow power and not the other way around, as in modern

---

[160] Rohrbaugh on Pliny's oft-quoted comment about Christians coming from *omnis ordinis:* "Is this a reference to class, as New Testament scholars often assume? Or is it a reference to a status stratification system Pliny is anxious to maintain?" ibid., 539 note 17.
[161] Ibid., 539 f.

capitalist societies. The Christians of the first century belonged, together with a vast majority of the population, to the powerless, who did not politically control the economic system, but were subject to the decisions of others. The fear of losing what position you had, or in other words the fear of downward mobility, was nearly universal.[162]

My first objection to Rohrbaugh's impressive analysis can be stated as a question: Would the application of his class level criteria make any great difference to the picture that Theissen and Meeks have arrived at with the help of a less complicated conceptual tool box? Secondly, the problem of conceptual confusion does not seem to me to have been decisively solved by Rohrbaugh, even if several things have become clearer. The difficulties of synthetical class and status conceptions, and the advantages of relational as compared to gradational approaches stand out very well. But Rohrbaugh himself cannot avoid gradational language, e.g., when he speaks of having a high social status, or of being in a powerless position. Substituting "powerless" for "lower class" does not camouflage the gradational thinking. It seems as if both the status system and the class system are gradational, after all.

The class system is said to be constituted of political and economic power. But even if it is true that the latter tended to follow the former, these two systems or categories of power are not identical. The relations between the three systems (status, power, class) are still confusing in Rohrbaugh's description. On the one hand, a millionaire could be in control over large economic resources, and yet be as far away from the centre of political power as the head of a noble, but ruined family. So, being upper class economically did not mean that a person was also highly placed in the status system, nor that he belonged among the upper strata of political power. But on the other hand, we know that in Roman society the peak of all three systems was located within that top 0.5 percent of the population that we encountered in the work of Alföldy. Curiously enough, Rohrbaugh's final analysis also has the same effect of telling us very little about the social level of the Christians. His unwillingness to discuss degrees of economic or political power or of social status makes him concentrate on the absolute, i.e., top level only. But, of course, economic control at provincial or city or village level existed and was a social reality. And hereditary status meant a lot for the social attitudes in a society so intent on the pursuit of honour—and honour existed outside the *ordines*.

---

[162] Ibid., 542 f.

If gradation is rigidly excluded, it is not possible to discuss the question of social level at all. The alternative seems to be to allow the gradational type of question, knowing that it is difficult to guard against subjective evaluations and that it also tends to introduce an anachronistic perspective. But all our analytical concepts like "class" and "status" are also modern. Historical research after all consists in putting our inevitably modern questions to the ancient texts, with our eyes wide open to the distorting effects of our analytical language, and a corresponding readiness to be corrected by the data themselves.

What has been achieved?

At the end of this critical survey of research concerning the issue of the social level of the first Christians, it seems appropriate to summarize the fruits of scholarly discussion. This chapter has not been aimed at proposing a solution to the material question of which social level the first Christians were located at, but I think one can point to some general conclusions in this field too. However, the most important advances in the continuous discussion of the issue concern the methodological dimensions, and this is where we will begin.

(1) A general methodological conclusion from the discussion presented above is that an inductive method (assembling the data, then finding the best theoretical interpretation of them) seems more appropriate and fruitful than a deductive one (where you start with a sociological theory and apply it to the data, or use it as a fact-finding instrument). This is especially the case if the theories or models from which search operations and deductions start are of a very general, grand-theory type; not seldom such theories have an inbuilt evolutionistic and reductionistic slant. On the other hand, a modified deductive approach, e.g., applying a clearly specified sociological hypothesis about the relation between types of religious movements and their social constituency, can be very useful as an heuristic guideline, indicating what kind of phenomena the researcher should look for.

(2) The evidence is too scant to allow a full social history or full social description of the "first Christians." There is good reason to guard against a facile optimism in regard to the possible results even of this basic fact-finding investigation. Is the fact that the "new consensus" actually mostly covers Pauline Christianity simply due to the scarcity

of historical evidence from other sources and the difficulty of evaluating and using the ones we have in the Gospels? It is true that the New Testament writings simply tell us more about Pauline Christianity, but there is something disconcerting about the lack of a good reconstructive method to apply to the Gospels. Until this lack has been filled, the degree of representativity of the new consensus must be considered to be lower than desirable.

(3) Romantic proletarian notions have been discarded; early Christianity is seen to be (a) more spread in different social strata, and (b) more a phenomenon of marginalized middle strata. Even Gager, who stands closer to the old consensus, feels the need to qualify the deprivation experienced by the first Christians—we are not back to Kautsky's proletarian movement or Deissmann's romantic picture of the lowly, but noble Christians. At no time or place was the Christian church a movement located primarily in the lowest stratum of society, as it attracted people from different social strata right from its inception.

(4) Scholarship has more and more learnt to avoid homogenizing the evidence. It is not unreasonable to agree with Theissen's general picture that many of the early Palestinian Jewish Christians belonged to a poor rural population, while their contemporary fellow Christians in the Hellenistic societies to the north and west of Palestine represented more a cross-section of urban society. The transition process behind this difference entailed several dimensions: the temporal (situations changed over time), the socioeconomic (a greater number of wealthy people became Christians when the movement really opened its doors to the Gentiles), the socioecological (the churches in Hellenistic societies were mostly urban), the sociopolitical (the Jewish Christians in Palestine increasingly became the socially downward-moving victims of nationalistic political struggle and oppression in the decades preceding and following the first Jewish-Roman war, while the situation of their Gentile Christian contemporaries was more peaceful), and sociocultural factors were also changed: Christianity became located in Hellenistic city culture, which meant more of an orientation toward and communication with the language, education, and values of the larger society and the ruling strata. Consequently, we can see a broader representation of different social levels within diaspora or Gentile Christianity, and the early Christians were better integrated in Greek-speaking Hellenistic society than they were in Palestine.

Not even in local Christian groups all members could be placed at the same social level. The very first Christian community in Jerusalem seems to have been constituted by at least two very different groups: one a group of marginalized, jobless Galileans, cut off from their families and social context and income, the other a group of fairly affluent, cultured, Greek-speaking, and international Jews, who had settled in Jerusalem. Social and ethnic differentiations were sometimes overcome within the church, and sometimes they were not. In Pauline Christianity there seems to have existed several social strata, related to one another in mutual support and cooperation (in Theissen's phrase a "patriarchalism of love"). The differentiation within the Jerusalem church was not solved in such a happy fashion as it may have been in, for example, Corinth.

All these observations add up to the necessity of a careful differentiation of the evidence concerning social location. A scholar must ask: from which time and place and ethnic segment does this evidence come? Which people does it concern, and of whom does it not tell anything? And how does this piece of evidence relate to the overall picture of change and diversity?

(5) Each Christian group has to be located in its own host society. This means, to begin with, that the Roman system of *ordines* has to be left outside this issue, as it pertains only to Roman and imperial aristocracy. Probably no Christian of the first century belonged to this top-level social stratum. For Pauline, and perhaps also Lucan, churches the host society was the surrounding Hellenistic urban society of the Eastern Empire, for 1 Peter a more agrarian backwater area in the inner parts of Asia Minor, etc. For Jewish Christianity we need a more systematic description of the social structure of Palestinian society, especially its rural areas. One difficulty in this task of seeing every writing and different Christian community against its own background is not only that we do not know enough about specific cities and areas and their social history in the first century, but also that we cannot with any certainty locate all New Testament writings in time and geography (cf. the Epistle to the Hebrews).

(6) Criteria for "social level" have been refined and made more precise. There is now a growing awareness that there need be no correlation between social level and literary culture, as Deissmann had surmised, when he concluded from an alleged low literary level of the New Testament writings to a low social level of the first Christians. Even disregarding the well-known fact that the NT writings are not homogeneous in literary level, it has to be stated that literary level is

not by itself a sufficient criterion to decide the social level of the writer (much less the readers).

Generally, much more attention has been given to ascertainable social facts, such as income level, type of occupation, civic position. But the conceptual apparatus needed to analyse the question of social location and social constituency has not yet become sufficiently clear and precise to allow a systematical comparison between the data and a set of criteria. "Social class" could still serve as an analytical concept of some importance, if duly refined. "Status" is also adequate, but should be operationalized into a set of applicable criteria; and it should not be equated with "class." Although much used by several scholars, "relative deprivation" is not possible to use as a criterion of social level, simply because it refers to subjective realities that are not measurable, and also because it is not stratum-specific.

(7) Social constituency is a many-dimensioned quality, primarily referring to group identity, more than individual status or class position. If we talk at all about the social level of the first Christians, we have to realize that this should not be understood as the mean or composite of all individual levels, but rather as referring to the location of several groups or house-communities related to each other.

The very task of trying to write the social history or describe the social structure of the earliest Christianity puts us into a closer contact with the society of which the early church was inevitably a part. This compels us to become more down-to-earth and more attentive to concrete historical details, and to the differences between data from different contexts. So the attempt will result in a more nuanced picture of the early church itself. We will also see more clearly than before the similarities between primitive Christianity and other religious movements, how "human" it was, or in other words how influenced by the social realities of its own time.

The work done and to be done on the issue of the social level of the earliest Christians also results in a better understanding of what we really ask about when looking for "social level." The complexity of this concept leads us to realize the complexity of the relation between church and society generally, and perhaps also to an awareness that even a successful classification of the first Christians along this specific and complex dimension is not the same as an explanation of the movement we are seeing more clearly. Elucidating and understanding the social constituency of the first-century church is an important task, but it does not tell us how it originated or why it attracted so many from different social strata.

3 Early Christianity as a Millenarian Sect

Two of the earliest attempts in applying sociological concepts and models to the understanding of early Christianity, both published 1975, used the comparative method, although in different ways. John G. Gager compared early Christianity to millenarian movements (mainly in Melanesia of our times), thus taking up and using the social scientific tradition of anthropological research. Robin Scroggs, on the other hand, compared the earliest church to a sect model constructed from an analysis of Christian sects in the Middle Ages and post-Reformation centuries. This model stood in a long scholarly tradition in the sociology of religion, all the way from Max Weber's first remarks on "church" and "sect."

There are undeniable similarities between the religious and social phenomena treated by these two social scientific traditions and signified by the terms "sect" and "millenarian movement." Not seldom sects are strongly millenarian in their outlook and behaviour, while millenarian movements often exhibit attitudes of exclusivity and protest toward society and its secular and religious authorities, attitudes that can well be characterized as sectarian. To take just one example of how close these two groups of phenomena are perceived to be, one could point to the work of the sociologist Bryan R. Wilson, *Magic and the Millennium* (1973), which all through its 500 pages treats of millennialism and sects. This is why I have allowed myself to use "millenarian sect" in the heading of this section. Methodologically, however, these two types of analytical approach are not identical, and biblical scholars who have applied these models to the New Testament usually choose one or the other. It will therefore be more appropriate to describe the research done in this field as proceeding along two separate lanes of scholarly tradition, one in the lane of anthropology, the other in the lane of sociology of religion.

The millenarian movement model applied to early Christianity

Early Christianity as a millenarian movement: Gager

When analysing the "earliest Christianity as a millenarian movement" in his seminal work *Kingdom and Community* (1975),[1] Gager followed the method he outlined in his introduction: "to examine specific problems in terms of theoretical models from recent work in the social sciences. In each case the model has been formulated independently of Christian evidence. My procedure will be to test them against information based on early Christian documents."[2] The models he used were taken from the discipline of cultural anthropology, especially the work of Kenelm Burridge and, to a lesser degree, of I. C. Jarvie, Yonina Talmon, and Peter Worsley, on millenarian cargo cults in Melanesia from our own century.[3]

Following Jarvie, Gager pointed to four basic traits common to all millenarian cults: (1) the promise of an imminent arrival of heaven on earth; (2) the overthrow or reversal of the present social order; (3) the communal life that is characterized by a strong release of emotional energy; and (4) the very brief life span of the movement. To these Gager himself added a fifth: (5) the central role of a messianic, prophetic, or charismatic leader.[4] Such movements typically arise among the disinherited (Worsley), and Gager proceeds to show that politically, economically, and religiously the situation in Palestine in the time of Jesus was ripe for the outbreak of such a movement: large segments of the population were politically alienated and repressed,

---

[1] John G. Gager, *Kingdom and Community: The Social World of Early Christianity*. Englewood Cliffs, New Jersey, 1975, 20-37. Another scholar who simultaneously and independently of Gager used the anthropological millenarian movement model in understanding the early Christian movement was Sheldon R. Isenberg, "Power Through Temple and Torah in Greco-Roman Palestine," in *Christianity, Judaism and Other Greco-Roman Cults*. FS Morton Smith, vol. II. Leiden, 1975, 24-52.

[2] Gager, *Kingdom and Community*, 12.

[3] Kenelm O. L. Burridge, *New Heaven, New Earth: A Study of Millenarian Activities*. Oxford, 1969; Gager explains on p. 36 f why he has chosen to rely on the work of Burridge. I. C. Jarvie, *The Revolution in Anthropology*. Chicago, 1967. Yoninna Talmon, "Pursuit of the Millennium: The Relation between Religious and Social Change" (originally in *Archives Européennes de Sociologie* 3, Paris, 1962; reprinted in W. Lessa and E. Vogt (eds.), *Reader in Comparative Religion: An Anthropological Approach*. 2d. ed., New York, 1965, 522-537). Peter Worsley, *The Trumpet Shall Sound. A Study of "Cargo" Cults in Melanesia*. New York, 1968 (2d. rev. ed., 1st ed. London, 1957).

[4] Gager, *Kingdom and Community*, 21. This is supported from Talmon, Worsley, and Burridge, idem, 28 f.

economically disadvantaged and made to feel like impure outsiders. The situation can be characterized as premillenarian. That this was the kind of situation to which Jesus addressed himself is clear from many parts of the gospel evidence.

But even this kind of situation needs a spark to ignite it or a catalyst to start the process, and this role is played by the charismatic prophet, who in this case was Jesus from Nazareth. The prophet typically articulates the needs and aspirations of the disinherited in a new vision of the world as it ought to be and soon will be. He gives new formulations of the old redemptive media, which in a Jewish context were the Torah and the temple cult, at the same time criticizing the old values and ways of access to the sacred centre of reality. "You have heard it said, but I say to you . . ." sounds a characteristic note of the revolutionary and literally radical proclamation of Jesus to the masses.

This new world is proleptically present in the community around the prophet, which understands itself as the true version of society, founded anew, in immediate contact with the Holy One. Life in the millenarian movement is strongly egalitarian and devoid of fixed structures, and traditional status distinctions concerning wealth, sex, and kinship are discarded; consequently it is seen both by adherents and opponents as a revolutionary movement. Jesus seems to have had and wanted a group of close followers, who left their ordinary lives behind and formed a new community around their master. This group is called blessed and inheritors of the coming kingdom.

What about the brief life span of the millenarian Jesus movement? Gager answers this question by claiming that the movement survived the death of its prophet, but that it continued in a different, nonmillenarian form as a vigorous missionary community—a transformation Gager interprets with the help of the sociological theory of cognitive dissonance (which is not treated here).

As for example Thomas F. Best has pointed out, Gager's theoretical models are taken from cultural contexts very far from first-century Palestine. It seems that the presupposition of comparability that lies behind the comparisons that Gager undertakes has been left undiscussed. As it is, the divide between Melanesian cargo cults in the twentieth century and the early Christians in the first is simply too great to permit any convincing analogies. The former can only be regarded as interesting illustrative material, but not as models with explanatory force.[5]

---

[5] Thomas F. Best, "The Sociological Study of the New Testament: Promise and Peril of a New Discipline" (*Scottish Journal of Theology* 36, 1983, 181-194), 189.

Christopher Rowland has also indicated a certain reluctance to use information from millenarian movements outside the Judaeo-Christian tradition, and suggested comparison with other examples, closer to the early church in outlook and better documented. What he is thinking of is especially radical movements in Europe of the sixteenth and seventeenth centuries, where the nonfulfillment of hopes was compensated by a complete spiritualization of what was once political utopianism.[6] While it is evident that there are interesting similarities between such movements and early Christianity, it seems that this suggestion would land the researcher in the opposite difficulty: a too great proximity. Similarities between sixteenth-century Christian movements and the early church can be more readily explained as attempts by the later Christians to emulate the New Testament ideal than as the influence of some universal millenarian pattern.

As a matter of fact, the distant comparison may not be so distant after all. In his scathing criticism of Gager's work,[7] Jonathan Z. Smith points out that Gager uses the work of the three anthropologists Kenelm Burridge, Peter Worsley, and I. C. Jarvie to construct his model of the millenarian movement without being aware of the deep theoretical differences among them. This points to a rather shallow acquaintance with the chosen model. Secondly, the four traits of millenarian movements outlined by Jarvie were not developed independently of Christian evidence, as

> they were derived from Norman Cohn's description of Palestinian Jewish eschatology, R. Eisler's description of early Christianity as "yet another millenarian movement," H. Zinsser's description of the Saint Vitus phenomenon and other Medieval Christian ecstatic movements, and Arnold J. Toynbee's characterization of Marxism as "pre-rabbinical, Maccabaean Jewish apocalypticism."[8]

It seems that Gager's claim to be using social scientific models that have been "formulated independently of Christian evidence" is unfounded. J. Z. Smith is right in concluding that what Gager has applied in his analysis of early Christianity is not so much an independent sociological model of universal application as a self-fulfilling prophecy.

---

[6] Christopher Rowland, "Reading the New Testament Sociologically: An Introduction" (*Theology* 88, 1985, 358-364), 360 f.

[7] J. Z. Smith, "Too Much Kingdom, Too Little Community" (*Zygon: Journal of Religion and Science* 13, 1978, 123-130).

[8] Ibid., 127 f.

Smith also finds Gager's use of the model inadequate. All the evidence concerning the poverty and powerlessness of Jesus' first followers is not presented, and as regards the ideology of poverty this is not fully discussed—it could point both to lack of riches and to the abandoning of riches, which belong in two different social backgrounds. And even if these people had been really disinherited, this fact in itself "can be only a barely necessary and scarcely sufficient cause" for their millenarian character.[9] The model does not explain the rise of the Christian movement and why its adherents did not become Essenes or Zealots instead. As a matter of fact, "all of the well-known Jewish groups (sects/philosophies) at the time of Jesus can be understood as millenarian groups," which means, of course, that this and other similar, all-inclusive comparative approaches are only useful for a preliminary categorization, but not for a more precise sociological analysis, that could distinguish between Jewish groups and movements of that time.[10]

Tidball has further criticized proponents of the millenarian interpretation of the Gospels for tending to make the evidence more homogeneous than it is: the eschatological aspect of Jesus' teaching is isolated and overemphasized, and all evidence showing him as more of a Jewish teacher and a leader of a group that he wanted to continue after his death is discarded.[11]

Finally, one notes that Gager makes no distinctions within early Christianity. It appears in his treatment to be one, homogeneous millenarian movement, all the way from the beginnings in the ministry of Jesus.

Millenarian characteristics in Pauline Christianity: Meeks
At the large symposium on apocalypticism in Uppsala in August 1979, Wayne A. Meeks gave a lecture in which he discussed whether Pauline Christianity can rightfully be called a millenarian movement.[12] He begins by noting that there exists no consensus between social scientists on "a unified theory of the functions of millenarian beliefs which could then generate a series of predictive hypotheses to be

---

[9] Ibid., 128.
[10] Richard A. Horsley, "Popular Prophetic Movements at the Time of Jesus, Their Principal Features and Social Origins" (*Journal for the Study of the New Testament* 26, 1986, 3-27), 11.
[11] Derek Tidball, *An Introduction to the Sociology of the New Testament.* Exeter, 1983, 37-40.
[12] Wayne A. Meeks, "Social Functions of Apocalyptic Language in Pauline Christianity" (in Hellholm (ed.), *Apocalypticism in the Mediterranean World* (1983), 687-706).

tested by our historical and exegetical research."[13] Instead he formulates six general theses, on which many social scientists could agree:

1. The meaning of millenarian (or rather: eschatological) beliefs must be understood from the function they serve for the groups that hold them.

2. Usually prophetic revelations provide the centre or ordering complex of beliefs.

3. These beliefs introduce innovations in a traditional society, often by new combinations of accepted traditions.

4. Members of millenarian movements have often experienced frustration of their access to social power and its media of expression.

5. The medium for change is primarily cognitive, i.e., a counter-interpretation of reality that makes sense of a world that seems to have gone mad. It is not first a compensation for (relative) deprivation, but aims at relieving cognitive dissonance.

6. These myths and beliefs pave the way for the building of a new plausibility structure, or in other words for the institutionalization of a new, alternative community.

From his detailed analyses of how the apocalyptic language is used in some of Paul's letters Meeks concludes that millenarian movement *is* a useful model in describing the Pauline communities. This is because we can clearly see that Paul fills the role of a millenarian prophet in relation to his communities by his skillful incorporation of the experiences (especially the adverse ones) of the communities into "a master complex of metaphors built upon the kerygma of the crucified Messiah, Son of God," and replicated in the experiences of both the apostle and other Christians. This belief system thus has a constitutive and not just a reflexive function in the life and development of the group.[14] Never one to throw himself wholeheartedly into any sociological perspective, Meeks adds on the last page of his article that only some aspects of Pauline Christianity are illuminated by such comparisons with ancient and modern apocalyptic movements.

Meeks utilizes his 1979 article in the final chapter of his *The First Urban Christians* (1983) where he uses "millenarian movement" as a comparative model, in order to sort and explain seemingly contradictory elements of Pauline Christianity.[15] Again he stresses that the deprivation behind millenarian movements is mainly an experience

---

[13] Ibid., 687.
[14] Ibid., 701.
[15] Meeks, *First Urban Christians*, 171-180.

of downward social mobility, which is perceived to be the result of deep-seated dislocations in the world as such. "Accordingly the millennial myth provides not just fantasies of reversal, but also a comprehensive picture of what is wrong and why, and of how life ought to be organized."[16]

The picture of the social level of Pauline Christians that Meeks arrived at in chapter 2 of his book does not fit the older concepts that eschatological beliefs (and millenarian movements generally) are simple compensations for social and economic deprivation; the Christians addressed by Paul do not seem to have suffered that kind of deprivation. Their social level accords better with the millenarian model's view that members of such movements suffer from cognitive dissonance, which Meeks understands as a feeling that their symbolic universe no longer makes sense, and get relief from adopting the apocalyptic worldview.[17] Meeks also takes over from the previous article his analyses of how apocalyptic language is used in 1 Thessalonians, Galatians, and 1 Corinthians, concluding that, in spite of different emphases, the central focus of all three letters was the solidarity and stability of the congregations. "This, too, fits our model of millenarian movements, in which the myth of the coming world-change supports both the shift from traditional social relations to the sect's special relations and also the internal institution-building of the sect."[18]

Both these arguments provide rather weak support for applying the model of millenarian movement. The first one, on the somewhat higher social location of Pauline Christians, is not an argument unless one has already accepted Meeks' underlying interpretation of how status inconsistency is connected with cognitive dissonance, which is then relieved by millenarianism. And unless "millenarian" refers to the contents of the Christian beliefs, it is hard to see anything specifically millenarian in the act of legitimating desired group behaviour from the group's central beliefs—any religious movement would do that.[19]

---

[16] Ibid., 173.

[17] For a strong criticism of the cognitive dissonance theory as a whole, see Cyril S. Rodd, "On Applying a Sociological Theory to Biblical Studies" (*Journal for the Study of the Old Testament* 19, 1981, 95-106), and Stanley Kent Stowers, "The Social Sciences and the Study of Early Christianity" (in W. S. Green (ed.), *Approaches to Ancient Judaism*, Atlanta, 1985, 149-181), 170-172.

[18] Meeks, *First Urban Christians*, 179.

[19] Christopher Rowland's use of the the term millenarian in his *Christian Origins* (1985) seems to bear no social scientific connotations at all, but is used more or less as a synonym to "apocalyptic" or "eschatologically oriented," e.g., 112 ff.

Intensified millenarianism in Thessalonica: Jewett
Robert Jewett summarizes the main thesis of *The Thessalonian Correspondence* (1986) in the preface of his book:

> While other Pauline churches were millenarian in the general sense,
> believing that they were part of a dawning new age and that the end
> of history would occur in the near future, only in Thessalonica do we
> encounter a group that proclaimed the actual arrival of the millennium
> and then proceeded to act on that assumption.[20]

In chapter 9, "The Millenarian Model," Jewett describes what he
considers to be the unusually close fit between the characteristics of
the Pauline congregation in Thessalonica and the millenarian model
put forward by social scientists, notably Yonina Talmon. The cultural
conditions conducive to millenarianism were there: pressures of economic dislocation, political powerlessness, and exploitation, together
with a religious vacuum caused by the taking over of the popular local
Cabirus cult by the higher social strata of Thessalonica. The expectation of a returning Cabirus, the champion of the poor, was therefore
"revitalized in the new and more compelling form of Christ. . . ." As
1 Thessalonians shows, a remarkable concentration on the apocalyptic
future was characteristic of the beliefs of the Thessalonian Christians,
including a high expectation of Christ's imminent return. Paul functioned partly as the millennial prophet of this group, although he
seems to have been criticized for an incomplete filling of this role, not
exhibiting a strong enough charismatic charge. The expectation of the
Saviour's immediate return seems to have led some to expect that
afflictions would no longer be possible, wherefore persecution and
deaths in the congregation caused a collapse in morale and trust,
which the apostle tried to answer in his first letter. One can also,
according to Jewett, see typical millenarian behaviour manifested in
Thessalonica's church: "claiming as a right the violation of traditional
sexual mores on grounds that the new age is present," the abandon-
ment of daily occupations by the "disorderly," experience of ecstatic
and highly emotional gatherings, and the resistance against both congregational leaders and the apostle.[21] The conclusion of Jewett is that
the millenarian model makes much better sense of the Thessalonian

---

[20] Robert Jewett, *The Thessalonian Correspondence: Pauline Rhetoric and Millenarian Piety*.
Philadelphia 1986, xiii.
[21] Ibid., 161-178. The quotations are from pp. 165 and 172.

correspondence than other models, like the "enthusiastic," "Gnostic," or "divine man" understanding of this church.

Jewett's application of the millenarian model is clearly an improvement over Gager's (which he refers to as pathbreaking).[22] Instead of speaking generally about early Christianity, he narrows the case to one specific congregation, and takes great care in filling in as complete a background as can be had concerning the political, economic, social, and religious conditions of this community. Jewett has also done a more thorough job, both on the social scientific side in describing how the beliefs, symbols, and typical behaviour patterns of a millenarian movement form a consistent whole, and exegetically in the comparison of the model with the New Testament material. It is not difficult to agree that there seems to be a very good fit between the millenarian model and the church in Thessalonica. One remaining question is, however, if Jewett's picture of an unruly, ecstatic, and radical movement that has sprung out of real, old-fashioned deprivation is not really a different kind of millenarianism from the rather refined variant depicted by Meeks, where deprivation seems to have more to do with existential *Angst*. Would Meeks agree to Jewett's description, and vice versa?

But granted that there is a good fit *between* the model and sociohistorical reality (especially in Thessalonica), the question remains what this fit really means, and what is explained by it. The methodological weakness of this undertaking as a whole is the same as the one pointed to in Gager's work. Early Christianity may not have been the first millenarian movement in the world, but it is clearly the most influential one. All later millenarian movements have been influenced by Judaeo-Christian apocalyptic. Jewett knows this, of course, but understands it only as an argument for the appropriateness of the model:

> Since Talmon shows that Judaism was the channel through which the millenarian tradition was passed to Christianity and Islam, and thence to the modern world, there is a *prima facie* relevance for a situation like Thessalonians where Jewish-Christian apocalyptic was so central.[23]

Jewett seems insensitive to the amount of circular reasoning specifically inherent in the attempt to explain the strongly apocalyptic early Christianity with the help of a set of characteristics, i.e., a model,

---

[22] Ibid., 162 note 10.

[23] Ibid., 162. In note 7 Hobsbawm is cited as saying that "classical millenarian movements occur only, or practically only, in countries affected by Judeo-Christian propaganda."

found in strongly apocalyptic movements, which all stand under the influence of the Judaeo-Christian heritage. The comparative method in this case consists of comparing early Christianity with early Christianity at one or two removes. To put it a bit exaggeratedly: how could the Thessalonian Christians *not* fit into the millenarian model—they practically created it!

I think Gager's (unfounded) claim to be using theoretical models that have not been influenced by the very data they are used to explain evidences a more careful approach to the use of social scientific work in New Testament studies. An ideal type of cross-cultural validity must be constructed from a sufficiently large number of empirical cases, which do not stand in a causal relation to each other, and then also be stripped of spatial and temporal markers.[24] But if Judaeo-Christian apocalyptic plays such a dominant part in the millenarian model, one could well raise the question whether there exists such a thing as a universal type of millenarian movement.[25]

The church-sect distinction applied to early Christianity

After a short introduction about the classical church-sect distinction, I will turn in chronological order to New Testament exegetes who have used it as an instrument in understanding early Christianity. I will both describe their work and attempt an evaluation of it, especially of its methodological dimension.

Classical sociology of religion on church and sect
The typology of "church" and "sect" originated in the work of Max Weber and his student Ernst Troeltsch.[26] Weber distinguished between

---

[24] Philip Francis Esler, *Community and Gospel in Luke-Acts. The Social and Political Motivations of Lucan Theology*. Cambridge, 1987, 14.

[25] Cf. Cyril S. Rodd, "On Applying" (note 17 above), 104: "The liability to error is increased when theories that operate at a high level of abstraction are applied directly and in their totality to a narrow and highly specific situation. This was my main criticism of Gager's use of Coser's theories about conflict, and it applies equally to the adoption of 'ideal types' such as 'sect', 'millenarian cult', or 'charismatic personality' and the immediate application of them to the Old or New Testaments. This is not what 'ideal types' were designed for."

[26] For a convenient summary of the research history of this sociological categorization, see Meredith B. McGuire, *Religion: The Social Context*. Belmont, Calif., 1981, ch. 5, "The Dynamics of Religious Collectivities." See also, from a more critical perspective, James A. Beckford, "Religious Organization" (*Current Sociology* vol. 21, No. 2, 1973 [publ. 1975], 12-18). The theoretical discussion in the dissertation of my colleague Curt Dahlgren has been of special help, idem, *MARANATA: En sociologisk studie av en sektrörelses uppkomst och utveckling*. [Maranatha: A Sociological Study of a Sect's Origin and Development]. Helsingborg, 1982, chapters 2 and 3 (7-48).

church and sect already in his famous work *Die Protestantische Ethik und der Geist des Kapitalismus,* which was published 1904 and 1905, and used the distinction several times in his later works. The church is the type of religious organization into which members are born, while the sect is that type of religious association into which one enters voluntarily and on the ground of religious qualification. There is an inevitable conflict between the two types. Weber's examples include the official management of the Confucian cult ("church") in relation to Buddhist, Taoist, and other sectarian pursuits of salvation, showing that the distinction is not simply a description of historical (Christian) data but an ideal type, an abstraction used for comparative analysis.

Troeltsch developed this into a typology, especially by adding much descriptive material from the history of the Christian church: the "church" accepts the world and society in which it lives, is conservative, and supports the values of the ruling classes. It recruits and embraces in principle everyone, from the cradle to the grave, and includes them into its salvific system (with a hierarchy, cult personnel, sacraments, and rites). The "sect" is the opposite: a small group of intensely religious people, into which one enters only by a conscious act of conversion and remains by adhering to a demanding group ethos and religious behaviour. The sect is often indifferent or critical of the evil world outside, does not identify with the higher classes, but recruits its members from the lower strata of society, and is typically anticlerical, antisacramental, and pronouncedly egalitarian. Not seldom it has started as a protest movement against the "church," which it considers as worldly and degenerated.

This basic two-part typology[27] was taken up especially by American scholars (H. Richard Niebuhr, E. T. Clark, R. A. Nisbet, Howard Becker, J. M. Yinger) and developed into a more detailed typology, with several intermediate types along the continuum between the universal church and the cult. Niebuhr put forward an influential hypothesis concerning the evolutionary tendencies of sects, and Bryan R. Wilson has described and classified a large number of various sects, arranging them in a sevenfold typology.

One of the pioneers in using sociology in New Testament exegesis was Gerd Theissen. But only once, in his earliest "sociological" essay,

---

[27] Troeltsch actually discussed two other types as well: mysticism, which is highly individualistic and subjective, uninterested in society and its problems and in forming any religious community, and the free church, which exists alongside other churches and accepts religious pluralism in society. Dahlgren, *Maranata,* 8 f.

does he refer to the concept of "sect," when he claims in passing that the three socially distinct forms of early Christian faith we meet in the first century (roaming radicalism, patriarchalism of love, and Gnostic radicalism) contain the beginnings of the three types that Ernst Troeltsch described through the whole history of the church: the sect, the institutional church, and spiritualism.[28] But Theissen neither defines the criteria that distinguishes these types from each other, nor uses the typology to investigate the relations between Judaism and the Christian movement. This may depend on his choice of perspective; his main interest is not the sociology of religious organization, but rather a situating of the early Christian movement against the background of ancient social history, and the use of a sociology of knowledge perspective in correlating belief and social situation.

Early Christianity as a Christian sect: Scroggs
When he wanted to describe "The Earliest Christian Communities as Sectarian Movement" in the *Festschrift* for Morton Smith (1975),[29] Robin Scroggs used the work that had been done in the sociology of religion since Max Weber and Ernst Troeltsch, ending with and relying upon the "well-defined sociological model" offered by Werner Stark, *Sectarian Religion* (London, 1967).[30] According to Stark the religious sect has seven characteristics, and Scroggs goes through them one by one to show that they fit "the earliest church directly stemming from the mission of Jesus," or in other words, the earliest Palestinian Christianity:[31]

1. The sect begins as a protest against economic and societal repression. The members of a sect are generally the disprivileged, a

---

[28] "Verfolgt man die Überlieferung der Worte Jesu im Urchristentum, so stösst man auf drei Sozialformen urchristlichen Glaubens: Wanderradikalismus, Liebespatriarchalismus und gnostischen Radikalismus. In ihnen sind jene drei Typen angelegt, deren Geschichte E. Troeltsch durch die ganze Christentumsgeschichte hindurch verfolgt hat: Sekte, Anstaltskirche und Spiritualismus." Gerd Theissen, "Wanderradikalismus. Literatursoziologische Aspekte der Überlieferung von Worten Jesu im Urchristentum" (*Zeitschrift für Theologie und Kirche* 70, 1973, 245-271; now in idem, *Studien*, 79-105), 104f.
[29] Robin Scroggs, "The Earliest Christian Communities as Sectarian Movement," in Jacob Neusner (ed.), *Christianity, Judaism and Other Greco-Roman Cults*. FS Morton Smith, vol. II. Leiden: Brill, 1975, 1-23.
[30] This is vol. 2 of Stark's multi-volume work *The Sociology of Religion*.
[31] Scroggs, "Sectarian Movement," 7. Scroggs focuses on the (early) synoptic traditions, and leaves the Acts and the Pauline letters aside, as he is interested in the preresurrection community called into existence by Jesus himself, which had not begun to move away from sect-type reality, as had later traditions. This earliest church clearly reflects an agrarian setting, idem, 8.

term that can include not only the destitute and hungry but also people who have been deprived of their status. First-century Palestine was a harsh milieu, where especially the numerous small peasants were alienated, not only economically but also culturally by the purity requirements of the Pharisaic party, which made them virtually untouchable. There was much mutual conflict and hostility, and Jesus tried to heal the deep breaches in his society, especially by caring for the poor and dispossessed.[32]

2. The sect rejects the view of reality taken for granted by the establishment, and tries to effect as much separation from the world as possible and form a counter-culture of its own. Scroggs here points to evidence concerning the hostility between Jesus and his family and his hometown, and especially against the establishment groups of Jewish society: the Pharisees, the wealthy, the intellectuals. Jesus and his adherents formed a group that proclaimed and lived out a reality different and separate from the outside society's.

3. The sect is egalitarian, having no hierarchy or organization. All are brothers and sisters, and the ordinary status differences of the larger society are abolished inside the sect. The early church was strongly egalitarian (cf. Gal 3:28), and distrustful of any church organization (as evidenced by Matthew 18 and 23).

4. The sect offers love and acceptance within the community, where the true life is to be found. This intense family feeling allows pent-up emotions to flow out, typically in glossolalia and other ecstatic phenomena. Here Scroggs points to expressions that manifest a conviction that God cares about you, especially if you are a nobody. Glossolalia and sharing of property are evidenced in early Christianity.

5. The sect is a voluntary association, which you have to make a committed decision to join; you are not born into it. This is self-evidently so in the early church.

6. The sect also asks a total commitment from its members. This commitment concerns moral behaviour and one's way of life, as well as the way one thinks and expresses doctrine. It is not difficult to find evidence of this in the early church; discipleship is likened to taking up one's cross, sell all one's possessions, not look back. The ethical demands are absolute.

---

[32] Scroggs admits that Jesus and some of his co-leaders were not of the peasant class, but finds this "an example of Stark's claim that sect leaders have to come from a slightly higher class when the protest-group is too abject to produce its own leadership," ibid., 12 f.

7. Some sects are adventist, i.e., they expect the imminent arrival of the kingdom of God on earth. It is a well-known fact that earliest Christianity was so oriented.

At the end of his essay Scroggs summarizes the profit from viewing, the early church in this way: "We now have a basically different gestalt from which to view the data." Our perspective has changed when we understand the New Testament documents, not primarily as theological products, but as expressions from "a group of people who have experienced the hurt of the world and the healing of communal acceptance."[33] To take one example of what this means, the Gospel of Mark shows that the death of Jesus was originally not interpreted theologically by the Christian sectarians as a victory over evil, or an expiation of the sins of the world. It stands out clearly as an act of the authorities, an execution on political charges. From the standpoint of sectarian reality, this fact is a twofold symbol: a symbol of the "natural" hostility of the world against all that is good, and a symbol of their own liberation from the norms of such an evil world. Understanding the early church with the help of this sociological distinction helps us see the world and its characteristically repressive social circumstances with the eyes of the early Christians, which is a very different thing from the way we affluent, middle-class, institutionally protected Christians see it.

Scroggs is well aware, both of the difficulties in finding reliable information about the beginning of the Christian movement in Palestinian society, and of the differences between this and other parts and periods of early Christianity. He himself points out that his analysis cannot be applied without alterations to the urban churches of the Hellenistic mission, although some of the characteristics, such as egality between the sexes, are clearly present in their earliest period too.[34] Thus there is a limitation to the religious sect model: it does not apply to early Christianity as a whole.

It could be questioned, though, whether even the early Palestinian Christianity is correctly described with the help of Stark's sect model. Was it really so separate, rejected, and particularistic as Scroggs depicts it? Günther Baumbach has pointed out that the characterization of first-century Jewish movements as "sects" in Troeltsch's sense fits the Essene communities, while it does not fit the apocalyptic groups so

---

[33] Ibid., 21.
[34] Adding this in a later article, "The Sociological Interpretation of the New Testament: The Present State of Research" (*New Testament Studies* 26, 1980, 164-179), 172 note 26.

well and still less the Pharisaic *chabhurot*.[35] If we compare the Essenes with the earliest Palestinian Christianity, it is easy to note several differences. In the early Jerusalem community of Christians the sharing of property was voluntary and aimed at supporting the poor members of the church; ascetic tendencies are missing; the Christian group observed the Torah and took part in the temple cult, and did not shut itself off from the wider Jewish context, but hoped to win their compatriots over to believing that Jesus was indeed the Messiah; their high, apocalyptic self-understanding did not entail a separation from the rest of Israel. Like the Pharisees the Christians had their own common meals, organized charity, and their own "oral Torah," the Jesus tradition, which functioned as a kind of "Jesus halacha." It is not an apposite classification to call primitive Christianity a sect, when it differs from Essenism in several respects, but is quite similar to the Pharisaic groups.

Further, the very term "sect," by being paired to "church" as its opposite, has acquired the connotation of a group in opposition to or deviance from the official church or religion. But as there existed no "official" or "normative" Judaism before A.D. 70 (or before Jamnia), against which more distinct groups stood out as deviant, more or less heretical sects, this terminology tends to import a distortive characterization into the allegedly neutral, ideal-typical classification.[36] Characterizing Palestinian Jewish Christianity as a sect would actually be more appropriate in describing its relation to Judaism in Palestine after A.D. 70 than before it!

Another question is whether this exercise in classification actually explains anything, or if it is not merely a fitting of early Christian phenomena into a classificatory grid, a description of old facts in a new terminology. There is something static and slightly uninteresting in pure classification, which Scroggs himself implicitly acknowledges when he moves beyond this to add conclusions about the symbolic interpretation of the death of Christ, which can hardly be said to be part of the sect typologization as such.

A further criticism against the study of Scroggs concerns the validity of his sociological instrument, the sect model of Werner Stark. As the deficiencies of this model are of a more general nature, and common

---

[35] Günther Baumbach, "Die Anfänge der Kirchwerdung im Urchristentum" (*Kairos* 24, 1982, 17-30). Baumbach's remarks are actually directed mainly against Theissen's characterization of early Palestinian Christianity as a sect, but concern the "sectarian" interpretation generally.

[36] Baumbach, "Anfänge," 21 f.

to much of the work on church and sect within the sociology of religion, a critical discussion of this matter will be postponed to a following section.

The community behind 1 Peter as a conversionist sect: Elliott
John Elliott took a close, sociologically oriented look at the First Epistle of Peter in his *A Home for the Homeless. A Sociological Exegesis of 1 Peter, Its Situation and Strategy* (1981). Taking as his starting point the investigation of Scroggs, Elliott finds a close similarity between the characteristics of a sect and the situation of the recipients of 1 Peter. But as he wants to have a more complete definition of a typical sect, he turns to the work of Bryan R. Wilson,[37] and starts his comparison by quoting Wilson's (1961) description of a "sect":

> The sect is a clearly defined community; it is of a size which permits only a minimal range of diversity of conduct; it seeks itself to rigidify a pattern of behaviour and to make coherent its structure of values; it contends actively against every other organization of values and ideals, and against every other social context possible for its adherents, offering itself as an all-embracing, divinely prescribed society. The sect is not only an ideological unit, seeking to enforce behaviour on those who accept belief, and seeking every occasion to draw the faithful apart from the rest of society and into the company of each other. . . . The sect, as a protest group, has always developed its own distinctive ethic, belief and practices, against the background of the wider society; its own protest is conditioned by the economic, social, ideological and religious circumstances prevailing at the time of its emergence and development.[38]

This accords very well with the situation of the Christians in northern Asia Minor to which 1 Peter is addressed: they are members of a clearly defined community, whose members see themselves as holy and elect. They have terminated their past familial, social, and religious ties, and now live in familial community, defined by their faith in Jesus as the Christ and Saviour, and by a demanding ethic, quite different from that of the surrounding society. They expect Jesus to

---

[37] John H. Elliott, *A Home for the Homeless: A Sociological Exegesis of 1 Peter, Its Situation and Strategy*. Philadelphia, 1981, 74-78. The works of Wilson referred to are his *Sects and Society* (1961), *Patterns of Sectarianism* (ed., 1967), *Religious Sects: A Sociological Study* (1970), and *Magic and the Millennium* (1973), which Elliott considers as offering a much improved version of Troeltsch's sect typology, 96 note 57.

[38] Bryan R. Wilson, *Sects and Society: A Sociological Study of the Elim Tabernacle, Christian Science, and Christadelphians*. Berkeley, 1961, p. 1. Quoted from Elliott, *A Home*, 75.

come back soon and bring in the full salvation, and until that day maintain a strict internal discipline, guarding against any assimilation with the outside.

According to Wilson's sevenfold sect typology, sects are distinguished from each other by their varying "responses to the world," i.e., in their way of deviating from and rejecting the prevalent values of society. The "conversionist response" is characterized by the basic assumption that the world is corrupt because men are corrupt: if men can be changed, then the world will be changed. This salvific change comes about through a profoundly felt, supernaturally wrought transformation of the human self, and this conversion experience is what the sect wants to spread to all others.[39] This experience gives both a subjective sense of salvation now and an assurance that complete salvation will follow in the future. Thus the sect offers means of enduring the tension with the world and even giving it a positive interpretation: being rejected by the world is proof of acceptance by God.

A closer look at the social situations where sects proliferate shows further similarities between the sect model and the historical background of 1 Peter: sects appeal to marginalized people and offer them a supportive, warm community that makes up for their various kinds of deprivation in the larger society. The sect promotes a high degree of group consciousness and solidarity among its members, and in order to do this it is important to keep the members separated from the world. Emphasizing a special religous status ("elect and holy") is one method, keeping up a demanding ethical code is another.

The problem for a conversionist sect, however, is that it cannot simply separate itself from the rest of the world, which it wants to win by its missionary enterprise. It must both present itself as attractive and joinable to outsiders, and maintain its own distinctiveness over against them. This type of ambivalence and tension in the attitude to the world outside is evident in 1 Peter, and it has often been commented by exegetes and explained by them as a tension between different theological conceptions in the mind of the author. But, claims Elliott, a much simpler and more realistic explanation is to understand this as the principal and unavoidable tension resulting from the conversionist sect's response to the world. The community behind 1 Peter cannot avoid experiencing this kind of tension, as it is socially determined by its specific relation to the outside world: the relation of a

---

[39] Wilson, *Magic and the Millennium*, 22.

conversionist sect.[40] As this tension is very difficult to uphold over time, the strain has begun to tell on the behaviour and the mood of the Christians addressed. Therefore, the authors of 1 Peter adopt a conscious socioreligious strategy:

> to counteract the demoralizing and disintegrating impact which such social tension and suffering had upon the Christian sect by reassuring its members of their distinctive communal identity, reminding them of the importance of maintaining discipline and cohesion *within* the brotherhood as well as separation from Gentile influences *without,* and by providing them with a sustaining and motivating rationale for continued faith and commitment.[41]

The Christians are, in short, to maintain the double character of a conversionist sect: an unflinching openness to the outside, together with a determined internal cohesion and distinctiveness from the outside, and accept the suffering that must follow.

Elliott has been criticized, with some justification, of allowing his conversionist sect model to influence the selection and interpretation of the evidence. It is hard to agree with Elliott, for example, that the letter recipients must have been *paroikoi* in the technical, legal meaning of that word, even before they became Christians, or that the terms *oikos* and *paroikoi* turn up at key points in the structure of the document.[42] Even if this is not the case, it does not invalidate the overall understanding of the situation of the addressees of this letter as evidencing the typical dilemma of a conversionist sect. I consider Elliott's demonstration of how this model explains the letter's well-known ambivalence in regard to the outside world to be proof of the value of applying sociological models to New Testament texts. This is because Elliott moves beyond a mere classification of phenomena to exhibiting that the inner dynamic of the model (the typical experiences and development of a conversionist sect) really helps to explain certain properties of the letter's content, rather better than conventional theological perspectives.

---

[40] Elliott, *A Home*, ch. 3 (pp. 101-164, esp. 102-112).

[41] Ibid., 148.

[42] For criticism of these and other points, see, e.g., Birger Olsson, "Ett hem för hemlösa. Om sociologisk exeges av NT" (*Svensk Exegetisk Årsbok* 49, 1984, 89-108), and the review by Colin J. Hemer in *Journal for the Study of the New Testament* 24 (1985), 120-123, who points out that we really know less about the complex historical situation in the interior of Asia Minor than Elliott presumes.

A further improvement in method consists in Elliott's use of Bryan R. Wilson's work on sects, which is characterized by a clear awareness of the cultural limitations and biases of the original church-sect typology, and a carefully reasoned attempt at substituting a more universal definition of the ideal type "sect." Wilson's sociological description and typology of sects has a higher level of generality than Stark's.

"Jesus sect" as partial description: Meeks
Already in 1972 Meeks made a hesitant reference to the Johannine community as a sect in his "The Man from Heaven in Johannine Sectarianism," stating that (but not how) his use of it differed from the classic definitions. It is clear, however, that the term referred to a small community in hostile isolation from the larger society, and one that had totalistic and exclusive claims.[43] In a later, short treatment of various ways of being separated from the Jewish communities, Meeks simply refers to this as an understanding of the Johannine community that is now widely accepted.[44]

In his important work *The First Urban Christians* (1983), where he synthesizes and evaluates much previous sociological work in the exegesis of Pauline letters, Meeks gives the impression of largely avoiding the concept "sect." Except for a mention or two, he uses it only when discussing the boundaries perceived to exist between the Pauline groups of Christians and the larger society.[45] In this section Meeks sees early Christianity as one of several Jewish sects, the others being the Pharisees and the members of the Qumran community. Also Paul and his congregations see themselves as a sect, sharply distinguished from the rest of humanity, the outsiders. The outside world is impure and unholy, but the Christian sect has been "washed" and "sanctified" by their baptism, so that they are undefiled. In spite of many signs of a rather strict separation from outsiders and a strong consciousness of being separate and special, the Pauline sectarian communities were remarkably open to outsiders, more conscious of the need to make a good impression on them, and more willing to

---

[43] (*Journal of Biblical Literature* 91, 1972, 44-72), 70.
[44] Meeks, "Breaking Away: Three New Testament Pictures of Christianity's Separation from the Jewish Communities" (J. Neusner and E. S. Frerichs (eds.), *"To See Ourselves as Others See Us": Christians, Jews, "Others" in Late Antiquity.* Chico, Califomia, 1985, 93-115), 103 note 27.
[45] Wayne A. Meeks, *The First Urban Christians*, 84-107, "The Fellowship and Its Boundaries." See 85 f, 89, 92, 97, 102, 106 f. The work of Bryan Wilson is mentioned on p. 85 note 65.

consort with them in ordinary social intercourse than sects usually
are (as evidenced by the Johannine community). Pauline Christianity
is thus not a very sectarian sect.

This ambivalence of closed and open boundaries to the world seems
to have made Meeks a bit apprehensive of a sectarian analysis of
Pauline Christianity. This is not necessary, as this trait of ambivalence
seems to point directly to the type of "conversionist sect" described
by Bryan R. Wilson in his *Magic and the Millenium* (1973), and well
utilized by John Elliott on 1 Peter (1981). The reader is not told why
Meeks does not use or even discuss this fruitful model, when he
knows of Wilson's and Elliott's work and is prepared to characterize
the Pauline Christians as a "sect." This interpretation of Pauline Christianity was taken up five years later by Margaret Y. MacDonald (see
below).

In his article on "Breaking Away" (1985) Meeks specified that the
sect character of Pauline Christianity did not mean that it had ever
broken loose from Jewish synagogues. "Socially, however, the Pauline
groups were never a sect of Judaism. They organized their lives independently from the Jewish associations of the cities where they
were founded, and apparently, so far as the evidence reveals, they
had little or no interaction with the Jews."[46]

In his *The Moral World of the First Christians* (1986), where Meeks
describes the *ethos* of the early Christianity, relating it to the great
Greco-Roman and Jewish traditions, he seems to have abandoned
much of his hesitation in calling it a sect.[47] The first sentence under
the subheading "A Messianic Sect in Israel" reads: "Christianity began
as a sect of Judaism, in the villages of Judea and Galilee." This is
immediately followed by pointing out the anachronism of such a
characterization and a statement that to call early Christianity a sect
means that it was a deviant movement within a cohesive culture that
was defined religiously.[48] The Christians stood within the great tradition of Judaism, as did the Essenes, the Pharisees, and the Thera-
peutae, but like them drew the boundaries of the sacred community

---

[46] Meeks, "Breaking Away," 106. The evidence in this case is simply an argument from
silence; we hear little about any contacts with organized Jewish communities, conflicts
are either internal or with the pagan society. For a different view, based on Gal and 2
Cor 11:24 f, which Meeks interprets as part of Paul's personal biography only, see A.
E. Harvey, "Forty Strokes Save One: Social Aspects of Judaizing and Apostasy"
(A. E. Harvey (ed.), *Alternative Approaches to New Testament Study*. London, 1985, 79-
96).—Meeks also describes the Matthean community as sectarian, idem, 113 f.
[47] Wayne A. Meeks, *The Moral World of the First Christians*. London, 1987 [first publ. in
USA 1986].
[48] Ibid., 98.

differently and more narrowly than the established leaders in Jerusalem. Major and early steps toward sectarian identity was the making of baptism into a ritual of initiation into a special community, and the frequent sharing of a communal meal, the Lord's Supper. Probably the Christians separated from other Jewish groups over the ritual observances of the law, even if they held some very basic beliefs in common with them, as regards God, the scriptures, and history. Early Christianity was one of several apocalyptic sects, but they connected their own identity and the fate of Israel and all human beings with the identity of one person, Jesus, whom they considered to be the Messiah, risen from the dead. This is the really decisive and divisive characteristic of the sect, which can consequently be called "the Jesus sect."[49]

In considering the "socioecology" of the sect, Meeks follows Theissen in seeing the life of wandering charismatic apostles or prophets as related to the hospitality of members of the wider society. The new movement (prophets and supporters) thus lived in a kind of symbiosis with its host culture, which necessitates a revision of the initial picture of how sect and society are related. The sect was not uniformly ascetical, but formed a two-level community, which could, and did, develop in various ways, depending on the local situation (or ecology). The author of Acts thought of the Christians as a sect of Israel, wherever they spread in the eastern cities. Probably the Christian sectarian groups often began within the Jewish community in each city, but were soon driven to a separate existence (as the Gospel of John witnesses), based on private houses, with their natural network of connections.[50] Meeks finally makes clear the inadequacy of all the important analogies:

> Something new was emerging in the private homes where believers in "Jesus the Christ" gathered. . . . The new thing was what we call "the church," but it is not easy to define it or to specify its newness. It was all the old things that observers in the first century might have seen in it: a Jewish sect, a club meeting in a household, an initiatory cult, a school. Yet it was more than the sum of those things, and different from the mere synthesis of their contradictory tendencies. . . . The early Christians themselves had a great deal of trouble deciding just what their movement was and what it ought to become.[51]

---

[49] Actually this name does not appear until the end of the chapter, 120.

[50] Ibid., 104 ff.

[51] Ibid., 119 f.

It is clear from the cautious way in which Meeks uses the terms "sect" and "sectarian" that he does not find this approach to be of the same explanatory importance as, for example, John Elliott. For the latter (conversionist), sect is a sociological model that really explains a whole New Testament text and shows the interplay between social situation and letter content. Meeks, on the other hand, uses "sect" more as one of several descriptive categories or analogies, all of which tell something important, and all of which are insufficient to grasp the full reality of early Christianity, even from the viewpoint of social description. This is probably part of Meeks' way of steering clear of what he characterizes as "the overenthusiasm for social theory and sociological 'laws' that occasionally threatens the good sense of exegetes."[52] On the other hand, one could ask against this commendable sobriety whether it is very useful to introduce a slightly inappropriate terminology (as Meeks clearly states it to be) without attempting to explain anything very specific with it.

Christianity as one of several Jewish sects: Rowland
The basic assumption of Christopher Rowland's *Christian Origins. An Account of the Setting and Character of the Most Important Messianic Sect of Judaism* (1985) is set out by himself in the preface of the book: "I have assumed that, in early Christianity, we are dealing with a Jewish messianic sect, which continued to be this throughout the bulk of the period we are considering."[53] He claims that pre-70 Judaism was so heterogeneous that it can be viewed as composed of many sects or differing groups.

> Unlike those who prefer to reserve the term 'sect' for the group which maintains a fairly strict exclusivism I have decided to use the terms sect and sectarianism to characterize Jewish religion before A.D. 70.[54]
>
> In all likelihood an observant Jew would have been a member of a sect, which set its own (stricter) entrance requirements, such as we find in the Dead Sea Scrolls or in the obligations laid upon members of the pharisaic fellowships. Refusal to accept the obligations of the sect might lead to exclusion from the sect or various kinds of punishment, but

---

[52] Wayne A. Meeks, "Understanding Early Christian Ethics" (*Journal of Biblical Literature* 105, 1986, 3-11), 6 note 10.
[53] Christopher Rowland, *Christian Origins. An Account of the Setting and Character of the Most Important Messianic Sect of Judaism.* London, 1985, xvii.
[54] Ibid., 65.

such rigid processes of exclusion would not have applied to the vast majority of Jews.[55]

It is thus impossible to speak of Judaism as a well-defined orthodoxy, against which Christianity stood out as evidently heretical, or clearly outside the pale. Belief in a Messiah, and in the claim that the Scriptures had actually been fulfilled were not unique for Christianity. The early Christian groups were simply more or less sectarian, just like other movements on the Jewish scene before A.D. 70. Pauline Christianity was more open than Johannine Christianity, but can nonetheless be characterized as a sect.[56] Rowland notes a greater formality and stress on non-enthusiastic tradition in the Jerusalem church, but considers this too as a sect.[57]

It is evident that Rowland knows of the sociological church-sect categorization, but that he refuses to apply the distinction. Instead he maintains that all of pre-70 Judaism was sectarian, and—as it belonged inside Judaism—all of early Christianity was sectarian too. This use of the term robs it of any sociological significance.

Christianity as sect and cult movement: Stark
Rodney Stark, who has worked extensively in surveying the contemporary religious scene in the U.S., has attempted to apply findings concerning the recruitment to different religious groups to the early Christianity.[58] He begins by criticizing the habit of sociologists of religion to view all new religions as phenomena of protest and compensation. One must allow for diversity here, and distinguish between sect movements and cult movements. The former occur by schism within a conventional religious body when persons desiring a more otherworldly version of the faith break away to "restore" the religion to a higher level of tension with its environment. These persons usually belong to lower social strata. Cult movements, on the other hand,

---

[55] Ibid., 223. Against the assumption that every observant Jew would have been member of a sect, see, e.g., Wayne A. Meeks, "Breaking Away," 93: "We should not fall into the trap of thinking that all, or even the majority, of Jews in Josephus' time belonged to one of the 'sects' he named, any more than a majority of non-Jews were Stoics, Platonists, or Epicureans."
[56] The language of Paul converting from one religion to another is anachronistic. Rather this event should be seen as "the transference of an individual from one Jewish sect to another, from the pharisaic sect to the Christian sect"; Rowland, *Origins*, 195.
[57] Ibid., 263.
[58] Rodney Stark, "The Class Basis of Early Christianity: Inferences from a Sociological Model" (*Sociological Analysis* 47, 1986, 216-225).

are new religions, with new ideas that are not intensifications or modifications of existing religions. In contemporary America this type of new religion (Mormons, Christian Science, Moonies, etc.) has appealed more to educated, well-to-do persons than to the disprivileged.

Stark starts his application to Christianity of the difference in social standing among recruits to sects and to cults by stating:

> During his ministry, Jesus seems to have been the leader of a sect movement within Judaism. . . . However, on the morning of the third day something happened which turned the Christian sect into a cult movement. It is unnecessary to believe in the Resurrection to see that *because the apostles believed in it, they were no longer part of a Jewish sect* [emphasis in the original]. From that time forth they were participants in a new religion, one that added far too much new culture to Judaism to be any longer an internal sect movement. Of course, the complete break between church and synagogue took many decades to occur.[59]

Whatever the relationship between Christianity and Judaism, in the larger context of the Roman Empire, it was the Pauline (or Gentile) church that triumphed and changed history. And there can be no doubt that Christianity wasn't a sect movement within conventional paganism. It was a new, deviant faith, a cult movement.

Stark goes on to add that, unless a convincing case can be made that basic social and psychological processes were different in the days of Rome than they are now, the early (Pauline) church just like other cult movements was based on a "relatively privileged constituency," and therefore had its greatest success with the middle and upper middle classes. Thus the new consensus discussed in the previous chapter receives support from what Stark calls "some very well-tested sociological propositions about the social basis of new religious movements. . . . If the early church was like all the other new religious movements for whom good data exist, it was *not* a proletarian movement, but was based on the more privilege[d] classes."[60]

---

[59] Ibid., 223 f.

[60] Ibid." 217. L. Michael White has responded to Stark's suggestions in "Sociological Analysis of Early Christian Groups: A Social Historian's Response" (*Sociological Analysis* 47, 1986, 249-266), and points to some possible conclusions, such as the necessity to distinguish between different parts and periods of early Christianity, the possibility of understanding Christian groups outside of their original Jewish environment as moving over into a cult-movement relation to society, and the importance of networks of patronage and benefaction in the growth of Christianity.

The perspective of Stark is similar to the one found in the article by Scroggs, and to Theissen's overall picture of the development of early Christianity: after a beginning in poverty-stricken, rural areas of Palestine, Christianity spreads into higher social strata as it moves further out into the diaspora. This interesting perspective results from making a sharper distinction between sect and cult, and taking into consideration the differing social locations of these two types. It is a reminder that the sociological typology or model must be clear-cut and validated in other sociological research. But the presupposition of a basic similarity between psychological and social processes in the first-century Roman Empire and twentieth-century U.S. is, of course, the weak point of the whole argument, and not likely to be validated.

Early Christianity between reform movement and sect: Esler
In his 1987 study of the social and political influences on Luke and Acts, *Community and Gospel in Luke-Acts. The Social and Political Motivation of Lucan Theology*, Philip Esler first applies the sect typology of Troeltsch to Luke-Acts.[61] His conclusion is that the Christian congregations behind these texts probably had a separate and sectarian existence apart from the Judaism they were once a part of. He then goes on to determine more closely which type of sectarianism is the dominant one in the Lucan community, with the help of Bryan R. Wilson's typology of sectarian responses to the world. There are only streaks of thaumaturgic response, and no revolutionist response (or, in theological terms, expectation of imminent *parousia*) whatsoever, while the conversionist response is clearly dominant in this community.

Now typological classifications like Troeltsch's and Wilson's are necessarily static, and simply describe existing differences. They belong at the second level of scientific research, classification, where phenomena are grouped according to criteria, so as to facilitate comparison, but do not explain the changes during the history of a religious movement. In order to understand and explain the change that has taken place between the inception of Christianity as a reform movement within Judaism and its existence as a separate sect in the later decades of the first century, one needs a sociological model concerning how sects originate and develop.[62] A model contains an idea of what probably, or usually, or inevitably happens with the phenomena that

---

[61] Philip Francis Esler, *Community and Gospel in Luke-Acts. The Social and Political Motivation of Lucan Theology.* Cambridge, 1987.
[62] See ibid., 6-12, for a clear and succinct description of the methodology of the social sciences.

are held together in the theory, and of how a change in one of the elements will affect the other elements, and can be described as "a related group of conceptualized phenomena with a 'mechanism', an inner dynamic, which has an explanatory and predictive function."[63] One such model is H. Richard Niebuhr's theory that sects are a first-generation phenomenon only, and inevitably develop into a more church-like type of religious organization.[64] The fact that some sects (e.g., Jehovah's Witnesses) neither accommodate to society, lose their millenarian fervour, nor become churches or even denominations, indicates that Niebuhr's theory does not have universal application. It is not thereby invalidated, but Esler considers the work of David Barrett on "independency" in African Christianity to provide material for a more helpful model for the development by which a reform movement turns into a sect.[65]

A religious reform movement arises as a result of a widespread dissatisfaction with the religious status quo in society, or in other words, with the "church." This dissatisfaction consists of a strong feeling that one has been deprived of or prevented from enjoying essential personal and religious values. A prophetic person arises who is capable of articulating and canalizing this vague religious hunger into words, rites, behaviour, and a way of life that are experienced as genuine and filled with holy spirit. This attack on the interpretational monopoly of the religious leaders usually creates increased tension and hostility, more reciprocal vilification, and eventually the application of naked force and outright persecution of the new religious minority, not seldom with the help of the judicial powers of society, who typically uphold the traditional, status-quo-protecting religion.[66] At some point in this process full separation is seen as inevitable, by one or both of the parties. The reform movement secedes or is pushed out from the church, and becomes a separate sect, a complete alternative to its parent community. A reform movement may sometimes be divided over the issue of separation, so that one part of it leaves and becomes a sect, while the other remains within the church.[67]

---

[63] Ibid., 50.

[64] H. Richard Niebuhr, *The Social Sources of Denominationalism*. New York, 1929.

[65] The work Esler refers to is David Barrett, *Schism and Renewal in Africa: An Analysis of Six Thousand Contemporary Religious Movements*. Nairobi, 1968; Esler, *Community and Gospel*, 50 f.

[66] Ibid., 18-23.

[67] Esler's example is the split of the Soatanana reform movement within the Lutheran church of Madagascar in 1955, where 10 percent remained in the church, and the rest became a separate sect. Ibid., 53 f.

This separation from the parent church has to be explained and legitimated to the sect's adherents, who need "strong assurance that their decision to convert and to adopt a different life-style had been the correct one."[68] This is often done by claiming that "we" in the sect are the real upholders of the original truth and spirituality of the old religion. Thus "we" are really those who represent and offer holiness, genuine contact with God, fidelity to the revealed truth, while all this has been diluted and distorted in the community from which "we" had to break loose.

One point at which the question of being or not being, in communion with the Jewish parent community surfaced in a very practical manner was the point of table-fellowship between Jews and Gentiles in the church. Normally, table-fellowship was such an important boundary-marker of Jewish identity to Jews in the centuries around the birth of Christ that eating together with necessarily polluting Gentiles was considered highly undesirable, if not impossible. This is clearly an important issue for Luke, as it is taken up and treated several times in Acts. This insistence alone indicates that eating with non-Jews had been a matter of intense controversy in the early church, and this is confirmed by Gal 2:11-14 and the discussion on what pollutes recorded in Mark 7 and Matthew 15.[69] The earliest evidence for conflict about this is found in Galatians 2, and Esler summarizes his interpretation of this text:

> The clash between Paul and the Jerusalem church is, therefore, one between a leader who has made a revolutionary leap to the realization that the old boundaries which preserved the Jewish *ethnos* from outside contamination have, in Christ, ceased to have any significance, since 'there is neither Jew nor Greek, . . . but you are all one in Christ Jesus' (Gal. 3:28), and, on the other hand, a group which, firmly believing in the election of the Jewish *ethnos*, wishes to restrict the power of the Gospel exclusively to Jews. In sociological terms, it is a clash between someone determined to establish a form of religious belief whose relationship to its mother church can only be described as sectarian, and others who see this new religious impulse as merely an intra-Judaic Messianic movement.[70]

Esler devotes the greater part of his book to the Lucan community, which lived in a time when the split between Judaism and Christianity

---

[68] Ibid., 16.

[69] Ibid., 71-109, ch. 4, "Table-fellowship."

[70] Ibid., 88 f. Esler thinks that Paul's position was defeated, but that such table-fellowship was taken up again in Antioch after Paul's death, and in the Lucan community, 106.

was already a fact (the eighties). He is especially interested in the energetic way Luke tries to legitimate this state of things, but this lies outside the scope of this chapter.

Methodologically, Esler's work is the most advanced so far. His three-stage approach of using sociological concepts for classification and sociological models for explanation introduces a much more sophisticated understanding of social scientific method in New Testament studies. It is certainly an improvement on the direct application of sociological distinctions on early Christianity as a whole, not simply because it is more sophisticated, but because it explains the barrenness of previous approaches. They have only proceeded to the pre-explanation level of research: the classification of phenomena. But a classification of early Christianity or a part of it as sectarian does not really explain anything! It does not even automatically engender a number of interesting and plausible hypotheses. This needs imagination and hard work, leading on to the fruitful toil of verification.

According to Bryan Wilson there are three different ways in which a sect can arise: it can develop around a local charismatic leader, it can arise through a schism within a religious group, and it can be the result of an organized revival movement.[71] Esler has chosen the second model: the Christian sect is a subgroup of Judaism that eventually secedes from its parent community. One almost gets the impression that this reform-movement could have remained in peaceful communion with the Jewish community for a longer time (perhaps indefinitely), if Paul and others had not precipitated a schism. It would be interesting to try out the first model as an alternative explanation, and ask whether it is really plausible to locate all the radicalism and charismatic creativity in Paul and hardly anything in Jesus. Was not already the earliest Jesus-movement and Jesus himself too radical, too "sectarian," as it were, to be contained within Judaism in the long run?

Perhaps one should also keep in mind that, while the Christian groups separated themselves from the larger, Jewish context and thus became more sectarian in relation to this background, their relation to the even larger society outside Judaism underwent the opposite change: they transformed their rather exclusive connections with the Jewish communities and became an open, outreaching, and strongly integrating religious movement, which was not "sectarian" at all![72]

---

[71] Bryan R. Wilson, "An Analysis of Sect Development" (*American Sociological Review* 24, 1959, 3-15).

[72] This is the perspective of Rodney Stark, Henneke Gülzow, and Gerd Theissen.

The term "sect" seems too narrow to account for all the dimensions of the change involved in the separation of early Christianity from Judaism.

Paul as creator of the Christian sect: Watson

Esler's model of how a reform-movement is transformed into a sect has also been used by Francis Watson, in *Paul, Judaism and the Gentiles: A Sociological Approach* (1986).[73] He also takes up a problem that Esler left after touching it: the question of what happened in the life and work of Paul, who was so "determined to establish a form of religious belief whose relationship to its mother church can only be described as sectarian." According to Watson, Paul began by preaching the gospel only to Jews, but with no success at all (cf. Gal 5:11). As a consequence of this failure, Paul and Barnabas as leaders of the Jewish Christian congregation at Antioch started a totally new approach. They gradually gave up the mission to the Jews and turned to the Gentiles, of whom they did not require full submission to the law: they were exempted from circumcision, the Jewish food-laws, the Sabbath and the feast-days of the Jewish calendar. This was done simply to make conversion easier for the Gentiles, and thus was originally not a matter of theological principle but of practical expediency, which was subsequently justified by theological arguments. All this, of course, meant the creation of Gentile Christian communities in sharp separation from the Jewish community, or in other words, the creation of a sect.[74]

This transformation of an originally intra-Jewish reform-movement into a sect was not accepted by the whole movement, but sparked strong conflict between the churches in Jerusalem and in Antioch—an incident of which we read Paul's report in Gal 2:11-14. In Antioch the new, "sectarian" mission approach was defeated—even Barnabas left it—but Paul continued it in new areas, farther to the west and north, with some success. The "Judaizing" opposition followed him

---

[73] Francis Watson, *Paul, Judaism and the Gentiles: A Sociological Approach*. Cambridge, 1986. A comparison between Watson (1986) and Esler (1987)—both were doctoral dissertations in Oxford 1984—shows that the former follows the latter as regards the sociological model used. Esler has worked out his model of sect in communication with the work done in sociology of religion (46-53), esp. by Bryan R. Wilson, whose sect typology is then applied to the data from Luke-Acts (53-65), and also with the help of a "sociological" analysis of African church history (65-70), while Watson simply refers to the work of Esler (Watson, 19 note 25 and 26), and shortly describes his sociological instruments on three pages (ibid., 38-41).

[74] Watson, *Paul, Judaism and the Gentiles*, 28-38.

into Galatia, and Paul seems to expect it turning up in Philippi too. This is why we meet such aggressive denunciation, antithesis, and reinterpretation of the Jewish heritage in the letters to these churches. In Rome Watson envisages the existence of two separate Christian congregations, one mainly Jewish and keeping to the law, the other mainly Gentile. The whole of Paul's letter to the Romans can be understood as one prolonged argument, persuading the former congregation to accept the latter, and with it, of course, also the Pauline interpretation of the law, the history of Israel, the work of God through Jesus, and the inclusion of the Gentiles into the people of God. This is a good example of what Watson considers to be his second sociological model, the typical three-part pattern of how a sectarian group legitimates its separation from a parent religious community, by (a) denunciation of the opponents, (b) antithesis (between them and us, then and now, unbelievers and the saved), and (c) reinterpretation of the religious traditions of the parent community so that they apply exclusively to the sect.[75]

From the perspective of method, Watson's analysis of Pauline history and letters represents an application of the methodological groundwork of Esler on a new material. He is even more distrustful of the source material than Esler (who discards Acts completely as a historical source), discounting also the information from Paul himself when necessary. The data have to give way for the model. This may account for the somewhat unpersuasive picture of the Pauline sect, starting as a one-man operation after the Antioch incident, and followed by other parts of the early church only after A.D. 70. This hypothesis demands a sharper separation from the Judaizing Christians than we see in Paul's letters. Paul's strenuous efforts to remain in contact with the church in Jerusalem and even establish a closer *koinonia* between his congregations and the center of the still Jewish reform-movement rather evidences a unity that has been strained but not broken.

Pauline Christianity as a conversionist sect: MacDonald
In her book *The Pauline Churches: A Socio-historical Study of Institutionalization in the Pauline and Deutero-Pauline Writings* (1988), Margaret Y. MacDonald has attempted to give a comprehensive interpretation of the institutionalization process of Pauline Christianity through its

---

[75] Ibid., 40. This model seems to be a systematisation of the legitimating strategies described in Esler, *Community and Gospel*, 16-23 and 66-70.

three successive stages, which are visible in the New Testament.[76] The genuine Pauline epistles represent what she terms the community-building institutionalization, while Colossians and Ephesians, written shortly after the Apostle's death, show the reader the same tradition in its community-stabilizing phase, and the Pastoral Epistles, which are dated between A.D. 100 and 140, evidence the community-protecting period of institutionalization. In all three periods the author analyses four elements: the attitude to the world, ministry, ritual, and belief. As part of the first element, she discusses the question whether Pauline Christianity can be characterized as a sect in its different stages.

MacDonald follows John Elliott in using Bryan R. Wilson's description of what a sect is and of what type of sectarian response to the world we meet in Pauline Christianity: it clearly corresponds to the type of conversionist sect. The Christians converted by Paul have undergone a powerful change and been set apart from an evil world, whose ways they have now left behind them. They have the Spirit and know God through Jesus, who has delivered them and will do so completely, when the present age soon comes to an end. The separation from the world is not complete, as marriages with non-Christians are permitted, as well as common meals, and the presence of outsiders in the assembly of the holy is possible. The boundaries are there, however, forcefully manifested in baptism and the Lord's supper. The typical conversionist sect tension between a desire for separation from the world and a desire for social respectability and attractiveness to the world is evidenced in these letters.[77]

The stage at which Pauline Christianity has arrived when Colossians and Ephesians were written can be characterized as "the growth of the sect," and these letters too evidence the duality between the language of separation and the language of belonging that Meeks has shown to be so typical of Paul's own letters. MacDonald concludes "that the term 'conversionist sect', employed to speak about Paul's communities in Part 1, remains an appropriate means of describing the communities of Colossians and Ephesians."[78] Turning finally to the church of the Pastoral Epistles, the author concludes, after having demonstrated the great differences between these documents and the earlier Pauline letters in regard to attitudes to the world, to the values

---

[76] Margaret Y. MacDonald, *The Pauline Churches: A Socio-historical Study of Institutionalization in the Pauline and Deutero-Pauline Writings.* Cambridge, 1988.
[77] Ibid., 32-42.
[78] Ibid., 99, cf. 121; "The growth of the sect" appears as a heading on page 97.

of the Greco-Roman society, to the role of slave-owners and women, and to wealth and ethics generally:

> With respect to Greco-Roman society as a whole, it is clear that the community of the Pastorals constitutes a sect. When one compares the community of the Pastorals with the communities that emerge from the authentic epistles and Colossians and Ephesians, however, it is possible to speak of a movement away from the sect-type, toward the church-type.[79]

This conclusion is somewhat ambivalent, mainly because it uses a double definition of "sect," first referring to a community that is deviant in relation to its host society, and secondly relating the same community to a scale of doctrinal and behavioural radicalism. The main conclusion, however, is that Pauline Christianity can be characterized as a sect well up into the second century. As regards the use of the church-sect typology, this investigation can be considered as continuing the work of Elliott, by extending it to a new group of New Testament texts.

Criticism of the church-sect typology

While many exegetes are rather careful in their treatment of the New Testament source material when they apply the church-sect distinction to it, they seem to be unaware of the problematical character of the sect model they are using. I consider it a scholar's duty to immerse himself or herself in the critical discussion of the model he or she has chosen as analytical instrument, instead of simply taking it over on trust, just because it comes from a sociologist. And in this case the criticism from sociologists against the church-sect dichotomy and its many refinements has been strong and persistent.

Cultural limitations
A thorough-going critique of the distinction is made by the sociologist most used by the above-mentioned scholars, namely Bryan R. Wilson. His basic criticism of the sect typification is that its Troeltschean background in medieval Christian history has influenced sociologists of religion for a long time, even after they imagined that they had refined

---

[79] Ibid., 200 f.

Troeltsch's typology and made it less culture-bound.[80] "Sect" is usually seen as a movement of protest against a larger "church," from which the sect has split off. But this is not generally the case, especially not if we move to third-world, non-Christian situations. The protest can also be levelled against the state, or the institutions of society, or even against particular groups in society. Further, what "religion" is has often been unconsciously determined by the picture of the Christian church, so that sects have often been measured by their degrees of organizational and/or doctrinal formalization. "But the conscious creation of formal and systematic organizations is in large measure a phenomenon that is culturally specific to western society."[81] And "perhaps the most important defect of the characterization of sects by doctrinal divergence from orthodoxy is that, like characterization in terms of organization, it puts too much emphasis on specifically Christian preoccupations."[82] Another feature inherited from Troeltsch is a strong tendency to dichotomizing analysis and description, which leads to simplification and emphasis on extreme manifestations in the understanding of the complex reality of sects. Here Wilson criticized Werner Stark especially, both for his excessive dichotomizing and for allowing the influence of a theological, normative judgment in his sociological work.[83] Wilson summarizes his criticism:

> We may, therefore, entirely with profit abandon both the traditional theological basis for sect classification in terms of doctrine, and the sociological attempts to distinguish new religious movements by the degree of institutionalization that they have achieved.[84]

It is clear then that the traditional church-sect distinction is not the neutral, cross-cultural, ideal-type sociological model claimed by many sociologists (and believed by some exegetes), but rather strongly limited to one specific culture, the Christian. This diminishes its general

---

[80] Actually Troeltsch's categorization was intended primarily for comparing and contrasting concrete historical developments in the Christian church rather than for creating a universal classification scheme, Roland Robertson, *The Sociological Interpretation of Religion*, Oxford, 1972, 116 f.

[81] Wilson, *Magic and the Millennium*, 13.

[82] Ibid., 16.

[83] Ibid., 15, with note 9, and esp. 16 note 10: "Some writers who regard their perspective as sociological betray the same normative theological perspective which very much diminishes, where it does not altogether destroy, the sociological value of their work. See, for example, W. Stark, *The Sociology of Religion* Vols. I-IV."

[84] Ibid., 16.

value, but becomes a very serious shortcoming when it is applied to early Christianity. I refer, of course, to the circular reasoning involved in using Christian sects of later ages to analyse and explain that very movement that they all wanted to imitate to the best of their capacity: New Testament Christianity![85] We have to conclude that the application of this typology actually may not be a sociological classification at all (much less an explanation), but simply a sophisticated mirroring of the early church in the mirror of church history—a history where early Christianity itself plays an important part. This is evidently a methodological flaw of some magnitude.

Analytical imperfections
Even if Bryan Wilson in *Magic and the Millennium* (1973) has attempted to clean the concept of sect from its cultural limitations by including many non-Christian examples from new religious movements in the third world and restricting himself to one sociological variable (response to the world[86]) in defining the types, the criticism of the distinction as analytically imperfect has not stopped. One could point to several fundamental critiques through the years,[87] but most of the critique is summarized in the essay by James A. Beckford, "Religious Organization."[88]

He begins by pointing out that a logical structure of contrasting dualities runs through most of the conventional usages of "church"

---

[85] Thomas F. Best, "The Sociological Study of the New Testament" (see note 5 above), 188 f.

[86] Wilson's description of the different responses seems to have a rather theological character anyway; cf. page 89 above.

[87] In my *Paul and Power. The Structure of Authority in the Primitive Church as Reflected in the Pauline Epistles*. Lund, 1978, 177 f note 68 (= Philadelphia, 1980, 175 note 68), I referred to the criticisms by Peter L. Berger, "The Sociological Study of Sectarianism" (*Social Research* 21, 1954, 467-485), Benton Johnson, "On Church and Sect" (*American Sociological Review* 28, 1963, 539-549), Alan W. Eister, "Toward a Radical Critique of Church–Sect Typologizing" (*Journal for the Scientific Study of Religion* 6, 1967, 85-90), and idem, "H. Richard Niebuhr and the Paradox of Religious Organization: A Radical Critique" (in Glock—Hammond (eds.), *Beyond the Classics? Essays in the Scientific Study of Religion*. New York, 1973, 355-408).
The criticism of Wilson's sect typology by Kippenberg, that it applies only to Christian sects, because (only) these apply no other membership conditions than formulated beliefs, builds on a misunderstanding of what Wilson means by different responses to the world, and is not correct concerning the entrance criteria of Christian sects either. Hans G. Kippenberg, "Ein Vergleich jüdischer, christlicher und gnostischer Apokalyptik" (in Hellholm (ed.), *Apocalypticism in the Mediterranean World*, Tübingen, 1983), 757 f.

[88] In *Current Sociology* vol. 21, No. 2, 1973 [publ. 1975], pp. 1-170.

and "sect." Each of the several dimensions is limited to two possibilities. One can group the numerous pairs of contrasts into three
categories: culturally determined, socially determined, and organizational. In the cultural dimension are found four pairs: purity *versus*
compromise in doctrines and ethics; immediacy of the sacred *versus*
intermediacy of it in churches; dogmatism *versus* doctrinal flexibility;
ascetical *versus* materialistic life-style. In the social dimension sociologists have suggested the following pairs of contrast: protest *versus*
accommodation to the prevailing social conditions; compensatory
functions of sects *versus* legitimizing functions of churches; exclusive
versus inclusive membership. If one turns to the dimension of organization, one can find three important contrasts that are considered to
distinguish sects from churches: small *versus* big; unstable, informal,
and simple organization of sects *versus* stable, formal, and complex
organization of churches; sects are said to be warm, primary social
groups *versus* the cold, impersonal churches. This abundance of dual
alternatives offers innumerable possibilities of confusion and of using
variables that are neither logically nor factually connected with each
other, but vary independently. It is also difficult to know whether the
typology aims at analysing phenomena at the collective or the individual level; often there is an unthinking switch from one to the other.
Not seldom definitions of church and sect may be composed of several
dimensions of opposed attributes, but explanation of collective processes and structures may be covertly framed in terms of only one
particular set of oppositions; or the emphasis may shift from one
attribute to another as the analysis proceeds. The time-factor is usually
disregarded, as is the purpose for which the type was originally constructed. From a logical and analytical point of view the "church-sect"
distinction is an arch-problematic concept that cannot be used without
a volume of modifications and necessary refinements, wherefore Beckford proposes a moratorium in the use of it.[89]

A further illustration of the analytical deficiencies of this whole
typology is offered by the way in which various scholars describe the
expansion and transition from rural Palestine to urban Hellenistic
society taking place in early Christianity. What Esler characterizes as
a transition from being an intra-Jewish renewal movement to becoming a sect, completely separate from its origin, Rodney Stark describes
as a transition from a sect to a cult movement! So, cutting loose from
the parent community changes the movement to a sect for Esler, while

---

[89] Ibid., 93-97.

Stark sees this as changing the sect to a cult. "Sect" is not a very distinct category.

Because of its historical and cultural limitations, the lack of precision in the construction of types, and the inherent tendency to static re-ification of the typology, the church-sect categorization of religious groups seems to be a rather doubtful instrument of analysis. The only thing that can be said in its defense is that it "has formed the basis for some of the most important work done in the sociology of religion."[90] But it seems to be time for a major revision of this badly flawed sociological model. And New Testament scholars need to be correspondingly more careful in their use of it—if they should not leave it aside altogether as blurring the understanding of the early church rather than making it clearer.

Explanatory power of the distinction

If one wants to assess the explanatory power of the church-sect distinction, it might be good to begin by taking a look at its power to discriminate among groups of different places and periods in early Christianity. Which parts of early Christianity are considered to be sectarian? The scholars differ in their answer to that question, naturally. Some make no distinctions at all but consider the whole movement to be sectarian (Gager, Meeks eventually, and Rowland; the latter includes all of pre-70 Judaism as well). Some would say that the movement in its earliest beginnings in Palestine had the characteristics of a sect, but that these did not prevail (Theissen, Scroggs, Rodney Stark). Others consider Pauline Christianity to be a clear example of a sect (Meeks), and even say that it is the first example of a sect in early Christianity (Watson, perhaps also Esler). One scholar characterizes Pauline Christianity all through the period A.D. 50–140 as a sect, albeit beginning to develop into a church-type movement at the end (MacDonald). Others too focus on rather late examples, like Lucan Christianity (Esler), rural Christians in northern Asia Minor in the last two decades of the first century (Elliott, who however can talk about the whole of early Christianity as a messianic sect[91]), and the Johannine community after A.D. 70 (Meeks).

This diversity seems first to allow the general conclusion that we find a low degree of scholarly continuity within this approach; many scholars do not bother to discuss the work of others, or do so only very briefly. Secondly, it seems obvious that all these scholars use the

---

[90] Meredith B. McGuire, *Religion: The Social Context*, 1981, Belmont, California, 110.
[91] Elliott, *A Home*, 72.

same term, but do not operate with the same category. Perhaps those who restrict the term to the earliest period consider the more radical, charismatic way of life and high-strung apocalyptic expectations evidenced in the beginning of the movement to be the true marks of a sect, while others refuse to speak of a sect unless there is a clear separation from the parent community. The most used category, the conversionist sect, which focuses on the ambivalence between keeping the world out and wanting the world in, is so wide that it permits all of these applications. We have to conclude that the category of "sect" has a very low degree of discriminatory power in the classification of different groups within early Christianity.

As the church-sect categorization is thought to enable clarification and explanation of the reality behind the New Testament texts, it is of interest to see what the scholars presented above have found it to explain. A few scholars do not use it to explain anything at all (Theissen, Rowland). Scroggs is one of the few who really makes explicit what he considers to be the profit of introducing the characterization of early Christianity as a sect, when he states that we now have a basically different gestalt from which to view the data. This means that the texts are freed from a crust of theologizing, and seen more as products of people living in repressive social circumstances, in an antagonistic outsider position over against all the authorities of society. In other words, our middle-class Christian reading glasses come off, and we see the first Christians more as they really were. I think this is quite to the point, and that Scroggs has formulated one of the real advantages brought to the study of the New Testament by a "sectarian" understanding of it.

Rodney Stark's short paper suggests a covariation between social location and a shift in worldview and type of religion, which offers some confirmation of the results of recent social historical investigations. Elliott's conversionist sect perspective serves to fill in the picture of the social life of its addressees, and explains not only why they are shunned by the larger society and so dependent on their own tight little communities, but also 1 Peter's ambivalence in world-view and attitude toward the non-Christians. MacDonald considers the well-known tendency of conversionist sects to be transformed in a more churchly direction to explain the fact that the Christianity of the Pastoral Epistles has moved closer to embrace the values of the surrounding world. This is a rare example of using Wilson's (additional) model of sect development on the New Testament. Esler and Watson, finally, use the sect perspective to explain the remarkable legitimating techniques of Luke and Paul, respectively.[92]

Even if all these explanations are credible in themselves, one has to note their wide diversity. This may, of course, be due to the fecundity of scholarly imagination, but it may also point to the same conclusion as above: when looking at the "sectarian" character of early Christianity, scholars are actually investigating rather different aspects of their object. "Sect" is not one category, but several, or, alternately, it is a very wide category, inside which the whole of first-century Christianity can be fitted.

The comparative method—possibilities and limitations

Our summary of the use of the comparative method that has been demonstrated in this chapter can start with Peter Burke's comments on it in his *Sociology and History:*

> One might say that comparisons are useful primarily because they enable us to see what is not there. Comparisons are also useful in the search for explanations. To see what varies with what makes it easier to understand the differences between one society and another. It was for this reason that Durkheim called the comparative method a kind of 'indirect experiment', without which it would be impossible to move from description to analysis. He distinguished two main kinds of comparison, between societies which were fundamentally the same in structure and between societies which were fundamentally different, but he considered both procedures to be of value.[93]

Burke points to what is the obvious usefulness of any type of comparison, even if it is not perfect from an analytical point of view: it enables us to see both similarities and differences of which we were not aware until the comparison showed them to us. But in order to

[92] Elizabeth Schüssler Fiorenza points to a further theoretical weakness: "When reconstructing the Jesus movement scholars seem to develop the heuristic model of 'sect or millenarian' movement over and against 'the world' and total culture, while in their description of the consolidation of the early Christian movement the sect-church model seems to loom large. Such a theoretical shift may be justified but it is not critically reflected." Idem, *In Memory of Her: A Feminist Theological Reconstruction of Christian Origins.* London, 1983, 80.

[93] Peter Burke, *Sociology and History,* London, 1980, 33. The distinction between the two kinds of comparison was made in Durkheim's *Les Règles de la méthode sociologique.* Paris, 1895, ch. 6.

be sure that what we see are real differences and similarities, we need a clear and well-constructed categorization of the phenomena—and this I consider that we are still lacking in the church-sect typology.

The deficiencies of this typology can be made clearer by using the distinction between monothetic and polythetic typologies.[94] A monothetic group of phenomena is so defined that the possession of a unique set of attributes is both sufficient and necessary for membership in the group. A polythetic group, on the other hand, is a group where most members share most attributes, but in which no single attribute is either necessary or sufficient for group membership. In a monothetic typology a phenomenon has to answer exactly to a set of, say, ten criteria to be included, while in a polythetic one it is enough if seven or eight out of ten characteristics are there; Wittgenstein termed this type of similarity "family resemblance." Now, the deficiency of the church-sect typology in my opinion is that it requires something like two or three similarities only, which is a too low degree of resemblance to make the typology workable and discriminating. No doubt many real and illuminating similarities and differences between various religious movements turn up in the process of comparison, and this makes for a limited fruitfulness of the enterprise anyway. But I contend that many are overlooked and not a few are spurious.

Durkheim's distinction between comparisons made between fundamentally similar societies and fundamentally different ones is familiar to those who have read Theissen's or Esler's comments on social scientific method.[95] Theissen points out that in the first case, the close comparison, the social situation is the common and constant element, and the different religious movements the variable answers to it. In the second case, where comparisons are made between distant societies, the differences in social situation are obvious, and the interest focuses on the corresponding structural similarities. The most used analogy is of course messianic-chiliastic or millenarian movements of different times and places, with their expectations of the end of the

---

[94] Burke, *Sociology and History*, 36 f. Burke actually talks about models, but since his definition of model—"an intellectual construct which simplifies reality in order to emphasise the recurrent, the constant and the typical, which it presents in the form of clusters of traits or attributes. In other words 'models' and 'types' are treated as synonyms" (Ibid., 35)—is very close to Esler's definition of a typology, and since I consider Esler's distinction between models and typologies to be valuable, I will here use Esler's terminology.

[95] Theissen, "Die soziologische Auswertung religiöser öberlieferungen," *Studien*, 51-53. Esler, *Community and Gospel*, 9-12.

world, messianic prophets, miraculous and ecstatic phenomena, and *parousia* disconfirmations. The drawback of this analogizing comparison is its lack of precision, as no phenomena are ever exactly the same. But the advantage is that it generates many interesting hypotheses.

Esler makes a similar point concerning what he terms distant comparison: it assists the sociological imagination in raising new questions and formulating new hypotheses. Close comparison, on the other hand, assists in the verification of hypotheses, and

> is analogous to an experiment where all conditions are kept constant, except for the variable whose behaviour is to be observed. For such a comparison of social data to be effective it is obviously necessary that the comparison be between two or more structures or institutions from contexts which are both similar culturally and not too distant chronologically. Otherwise the comparison will be too artificial to contribute to the verification of hypotheses.[96]

Behind the attempt at finding structural similarities between widely separate cultures lies, I suspect, the functionalist assumption that all human cultures are basically similar at some deep, functional level, which is independent of people's beliefs and motifs.[97] And one could ask critically, whether the hidden goal (or assumption!) behind many distant comparisons, is not simply the establishing of generalizations of this universal, ideal-typical kind.

It is evident that the comparisons made above between early Christianity and the sect typologies of Troeltsch and Wilson, and Esler's model of sect development, are not of the close kind.[98] The comparisons have not been made in order to verify any hypotheses, as they are all of the distant kind where one looks for new hypotheses and questions to put to the New Testament data. This means that what we should expect from the comparative application of the church-sect typology is not verification but rather interesting new ideas and hypotheses for future work. Perhaps this is what the church-sect typology and millenarian model are really good for; but then this goal

---

[96] Esler, ibid., 10.

[97] See the perceptive critique of this position in Stanley Kent Stowers, "The Social Sciences and the Study of Early Christianity" in W. S. Green (ed.), *Approaches to Ancient Judaism*, Atlanta, 1985, 149-181), esp. 155 f.

[98] Theissen has attempted such comparisons in his *Soziologie der Jesusbewegung* (1977), and in "Wir haben alles verlassen' (Mc. X, 28). Nachfolge und soziale Entwurzelung in der jüdisch-palästinischen Gesellschaft des 1. Jahrhunderts n. Chr." (*Novum Testamentum* 19, 1977, 161-196; now in idem, *Studien*, 106-141).

should be kept in mind and not misunderstood as delivering explanations.

The comparative method is in itself so fruitful that one learns much, simply by beginning to use it, even if the categories at hand are rather primitive. This explains why the research described in this chapter has brought forth many new and interesting results. But probably they would be more numerous and more assured, if the classifications were improved beyond the state of the church-sect typology.

4 Correlations between Symbolic and Social Structures

Sociology of knowledge—some New Testament applications

One of the most promising—and, as will be shown, most difficult—approaches in New Testament sociology uses the insights of the sociology of knowledge in attempting to find correlations between expressions of faith and the underlying social situation or structure.[1]

We have already met a number of alleged correlations of this type in the previous discussion. John Gager suggested that millenarian beliefs and social distress are correlated, and also made some use of Weber's idea about elective affinity between different social strata and their various types of religion, when he concluded that early Christianity was a typical lower middle-class religion. Rodney Stark found probable a correlation between low social position and a sectarian protest movement on the one hand, and between the "cult movement" and people in more affluent strata on the other hand. Philip Esler and Francis Watson both proposed that theology must be seen in strong correlation with the needs of a specific social situation, if it is to be understood correctly. A borderline case is the one depicted by John Elliott, when he posits a conscious "strategy" on the part of the authors of 1 Peter. They know the dilemma of their addressees, and this has shaped their two-pronged approach: emphasizing both faithfulness to the calling to be the elect and holy of God, and the effort to impress and win the outsiders. As the "fit" between social reality and religious language in 1 Peter is the result of conscious planning and problem-solving, it is not really analogous to the types of "natural fit" that Meeks and Theissen have suggested (see below). The very phrase

---

[1] Among them who consider it promising are Jonathan Z. Smith, "The Social Description of Early Christianity" (*Religious Studies Review* 1, 1975, 19-25), 21; Robin Scroggs, "The Sociological Interpretation of the New Testament: The Present State of Research" (*New Testament Studies* 26, 1980, 164-179), 175-177, and John G. Gager, "Shall We Marry Our Enemies? Sociology and the New Testament" (*Interpretation* 36, 1982, 256-265), 263 f. All three point to the article of Meeks on Johannine sectarianism (1972) as the prime example of this approach; this is discussed below.

"natural fit" indicates that the similarity or correlation between social structure and the structure of belief is more unplanned, selfgrowing, and situated at a deep connecting level.

For this reason, and also because the work of Meeks and Theissen in this field is very well known, interesting, and path-breaking, I will concentrate on their contributions in the following.

The Synoptic Gospels—a reflection of the wandering charismatics
Probably any reader of Gerd Theissen's work will be impressed by the continuity of his analytical perspectives throughout a remarkable series of publications. As one reads through his essays in *Studien zur Soziologie des Urchristentums* (1979, ²1983), from the earliest ("Wanderradikalismus," 1973)[2] to the latest ("Christologie und soziale Erfahrung" from 1983), complementing this with the sociological part of *Urchristliche Wundergeschichten* (1974), and with *Soziologie der Jesusbewegung* (1977), one notices that through all the various texts analysed and the many different sociological perspectives applied, Theissen's total perspective remains the same. Modifications there are, and much added material over the years, but the main lines of his sociological perspective have been consistent.

Among those constant features belongs Theissen's fundamentally form critical view of the New Testament, especially the gospel material. He explicitly refers his own understanding and execution of the sociology of literature to that of Rudolf Bultmann. The basic idea of finding the "Sitz im Leben" of these texts through constructive, analytical, and comparative conclusions, which is so dominant both in Theissen's essay on the methodology of sociological fact-finding in the New Testament, and in his application of these methods, comes straight out of the first few pages of Bultmann's *Geschichte der synoptischen Tradition* (1921).[3] To analyse the New Testament from a sociology of literature perspective means then to ask for the intentions *and* for the social conditions of typical, interpersonal behaviour of the authors, tradition carriers, and recipients of New Testament texts. Traditional form criticism focused on the former aspect, the intentions, which made it concentrate on religious and churchly type situations, but nothing prevents a broadening of the original task to include social conditions generally.

---

[2] Actually given as his "Habilitationsvortrag" in November 1972.
[3] Gerd Theissen, "Die soziologische Auswertung religiöser Überlieferungen" *(Studien,* 35-54), 36 note 4, and idem, "Wanderradikalismus" *(Studien,* 79-105),82.

The transmission of the words of Jesus (and the whole Jesus tradition) is a sociological problem, because it began as an oral tradition. Jesus did not leave a written deposit of teaching, and the tradition from him and about him was, like any other oral tradition, left at the mercy of its transmitters and receivers, as Theissen puts it.[4] Its preservation was bound to certain social conditions, such as (a) an anchoring of the tradition in a repeated, typical, interpersonal behaviour pattern of the transmitters, which was relatively independent of individual preferences, (b) an interest from the side of the passive tradition preservers, who must want to hear the traditions and be guided, edified, etc., by them; if nobody even attempts to observe ethical instructions, it is unlikely that they will be transmitted for a very long time, and (c) a sociological continuity between Jesus and the transmitters of his words. Those who were the disciples of Jesus during his lifetime became his preachers after his death, and continued his life-style as wandering charismatics.[5] One can assume that the words of Jesus were revered and practised in this group, which does not preclude that they were also modified to approximate the actual behaviour of the disciples.

Now, the question is which type of people in which type of social conditions can have transmitted, for thirty years or more, words from Jesus to the effect that no one who does not hate his own family can be his disciple, that one has to leave one's house, work, family and follow him, that property is an effective hindrance for entering the kingdom, etc. Theissen's answer is the thesis that this ethical radicalism, which we find especially in the Q material, is wandering radicalism, i.e., a radicalism carried and practised by a group of people who lived like their master, in charismatic poverty, walking from place to place to preach the advent of the kingdom of God, pronouncing blessing and healing on those who receive them, and the judgment of God on those who don't. These charismatic apostles and prophets were the only ones who were free to really practise what Jesus had taught, and that is why they were the transmitters of the tradition from Jesus, himself the first wandering charismatic.[6]

Thus, if the words in a gospel text are authentic words from Jesus, we can assume that the transmitters have shaped their lives in accordance with the tradition, and if they are not, we must assume that

---

[4] "Wanderradikalismus," 81: "an die Interessen ihrer Tradenten und Adressaten ausgeliefert."

[5] Theissen, *Jesusbewegung,* 12 note 4. Theissen is here less skeptical than Bultmann, who sees a sharp discontinuity between Jesus and the early church.

[6] "Wanderradikalismus," 82-91.

the transmitters have formed the tradition in accordance with their own way of life. Either way, Theissen's basic assumption is that of an agreement, or correlation, between the content of the tradition and the way of life of its transmitters.[7] Theissen is, at least in principle, more open than traditional form criticism for considering the Jesus tradition authentic, or in other words, willing to accept some degree of correlation between the tradition and Jesus, although this is not what his work is about. But he has no hesitations whatsoever about the correlation between the gospel tradition and the social situation of its transmitters, the pre-70, Syro-Palestine wandering charismatics.[8] This is especially evident in one of the most marked theses of Theissen, that there exists a "structural homology" between the behaviour of the first Christians and the role of the Son of Man.[9] The Son of Man has the role of an outsider, both positively and negatively. He stands above the norms of the society, and can break the Sabbath rules or disregard fasting—and so can his disciples. He is also homeless and shunned, and so are his followers. Evidently, the Son of Man christology had an important social function: to interpret and justify the social situation of the wandering charismatics, who were authorities in the small groups of believers and deviant outsiders in the larger society. The tension between (future) exaltation and (present) disgrace in the Son of Man christology is structurally homologous with the role-conflict of the wandering charismatics. The connection is so close that Theissen himself asks whether the "Son of Man" perhaps was only the externalized super-ego of the wandering charismatics: while trying to shape their lives in "imitation" of His, in reality the picture of the Son of Man was formed after their social role.[10]

---

[7] *Jesusbewegung*, 12.

[8] For this date and place, see e.g., *Jesusbewegung*, 9, and "Gewaltverzicht und Feindesliebe (Mt 5,38-48/Lk 6,27-38) und deren sozialgeschichtlicher Hintergrund" (*Studien*, 1979, 160-197), 184. From "Wanderradikalismus," 86-89, and *Jesusbewegung*, 15 f, it appears that the phenomenon of wandering charismatics continued well into the first half of the second century.

[9] There seems to be some disagreement as to what is meant by a structural homology. Theissen, leaning on L. Goldmann's "genetical structuralism" approach to the sociology of literature, defines it as a structural agreement between social realities and spiritual phenomena (*Jesusbewegung*, 28 note 8). But according to Klaus Berger there is no direct correlation between statements in a text and sociological data; the correlation is mediated through the symbolic universe ("Weltanschauung") of the group that produces or receives the text. Structural homology is thus a relation between the symbolic universe and literary contents. Klaus Berger, *Exegese* (²1984), 234.

[10] Theissen, *Jesusbewegung*, 28-30. Theissen's answer is hardly sufficient to ward off this fatal identification: the judgment parable of Mt 25, 31-46 shows that the behaviour that will be rewarded is active love, independent of any conscious belief in the "Son of Man."

In his 1979 article on the sociohistorical background of the gospel traditions about nonviolence and the love of enemies, Theissen shows how a teaching that he considers to be from Jesus himself has been received and somewhat changed in different social situations.[11] The special Matthean emphases point to the situation of Palestinian Jewish society during and after the war with the Romans A.D. 66–70, while the accents of Luke's own material indicate that love of enemies was connected with problems concerning the lending of money and the duty of rich Christians to support poor ones. The Q material underlines the need to love and bless people who hate and illtreat the disciples, a situation pointing to the experiences of the wandering charismatics. The source and basis of these applications is the demands of Jesus, formulated in a highly general, apodictic way, impressive and helpful alike in many differing situations. One could perhaps call this an ongoing (dialectic?) correlation between the tradition and the social situation of early Christianity as it developed and changed.[12]

It seems, to begin with, that Theissen is not so cautious in his historical groundwork as his own methodology requires. His evidence for the social situation with which the Gospels correlate, i.e., the existence and life-style of the wandering charismatics of the Jesus movement, consists of three parts: constructive, analytical, and comparative conclusions. The analytical conclusions presuppose that such a correlation exists, and can therefore not be allowed as evidence for it, which leaves us with the other two types. As comparative evidence Theissen points to the wandering Cynic philosophers, admitting however that this analogy brings us outside Jewish Palestine. The constructive evidence consists in assembling all early Christian examples of apostles or prophets who wander or travel; most of the examples come from the Acts of the Apostles and Didache, both of which are non-Palestinian and late sources. The independent historical basis for the existence of this leading group in the first decades seems rather slender, especially if we withdraw Peter, Paul, and Barnabas from the examples, as none of them is true to the type Theissen has described. The case rests, then, mainly on the analytical conclusions drawn from

---

[11] Gerd Theissen, "Gewaltverzicht."

[12] The essay "Christologie und soziale Erfahrung. Wissenssoziologische Aspekte paulinischer Christologie" which was first published in 1983 (*Studien*, 318-330), consists of a discussion of the "plausibility basis" (a concept from Berger and Luckmann) of two themes in Pauline christology. When "plausibility basis" is made more or less synonymous with "background," as it is here, the meaning of "correlation" also becomes very attenuated.

the Synoptic Gospels (none of which in their finished form has a certain pre-70, Palestinian provenance!), which is another way of saying that it rests on the presupposition that the correlation Theissen uses is a fact.

Anyone criticizing this presupposition will at the same time have to attack basic postulates of form criticism. A full-scale criticism of such a dominant scholarly tradition is obviously a taller order than can be met in this little book.[13] But one can at least try to point out some weaknesses of form criticism as a sociology of knowledge.

One such weak point is the assumption of a simple, one-to-one correspondence between a text or type of text and the underlying social situation of its carriers.[14] Even Bultmann's own suggestions that we could conclude from a conflict between Jesus and the Pharisees concerning the former's authority to forgive sins (Mk 2) to a repeated, typical pattern in the life of the early church of forgiving sins and having to defend this took some believing. But Theissen sometimes goes further and sees the *contents* of the narratives about Jesus as more or less a description of the life of the Jesus movement.[15] He can, for example, write about the movement's ambivalence toward wealth

---

[13] An important impulse toward rethinking the basic postulates of form criticism is to be found in the work of my teacher Birger Gerhardsson, from his *Memory and Manuscript* (1961) and onward. Regrettably few have grappled with what he really writes. Some newer literature on and discussion of form criticism can be found in Walter Schmithals, 'Kritik der Formkritik" (*Zeitschrift für Theologie und Kirche* 77, 1980, 149-185); Reiner Blank, *Analyse und Kritik der formgeschichtlichen Arbeiten von Martin Dibelius und Rudolf Bultmann* [Diss. Basel 1978]. Basel, 1981; Peter Stuhlmacher (ed.), *Das Evangelium und die Evangelien* (WUNT 28). Tübingen, 1982; Klaus Berger, *Formgeschichte des Neuen Testaments*. Heidelberg, 1984; Alfred Zimmermann, *Die urchristlichen Lehrer* (WUNT 2. Reihe 12). Tübingen, 1984; Georg Schelbert, "Wo steht die Formgeschichte?" (*Theologische Berichte XIII. Methoden der Evangelienexegese.* 1985, 11-39); Hermann-Josef Venetz, "Der Beitrag der Soziologie zur Lektüre des Neuen Testaments. Ein Bericht" (ibid., 87-121).

[14] "We have to beware of assuming a one-to-one relationship between genre and sociolinguistic function," Lars Hartman, "Survey of the Problem of Apocalyptic Genre" (in Hellholm (ed.), *Apocalypticism in the Mediterranean World*, 329-343), 335, with further literature; cf. idem, "Till frägan om evangeliernas litterära genre" (*Annales Academias Regiae Scientiarum Upsaliensis* 21, 1978, 5-22), 17. In "Some Unorthodox Thoughts on the 'Household-Code Form' " (Neusner et al (eds.), *The Social World of Formative-Christianity and Judaism.* FS H. C. Kee. Philadelphia, 1988, 219-232), 229 f, Hartman has extended his criticism of the form critical idea that a specific literary form must have a specific social situation behind it to a text in the Pauline tradition.

[15] This is probably due to the high degree of plasticity or malleability that Theissen and form critics generally ascribe to the gospel tradition, sometimes referring to a complete lack of interest in history prevailing in the intensely apocalyptic early Jesus movement. This is also an axiom whose historical plausibility has been contested by a number oi scholars (Roloff, Schürmann, Stuhlmacher).

and property: One criticized the rich (Mk 10:25; Lk 6:24 f), but profited from them. One let oneself be supported by the affluent wife of a Herodian officeholder (Lk 8:3), by Joseph from Arimathea (Mk 15:43), by a rich sinner (Lk 7:36 ff) as well as by the chief tax collector Zacchaeus (Lk 19:1 ff). "Make friends for yourselves by means of unrighteous mammon," goes the maxim (Lk 16:9).[16] So these names and persons from the Gospels belong just as well in the life of the Jesus movement (A.D. 30–70, Palestine and Syria) as in the life of Jesus, or maybe even better!

This rather unprincipled application of the correlation principle reveals that the basic assumption conceals more and may be more questionable than it first appears. Theissen refers to the thirty years of oral tradition (a form critical axiom which no longer stands uncontested) as a chasm that could only be bridged by the interest of the movement members in finding support for their own behaviour; everything else that Jesus might have said and done just fell away during this passage. This pattern may be true concerning the transmission of folklore, which is mostly "low-intensity" literature for didactic purposes and pleasure, and is passed from generation to generation—what is not interesting will not survive.[17] But is it really probable that traditions about Jesus were preserved *only* because they were in agreement with the behaviour patterns of the Jesus-believers? It seems possible, to say the least, to think of other preservation factors operative during this one generation, for example the personal continuity between Jesus and his disciples that Theissen himself believes to have been a historical fact. Would not a group of dedicated followers of Jesus, who did not merely think him the best teacher in the world, but also believed that he had actually been resurrected from the dead by God to show that he was indeed the Messiah and Lord of Israel, regard his words as worth preserving just because he had said them? Even if it is quite explicit and conscious, such a belief in Jesus is, of course, sociologically effective, simply because it too shapes group attitudes and behaviour patterns. To be sociologically effective is not a prerogative of the more latent interests of legitimation and group preservation.

The possible operation of several different preservation factors opens for a discussion concerning various degrees and types of correlation. The postulate of complete and positive correlation between

---

[16] Theissen, *Jesusbewegung*, 39 f.

[17] The main issue in the work of Birger Gerhardsson is whether form criticism really found the historically most plausible historical analogy to the transmission of the gospel tradition in the transmission of folkloristic material, not whether form criticism is too sceptical or not.

a text and the social group that carries and receives it is implausible. To read the gospel narratives as if they were uniformly allegories of early church life is, if nothing else, somewhat unimaginative. A text can just as well be standing in a negative correlation to the situation of the receivers, i.e., challenge or try to change it.[18] And the uncertainty concerning what type of correlation we encounter applies especially where the texts use symbolic language, which often is a kind of double talk that has metaphorical and distant references, or may be charged with irony.[19] In practise this means that one should at least ask oneself if the correlation between the analysed text and its social situation is complete or partial, positive or negative.

The Gospel of John shaped by a sectarian situation
In 1972 Wayne Meeks published an article on "The Man from Heaven in Johannine Sectarianism" where he attempted to show that several aspects of the fourth gospel could be understood better with the help of sociology of knowledge than from the traditional, history of ideas perspective. The latter usually reduces mythical language to theological categories, "and *historical* judgments are then made on the basis of the presumed *logical* priority of one or the other of these categories."[20] After a careful description of the central descent/ascent motif in the gospel, Meeks concluded that this does not really function as a symbol of unity, as has been held, but is always in John connected with contrast, foreignness, division, and judgment. It serves to underline and express the strangeness of Jesus, who cannot be comprehended even by sympathetic Jews like Nicodemus or the Baptist. The whole gospel is a closed system of metaphors, which must be accepted totally or will not be understood at all.

The story of Jesus in this gospel is the story of a progressive alienation from the Jewish community, and Meeks follows Louis Martyn in stating that there can be no question "that the actual trauma of the Johannine community's separation from the synagogue and its continuing hostile relationships with the synagogue come clearly to expression here."[21] The social situation of the community is mirrored in its depiction of Jesus over against his unbelieving people, and "one of the primary functions of the book, therefore, must have been to

---

[18] Cf. Abraham J. Malherbe, *Social Aspects of Early Christianity*, 1977, 13 f.
[19] Christopher Tuckett, *Reading the New Testament*, 136 ff.
[20] Wayne A. Meeks, "The Man from Heaven in Johannine Sectarianism" (*Journal of Biblical Literature* 91, 1972, 44-72), 46 f; emphasis in the original.
[21] Ibid., 69.

provide a reinforcement for the community's social identity, which appears to have been largely negative. It provided a symbolic universe which gave religious legitimacy, a theodicy, to the group's actual isolation from the larger society."[22]

Meeks envisages a continuing dialectic between the group's historical experience and their symbolic world: the christological claims of these Christians alienated them from the other Jews in the synagogue, and finally expelled them; this experience was then projected onto the story of Jesus, who was increasingly depicted as the Stranger, never accepted by his own ("the Jews") and totally incomprehensible to them; these more extreme christological motifs and the accompanying totalistic and exclusive claims[23] drove the Johannine group into further sectarian isolation. "It is a case of continual, harmonic reinforcement between social experience and ideology."[24]

This essay has been much admired and seen by several other scholars as opening up a new and fruitful approach. Jonathan Z. Smith thought it to be the most creative study of early Christian materials as the creation of a social world, and characterized Meeks' conclusions as "the results of a happy combination of exegetical and sociological sophistication."[25] And Robin Scroggs considered Meeks' article to be an illustration of the "immense possibilities" of the most important approach within the field of sociology, viz., the sociology of knowledge.[26]

In an article from 1985, where Meeks discusses the separation of the Johannine, Pauline, and Matthean Christian groups from the Jewish communities, he could also state that his ideas from 1972 have been widely recognized in recent scholarship, both his characterization of this group as a sect, and the idea that the rupture with "the Jews" shaped the Johannine group's language and their perception of the world. What is added in this article is an attempt at localizing

---

[22] Ibid., 70. The terminology here is borrowed from Peter L. Berger's and Thomas Luckmann's sociology of knowledge, and this probably constitutes the first use of these perspectives in New Testament studies.

[23] As Meeks puts it in a later work: "the leaders of the Christian [Johannine] community despised secret believers in Jesus who wanted to remain in the Jewish community." Idem, *The Moral World of the First Christians*. London, 1987 [first publ. in USA 1986], 109.

[24] Ibid., 50 and 71.

[25] J. Z. Smith, "The Social Description of Early Christianity," 21.

[26] Scroggs, "State of Research," 176. Cf. also Gager's remarks on Meeks' 1972 article in "Marry Our Enemies?," 264, and the discussion of it in Dennis C. Duling, "Insights from Sociology for New Testament Christology: A Test Case" *(Society of Biblical Literature 1985 Seminar Papers* 24, 1985, 351-368).

the Johannine community. With others Meeks locates it in an urban milieu, most probably in towns of Lower Galilee or its vicinity, where there was a relatively large presence of Judaean, Galilean, and Samaritan immigrants.[27] Meeks also thinks that by the time the Johannine letters were written, the community had left the synagogues and the wish to belong to them, and retreated into their own house-churches.[28]

But as all pathbreaking works this important essay has also been criticized. Klaus Berger disputes that John's puzzling imagery is evidence for a closed system of metaphors, which made the book totally incomprehensible to any but the "insiders" of the Johannine community. This is a misunderstanding of the implied reader of the gospel, who is not left in the position of Nicodemus, but rather given instructive examples of how Jesus should not be (mis)understood. These are just the kind of hints that would not be needed in a book for insiders only, and one meant to be incomprehensible to others. And compared with Gnostic writings, or even with Romans 8, it is not very difficult to grasp the meaning of John's metaphorical language. Further, the Johannine group seems to have understood itself, not so much as a tightly knit family of "brothers," but rather as a group of "friends" and "disciples"—a self-understanding that points in the direction of the ancient philosophical schools. This, together with the fact that the gospel presupposes and reworks synoptic material, and tries to initiate the readers into a deeper understanding of what they already know of Jesus, makes Berger conclude that this gospel had a much wider appeal and served the integration of several groups with different backgrounds.[29]

Even if Berger's suggestion of seeing the Johannine community as more of a "school" is not followed, one can feel hesitant about the method of Meeks. At the root of the whole construction lies a piece of psychologization: a christology of a God-sent Saviour who is incomprehensible and rejected by his people must reflect a feeling among those who believe in Jesus of being uncomprehended, disbelieved, and rejected. This psychologization is then sociologized: that feeling must be a reflection of their actual experiences of social

---

[27] Wayne A. Meeks, "Breaking Away: Three New Testament Pictures of Christianity's Separation from the Jewish Communities," in J. Neusner and E. S. Frerichs (eds.), *"To See Ourselves as Others See Us": Christians, Jews, 'Others' in Late Antiquity*. Chico, Califomia, 1985, 93-115), 94 and 103.

[28] "Breaking Away," 103 f, and Idem, *Moral World*, 109 f.

[29] Klaus Berger, *Exegese des Neuen Testaments: Neue Wege vom Text zur Auslegung*. Heidelberg, 1977, ²1984, 230 f.

relations with the surrounding nonbelievers; *ergo*, they were a har-
rassed minority, a typical sect. It sounds plausible, but how secure is
the psychologization at the root? Perhaps there could be alternative
explanations. As Baasland has pointed out, what Meeks actually does
is to elucidate one unknown (the Johannine group) with another (the
social situation presupposed by their gospel).[30] This would seem to
be a variant of a circular type of reasoning: first one reconstructs a
specific social situation (about which nothing else is known) out of a
religious, mainly theological or hortatory text, then one turns around
and interprets the meaning of the text with the help of the situation
that one now "knows." The only legitimate procedure is to reverse
this procedure and work inductively, i.e., to start from sociologically
relevant data that exist independent of the theological text, and investigate whether they "fit" structures in the symbolical world.[31]

Finally, the value of this sociological interpretation has been questioned also from another point of view: does it do anything else than
retell what we already knew, but in a new terminology? The mere
fact that sociological models can be made to fit the New Testament
data is no proof of their validity. As it stands, the sociological com-
ponent of Meeks' article does not add anything to his interpretation
of the Gospel of John, but merely reinforces the interpretation he had
already chosen.[32]

Status inconsistency and Pauline Christianity
Meeks also turned to a comprehensive analysis of Pauline Christianity,
ranging over wide fields of sociological analysis, eventually published
as what has rightly been lauded as the best book on the social world
of Paul and Pauline Christianity, *The First Urban Christians* (1983). In

---

[30] Ernst Baasland, "Urkristendommen i sosiologiens lys" (*Tidskrift for Teologi og Kirke*
54, 1984, 45-57), 57 note 29.

[31] "Only when one already has sociological data, is it possible to correlate social situations
and texts (Erst wenn man über soziologische Daten verfügt, kann man soziale Situ-
ationen und Texte korrelieren)." Gerd Theissen, "Die soziologische Auswertung religiöser Überlieferungen," *Studien*, 50 note 31. Cf. what Peter Lampe has formulated in
another context: "It is methodologically illegitimate to conclude to the social situation
of the Gnostic simply from the structure of his theological system (Denkgebäude)
because one has certain preconceived (Weberian) ideas about correlations between
"social conditions" and "metaphysical doctrines." The procedure must be inverted."
Peter Lampe, *Die stadtrömischen Christen in den ersten beiden Jahrhunderten: Untersuchungen
zur Sozialgeschichte* (WUNT Reihe 2, 18) (English trans. forthcoming from Fortress Press).
2. Aufl. Tübingen, 1989, 252.

[32] Christopher Tuckett, *Reading the New Testament: Methods of Interpretation*. London,
1987, 145 ff.

this book he discussed a number of social-science perspectives on this part of early Christianity, such as its social historical context, social stratification, conflict resolution procedures and governance, internal social organization, the function of rituals, and the interplay of belief and social situation. On this last question he put forward a very interesting hypothesis in a prepublication article, "The Social Context of Pauline Theology." He summarized:

> A significant number of the people who were converted to the Christianity of the Pauline circle had experienced ambiguities in their social status. They were restless, mobile people. In the teaching and rituals of the new movement they discovered a powerfully ambivalent constellation of symbols—the crucifixion of the Son of God—that confirmed and transformed aspects of their experience. Furthermore, the small groups into which they were initiated were more closely knit and promoted a much more intense and emotional kind of interaction among members than did the ordinary clubs and cultic associations. Yet these groups were also unusual in the degree to which they mixed together people of different social levels. In these groups the people we have noticed found new channels for the energies and skills that had already made them into crossers of social boundaries. They exercised power within these groups, in ways that were not readily accessible to them in the "outside" society, and these new experiences of authority were confirmed by beliefs about the way God shows *his* power now and about the ways he would very soon transform the whole world.[33]

Meeks leaves open the question of cause and effect in this "natural fit" or "structural analogy" between the Corinthian congregation's social structure (several prominent members exhibited status inconsistency) and its paradoxical and antithetical central belief that the Son of God himself had been incarnated, rejected by the larger society, but confirmed by God in the resurrection. These persons can have felt attracted to a movement whose beliefs and rituals helped make sense of their own tension-laden social experience. And/Or their experience can have contributed to the selection and shaping of such beliefs.[34]

Nonetheless, it is hard to avoid the impression that this hypothesis actually builds on the presupposition that religion functions as a compensation for various kinds of deprivation among the leading stratum

---

[33] Wayne A. Meeks, "The Social Context of Pauline Theology" (*Interpretation* 36, 1982, 266-277), 275 f.
[34] Ibid., 272.

of Pauline Christians: (a) The pattern of Christ's life offers an interpretation of their own social frustrations, which makes sense of the
world and gives their lives a meaning that they have lacked before;
(b) the warm atmosphere of the Christian group gives them a sense
of belonging that they have lacked before; (c) these groups' need of
competent leadership fits with their need to deploy their energy and
skill, and to have legitimate power over others, needs that have hith-
erto not been satisfied. The hypothesis in this form is then a combination of a sociology of knowledge perspective and one from
motivation psychology.

In his book, *The First Urban Christians* (1983), Meeks returned to the
hypothesis concerning status inconsistency. This concept is discussed
and defined at the beginning of chapter 2 ("The Social Level of the
First Christians"), where Meeks explains why both social class and
ordo are unusable categories in forming a picture of stratification in
the Greco-Roman cities.[35] He goes on to mention that persons in
present-day American society who suffer from status inconsistency
(being ranked high on some status variables, low on others) tend to
search for ways of removing this inconsistency by changing the society, themselves, or perceptions of themselves. This might lead on
to the hypothesis that people of low status consistency in ancient
times would be similarly minded, and thus more prone to radically
change their situation and self-perception than the normal citizen. We
cannot assume that ancient mentality as regards self-perception and
motivation was the same as our individualistic, post-Augustinian and
post-Freudian one, but Meeks is optimistic concerning the applica-
bility of these modern results, considering the theories about status
inconsistency to have "great heuristic power."[36]

At the end of this chapter Meeks adds up his analysis of the prosopographical and indirect evidence concerning the social level of the
first Pauline Christians as confirming the emerging consensus that a
Pauline congregation reflected a fair cross-section of urban society,
and that one could find evidence of divergent rankings in the different

---

35 Meeks, *Urban*, 53-55.

36 And so are others in his wake, like Loveday Alexander: "Many scientific authors
[among which Luke could be placed] probably exhibited the kind of 'high status inconsistency' identified by Wayne Meeks as critical in forming, the self-understanding
of early Pauline Christianity. Whatever the social standing of their subject-matter (rhetoric, for example, would rank high), its teachers and practitioners themselves would
tend to be slaves or freedmen in great households, Greeks in Roman society, men
obliged to support themselves by the exercise of their profession." Idem, "Luke's Preface
in the Context of Greek Preface-Writing" (*Novum Testamentum* 18, 1986), 70.

dimensions of status, especially among the leading members. Meeks adds a generalization of his own: that the most active and prominent members of Paul's circle are people of high status inconsistency, and asks whether this is more than accidental, i.e., whether this is a natural fit, or simply an accidence of the record.[37] At the last but one page of his book Meeks almost turns the question into a sociological hypothesis: this was an important factor in bringing about their conversion to Christianity. But he does it in the form of a double-sided question: Does it seem plausible that the symbol world of (Pauline) Christianity would attract status inconsistents? Or, inversely, would their experiences tend to reinforce just those paradoxical and dialectical symbols?[38]

The method of putting forward a hypothesis in the form of contrasting pairs of questions is an elegant way of showing how tentative the suggestion is, and can naturally be understood as evidence that Meeks has grown increasingly more cautious in making statements about correlations.[39] But it is also a way of suggesting the dialectic between social experiences and theological formulation (cf. the term "reinforce"). As Meeks put it in 1972: "It is a case of continual, harmonic reinforcement between social experience and ideology."[40] There is no mistaking that, however guardedly formulated, Meeks considers the correlation between beliefs and social situation to be there, also in Pauline Christianity.

Criticism of the status inconsistency hypothesis

The hypothesis of status inconsistency and its correlations in the theology of Pauline communities has called forth a small flood of interested and critical comments—a sure sign that something new and eye-opening has been presented in our discipline. Perhaps it is worth keeping in mind that in a scholarly context the trivial or evidently false hardly calls for any comment, and that serious criticism is in fact a mark of respect. When other scholars are impressed, they really have to think the subject through in a more radical fashion, and consequently come up with more radical criticism.

We have seen that Meeks' central thesis is that the leading members of the Pauline congregations suffered from status inconsistency, leading to a state of cognitive dissonance (a term that Meeks interprets

---

[37] Meeks, *Urban*, 73.
[38] Ibid., 191.
[39] Pointed out among others by Tuckett, *Reading the New Testament*, 149 note 24.
[40] See note 24 above.

as some kind of deprivation: a feeling that the world itself is out of joint and they with it), which was relieved by entering the Christian millenarian sect. To begin with, the problem of Meeks' thesis is that in reality it is much more than a heuristic tool. "The theory is paradigmatic. It provides the primary explanation for the existence of Pauline Christianity."[41] Evidently it is quite important for Meeks, as it returns more than once in his work, is made part of his application of the millenarian movement or sect model, and seems to make explanations of why people became Christians in terms of convictions and motives superfluous.

Not a few reviewers have registered some doubts about the historicity of status inconsistency as such. One could, for example, ask whether it has really been proved by Meeks to exist, or simply stands as an interesting suggestion concerning a future line of research. The very fact that status is not a one-dimensional factor makes such a historical investigation very difficult, even if we had the source material necessary for it, and we don't.[42] Another question concerns the representativity of the people uncovered in the prosopographical analysis: status discrepancy can be felt just as well by persons of downward mobility who did not become leaders! To how many Christians in these congregations would Meeks' hypothesis apply?[43] And what about the appropriateness of conversion to Christianity as a remedy for this kind of plight: if the higher standing persons wanted to reduce their status inconsistency, why did they join a group that would lower their prestige in the eyes of the world and thus aggravate their problem?[44]

Several commentators consider the psychology behind Meeks' reasoning about status inconsistency and its probable effects as much too modern.[45] In no single case can it be directly proved that the

---

[41] Stanley Kent Stowers, "The Social Sciences and the Study of Early Christianity" (in W. S. Green (ed.), *Approaches to Ancient Judaism*. Atlanta, 1985, 149-181), 170.

[42] Georg Schöllgen, "Was wissen wir Über die Sozialstruktur der paulinischen Gemeinden?" *(New Testament Studies* 34, 1988, 71-82), 78-80. Meeks summarizes the evidence very shortly on pages 73 and 191 in *The First Urban Christians* (1983).

[43] Gerd Theissen, "Review of The First Urban Christians by Wayne A. Meeks" *(Journal of Religion* 65, 1985, 111-113), 111. John H. Elliott, "Review of The First Urban Christians by Wayne A. Meeks" *(Religious Studies Review* 11, 1985, 329-335), 331. Richard L. Rohrbaugh, " 'Social Location of Thought' as a Heuristic Construct in New Testament Study" *(Journal for the Study of the New Testament* 30, 1987, 103-119), 110 f.

[44] Theissen, "Review Meeks," ibid. Elliott argues that this was the effect of becoming Christians for the receivers of 1 Peter.

[45] E.g. Bruce J. Malina, "Review of The First Urban Christians by Wayne A. Meeks" *(Journal of Biblical Literature* 104, 1985, 346-349). Edward A. Tiryakian, "Review of The First Urban Christians by Wayne A. Meeks" *(American Journal of Sociology* 90, 1985, 1138-1140). Rohrbaugh, "Social Location," 110, 118 note 30.

alleged status inconsistency was noticed by those who are said to have felt it or by the surrounding society, and even less that it was considered by them as painful.[46] The idea that they did is based on what Rohrbaugh terms "sociocentrism": the tendency to see things the other side of the industrial revolution as if that revolution changed nothing in our patterns of social perception.[47] This opens up a further question concerning whether status inconsistency was really a promi- nent driving force in the social situation Meeks is describing. Rohr- baugh contends that the fear of downward mobility (which was almost universal) may not have had so much to do with social aspirations as with a more fundamental anxiety for one's life. It is more likely

> that the theological message of the text [NT] is to be understood as speaking to persons who are not so much thwarted in their social aspirations as they are frightened by the precarious nature of their position in the world. Whatever influence the desire for social prestige may have had on both early Christianity and the New Testament, it was probably of modest proportions alongside the hope for an alter- native future, for a new and different kingdom.[48]

Elliott criticizes Meeks for not making the role of theory in his hypothesis on status inconsistency explicit:

> On the one hand, his analysis of the correlation of belief and behavior rests on the theoretical assumptions that religious beliefs are determined in their force and meaning by specific social contexts, that such beliefs reflect specific perceptions of social reality and simultaneously contrib- ute toward the actualization of specific social goals, and that therefore it is possible and necessary to inquire concerning the various social functions of belief systems.

For some reason Meeks thinks that he is avoiding strong theoretical assumptions, but it is quite the opposite:

> It is precisely these sociological assumptions which suggest the new questions he asks, the data he gathers, and the correlations he seeks, and gives them imaginative power and explanatory potential.

---

[46] Schöllgen, "Was wissen wir?," 79.

[47] Rohrbaugh, "Social Location," 113.

[48] Richard L. Rohrbaugh, "Methodological Considerations in the Debate over the Social Class Status of Early Christians" (*Journal of the American Academy of Religion* 52, 1984, 519-546), 543.

And Elliott goes on to point out that Meeks' work should have profited from a clear articulation and discussion of the underlying theory and assumptions, as this would have shown the underlying theoretical framework and also made it easier to look for corroborating evidence from other social scientific research.[49]

In his thorough criticism of Meeks' work, Stanley Kent Stowers concludes by pointing to one general characteristic of his theories, which comes to the fore, e.g., in his chapter on ritual. The remarkable thing about Meeks' understanding of ritual as evidence of a latent structuring social situation is that it seems largely unnecessary, as the functions are so explicitly there in the Pauline texts. The function of baptism and Eucharist as creating and shaping unity in the congregation is among the most explicit of Paul's aims in referring to them. And the same goes for the belief structures that Meeks takes up in his last chapter: what he considers as only latent functions of these beliefs is actually enjoined as an ideal or at least already implicit in the concepts themselves. The correlation between belief structures and behaviour structures is thus part of the apostle's manifest intention, not something that can only be unearthed through a sociology of knowledge analysis.[50]

Sociology of knowledge—some critical perspectives

The application of perspectives from the sociology of knowledge to New Testament texts also raises some problems that do not concern merely the few examples that have been discussed above. We will now turn to some of these general methodological problems.

Symmetry or asymmetry in correlation?
Theissen himself has given us a valuable discussion concerning the principles of analytical conclusions, i.e., conclusions from different types of indirect information, such as historical occurrences, explicit or implicit norms, and symbols of religious belief.[51] Concerning the latter, which is evidently topical when one is discussing relations between beliefs and social situation, Theissen states that it is the most difficult of all analytical conclusions. This is because it is impossible to decide at the outset whether there exists symmetry or asymmetry

[49] John H. Elliott, "Review of The First Urban Christians by Wayne A. Meeks" (*Religious Studies Review* 11, 1985, 329-335), 333.
[50] Stowers, "The Social Sciences," 168-176.
[51] Gerd Theissen, "Die soziologische Auswertung," 40-51.

between symbol and social reality.[52] When, for example, the apostle Paul uses the Body as a symbol for the church, this will have to be interpreted as simultaneously an indicative and an imperative. This means that this symbol is both a description of a tight-knit community (evidence of a symmetry between symbol and reality) *and* an exhortation to be and become such a community (some lack of symmetry between symbol and reality). But there is nothing in the symbol itself to tell us on which aspect we should put the emphasis, the symmetrical or asymmetrical.

If we turn to the metaphorical language of Jesus' parables, this gives us clues about the socioecological background of this tradition. We learn about landowners, day-labourers, debtors, shepherds, housewives, and others in a rural Palestinian setting. But to draw conclusions from this general background to the social location of the speaker or the tradition-carriers is much more difficult. It is notable, for example, that many of Jesus' parables tell about lords and kings, and that in such parables things are usually seen from their perspective. Does this show that Jesus came from or had sympathies with the upper class? There are other and more probable explanations. But then one should, of course, also beware of naive assumptions of symmetry between the predominantly rural imagery and the character of the Jesus-movement.

Turning to the third kind of symbols, the mythical ones, where not social realities are depicted, but God and heavenly realities are spoken of directly (although of course in anthropomorphic language),[53] Theissen introduces the concept of "symbolical intensification" (Steigerung). In poetical symbols everyday realities are given in concentrated form, but in mythical symbols they are so intensified that empirical reality is transcended. Sometimes this functions as an intensification of experiences of an ordinary kind, as when demonic dominion is

---

[52] Ibid., 46.

[53] "Anders als poetische Bilder stellen sie keine soziale Realität dar, die dann als Ganzes für etwas anderes transparent werden soll, sie thematisieren sehr viel direkter dies 'Andere': das Handeln von Göttern, Engeln und Dämonen. Sie benutzen dazu freilich auch Bilder aus dem vertrauten sozialen Leben: Gott wird etwa als König vorgestellt, die Engel als sein Hofstaat." Ibid., 47.

In his article "Ein Vergleich jüdischer, christlicher und gnostischer Apokalyptik," in Hellholm (ed.), *Apocalypticism in the Mediterranean World*. Tübingen, 1983, 751-768), Hans Kippenberg accuses Theissen of a positivistic attitude to mythical symbols. He misunderstands Theissen as saying that mythical symbols have no relation to empirical reality, and that only empirically observable relations between human beings constitute a social reality.

coloured by the negative experiences of political oppression (cf. the demon in Mk 5:9 f who calls himself "Legion" and wants to stay in the land). But the symbolical intensifications can also serve as a method of transcending earthly reality altogether, which means that mythical symbols can function both as an intensification of and a denial of empirical experience. This character of possible ambivalence makes it hard to correlate mythical symbols with a social situation, even if we knew that situation. When the symbols are our only or most important means of information about the social situation, we must state that nothing can be known about it.

Mythical symbols can be analysed sociologically in several ways. One can start (a) in their semantical dimension, and attempt conclusions from what human realities are used (e.g., the human body, or family, or artefacts) to the social situation of those who use the myths and symbols. But very often mythical images reflect an earlier stage of culture (as when God is called a king, although the political organization has changed to a republic, or sacrifices his son, although this is not considered ethical among humans any longer). This is a reminder that symbols and metaphors quickly begin to live their own, independent life, in which they are open for new contents and interpretations. Another approach (b) is to look for structural homologies between social reality and religious imagery, especially in their "syntagmatic" properties (what happens between the elements of the imagery and of the situation). For example, the integration between dfferent religious traditions can be mirrored in genealogies of the gods, who are thus reconciled into one coherent system. One important example that Theissen mentions is the structural homology between the foreignness of the Logos in this world and the foreignness of the Johannine community in this world that Meeks demonstrated in his famous article from 1972. Finally, one can start (c) in the paradigmatic dimension of myths, exploring the timeless relations and oppositions between their elements (Lévi-Strauss considered fundamental societal conflicts to be mirrored in such oppositions).

After having given this detailed description of different ways to draw conclusions from mythical symbols to social realities behind them, Theissen concludes by stating emphatically that this kind of analytical approach is so problematic that one should try every other approach first.[54] But this precariousness characterizes all analytical

---

[54] "Insgesamt wird man den Rückschluss aus mythischen Symbolen für den problematischsten Weg einer soziologischen Analyse religiöser Traditionen halten müssen. Es empfiehlt sich, immer erst alle anderen Rückschlussverfahren zu erproben." Theissen, "Die soziologische Auswertung," 49.

conclusions. That also narrative texts may oscillate between a descriptive and a prescriptive (or even symbolical) meaning is a commonplace since decades in redaction criticism (cf. terms like "Lucan tendency"). Theissen himself mentions that there is always a gap between norms and social reality, which means that the information value of norms concerning behaviour patterns can neither be put at 100 percent nor at 0 percent, or in other words, we don't know and can't know which degree of symmetry pertains to them. In treating Gospel material (and some would add the Acts as well) one meets the further difficulty of not knowing what the Gospels are. Are they records of historical occurrences? or norms, explicit and implicit? or symbolical texts? A form critic would perhaps say both yes and no to all these alternatives. The main conclusion from this discussion about the degree of symmetry between biblical texts and social situations must be that judgments about such correlations are necessarily tentative and uncertain, simply because of the complex and multidimensional character of texts.

Conclusions from the multifunctionality of beliefs

It has been noted by more than one biblical scholar that theological traditions or belief complexes often function in several different contexts. For example, Paul Hanson has shown that apocalyptic can be used by persons in different social situations. Some use it in a crisis, other users belong to the mainstream tradition, yet others employ it from an interest in speculative thought. It can also be used for different purposes: (1) to legitimate a period of nonfulfillment and waiting, (2) to give some compensation for present hardships by holding out the hope of a better world, (3) as a utopian spur to action. From the perspective of integrating the adherent in society, one can note that both (1) and (2) are status quo-retaining, while (3) is more revolutionary.[55]

In a similar way Wayne Meeks demonstrated that apocalyptic language can have at least seven different functions in Pauline letters.[56] Probably all these instances of apocalyptic language function together as parts of a larger symbol-complex, which serves as the organizing center of the new community. But this center is flexible. Meeks stresses that the apocalyptic tradition can be used (in Galatians) to warrant

[55] Christopher Rowland, "Reading," 361-363.
[56] Wayne A. Meeks, "Social Functions of Apocalyptic Language in Pauline Christianity," in Hellholm (ed.), *Apocalypticism in the Mediterranean* World (1983), 687-706, listed on page 700. Cf. also idem, *The First Urban Christians*, 174-179.

innovations deviating from previous norms, but also (in 1 Corinthians) to resist deviant behaviour that disrupted the community. Clearly, there exists a dialectic between apocalyptic tradition and social situation, as the former is not correlated with the latter in any uniform way, even if the unifying function or focus is the solidarity and stability of the congregations.[57] In another article Meeks pointed in similar fashion to five different social functions that the crucifixion-and-resurrection complex served in the life of the Pauline movement, and summarized:

> We see that the implications of belief were not automatic. The spelling out of the meaning of even so central a belief as the resurrection of Christ was a dialectical process. What we may crudely call its social consequences were an integral part of that process. So, also, the social world which had shaped the lives and minds of the members of the Christian groups must have played a role in the process.[58]

I think that Meeks and others are quite correct in observing that one and the same belief complex could be put to several, quite different uses in the overall task of consolidating the symbolic universe and the social world of the early Christians. If we allow an unwieldy word for this, it could be termed the multifunctionality of beliefs. This multifunctionality also has to do with the dialectical use these central beliefs were put to. Probably many meanings evolved only when the social situation called for a new interpretation or deeper understanding of the faith that had already been transmitted and received.

But which are the implications of this multifunctional, dialectic character of beliefs for the possibility of correlating them with specific social situations? Sociological functionalism of a cruder type, assuming a one-to-one relation between beliefs and their social functions ("This

[57] Peter Lampe has shown the same kind of dialectic, or interplay, between three factors (using an apocalyptic tradition, standing in a stratum-specific ethos, and experience of the actual situation) to be operative in the variant apocalyptic traditions in the crisis situation of the 160s B.C., and those used in the Apocalypse of John; Peter Lampe, "Die Apokalyptiker—ihre Situation und ihr Handeln," in *Eschatologie und Friedenshandeln: Exegetische Beiträge zur Frage christlicher Friedensverantwortung*, Mit Beiträgen von U. Luz, J. Kegler, P. Lampe, P. Hoffmann (Stuttgarter Bibelstudien 101), Stuttgart, 1982, 59-114).
[58] Wayne A. Meeks, "The Social Context of Pauline Theology" (*Interpretation* 36, 1982, 266-277), 272-275; quotation from 275. For a similar, independent interpretation cf. Stephen C. Barton, "Paul and the Cross: A Sociological Approach" (*Theology* 85, 1982, 13-19), which was followed up in Idem, "Paul and the Resurrection: A Sociological Approach" (*Religion* 14, 1984, 67-75).

belief might have had this function, and filled that need of the group") is no longer plausible. But one could ask whether it is any improvement to state that "This belief complex had at least these five or six functions." If a complex of beliefs develops in constant interaction with different situations, this means, of course, that one cannot read backward from the finished theological product to the situation that shaped it, because this could be any of five or six situations! Or in other words, if the gospel of the crucified and resurrected Jesus Christ filled the spiritual hunger and relieved the social distress and anxiety of rich and poor, men and women, slaves and free, Jews and Gentiles, if it could stimulate ethical innovations like commensality, and curb too radical innovations, if it increased the authority of the apostle and served to define the boundaries of the community and made sense of suffering and gave hope of life eternal, one must ask whether it actually does not correlate with all of human life.

And as the process of correlation very likely is a dialectical one, this increases the impossibility of concluding to the social situation from the end result. One original social situation can lead to several different results, because the intervening interactive factors need not be the same. And the same end result can, at least in theory, have been reached by several different routes. It seems inevitable that, once we leave the primitive idea of strong, direct correlation between ideas and social basis of an almost deterministic kind, we are bereft of the possibility to say anything much about correlations at all.

The assumption of intercultural commensurability
Stanley Kent Stowers has made a superb methodological analysis of the question how sociological models can be applied to ancient cultures, and related this to the ongoing discussion concerning commensurability between different societies and cultures.[59] Such a commensurability is often simply assumed, not only by functionalist sociologists and philosophers, but also by exegetes who take a sociological model, like Bryan Wilson's sect model, and apply it to early Christianity. But the idea that all societies are fundamentally similar and can easily be compared with each other is philosophically and methodologically naive and unfounded.[60]

---

[59] Stanley Kent Stowers, 'The Social Sciences and the Study of Early Christianity" (1985), see note 41 above.
[60] Cf. T. O. Beidelman's critique of the facile assumption that twentieth-century sociological concepts and models (like "trickster") can function as some kind of universals in comparing different societies and cultures, in idem, "The moral imagination of the Kaguru: some thoughts on tricksters, translation and comparative analysis" (*American Ethnologist* 7, 1980, 27-42).

Functionalist sociologists consider that social phenomena and society as a whole can be analysed quite independently of what the actors think. Their ideas, norms, beliefs, and motives may seem to govern the social life, and is so understood by themselves, but actually they simply veil the real process, which follows its own, latent, functional laws. The last few decades of discussion within the philosophy of science and of history has, however, led to a growing recognition that the functionalist axiom that the thinking of the actors should be excluded from sociological explanations lacks foundation. Explanations must begin in the motives, norms, and beliefs of the actors themselves, and only thereafter proceed to introduce causal explanations for what cannot be explained by recourse to the symbolic universe of the actors. This means that each group and society has to be analysed as a moral community in itself, a community with aims that form and govern its social behaviour—and this is what is often lacking in sociological studies of early Christianity.

Both the studies of Theissen and Meeks are vitiated by the functionalist axiom of the invisible social laws that operate independently of what the actors want or think. Stowers pointed out above (page 127) that Meeks seems to think that the latent functions of rituals and beliefs to relieve social malaise are the really operative ones in the social life of the early Christians—an indication of the degree to which the functionalist axiom determines his analysis.[61] In Theissen's form critical sociology of knowledge the idea of the latent functions appears in the form of devaluing the role of explicit belief and conscious effort in the preservation of the Jesus' tradition. The latent, self-legitimating interests of the followers are considered to have exclusive selective and shaping power over this tradition, which is why it is such a faithful mirror of their social situation and their role patterns.

Direct correlation and the social location of thought
In his article " 'Social Location of Thought' as a Heuristic Construct in New Testament Study" (1987), Rohrbaugh gives an incisive analysis of some basic concepts and postulates of the sociology of knowledge and how these affect the attempts of exegetes to find correlations between texts and their social contexts. He states that one must begin by knowing what is meant by a social location of thought. "In fact, social structures and belief do frequently seem to be related, though in a complex and apparently unsystematic way."[62] The fundamental

---

[61] Stowers, "The Social Sciences," 176.
[62] Rohrbaugh, "Social Location," 104.

idea, which is especially emphasized in Marxist sociology, is that all knowledge or belief has a social base, whether it be class, generations, occupational groups, sects, parties, or even processes like competition or conflict. Many proposed groups (such as "ascetics" or "Pauline Christians") are difficult to define, frequently overlap with other locations, and are consequently hard to correlate with particular ideas. A closer analysis reveals that most groups or strata designed as social locations are made by arbitrary definitions of researchers, and not anchored to the conceptions of the participants themselves. This is even more so, when we are separated from the research object by a great temporal and cultural distance—our analytical divisions of society into groups and strata are inevitably modern.

When looking at Meeks' analyses Rohrbaugh recognises these typical problems. Were the Pauline Christians homogeneous enough to be regarded as a separate group, a distinct social location? How do we know that, simply from reading Paul's letters, many may have disagreed with him or found other, unmentioned parts of the belief important? Of course, Paul's ideas must have made sense to some people ("correlated" with their situation), but "it is almost impossible to construct social locations with the use of inferences drawn from the thought of a single author."[63] Meeks' attempt to describe their pre-Christian profile and explain why they were drawn together into one group with the help of sociological concepts like "status inconsistency," "millenarian movement," and "cognitive dissonance" is criticized by Rohrbaugh, as we saw above, as being strongly coloured by anachronistic, sociocentric assumptions about how people must have felt and reacted.

We have to understand that social location is what Peter Berger and Thomas Luckmann called a "plausibility structure," a socially constructed province of meaning. This means that it is a mental construct, a picture of the world that is socially produced and maintained, but not a set of social conditions.

> The social base is not the cause of other ideas, but the context in which other ideas are interpreted and understood as realistic possibilities. Few contemporary sociologists of knowledge would assume it is possible to locate the causal origins of particular ideas as if a social location 'accounts

---

[63] Ibid., 111. Rohrbaugh points out that Meeks sees "correlation" evident in consistency of belief and social practice, while this term in sociological parlance means the "correlation" between a person's position in a social order and his/her thought and actions, whether the latter are consistent with each other or not, 117 note 24.

for' ideas that emerge in it. . . . Even Marxists, who routinely assume
a correlation between the ideas of a group and that group's social interests, shy away from rigid notions of causality. Social locations are
heuristic constructs, not explanatory ones.[64]

Of course, this criticism does not mean that the quest for correlations
between texts and social situations is in itself invalid or hopeless. It
means, however, that we are once again brought back to the need of
starting such a quest from good factual knowledge about social data,
and to the realization of how complex and subtle such relationships
typically are.

Perhaps one could generalize beyond the criticisms of Rohrbaugh
and Stowers, and say that the idea of a single-factor, direct, causal
relationship between social life and human thinking has been pro-
gressively pushed back in sociology, and been substituted by richer
and more complex models. To mention one example, the simple base/
superstructure theory, which sees all ideology and all cultural expressions as reflections or outworkings of a deeper social dynamic
that is located in the socioeconomic system, is today seen to be too
crude and unrealistic, even if it has got hold of an essential characteristic of social life.[65] This development should incite a certain caution
in biblical scholars as regards the taking over of undeveloped, sim-
plistic sociological models, both from sociology proper (e.g., sociocentric functionalism) and from the exegetical tradition itself (form
criticism).

---

[64] Ibid., 114, referring to Barry Barnes, *Interests and Growth of Knowledge*, London, Henley,
and Boston, 1977, esp. chapter 3 on the problem of imputation. Barnes finds a much
weaker connection between knowledge and social structure than that normally asserted
by writings in the sociology of knowledge tradition, and considers it impossible to
assume any general theory that sets even particular social interest into direct correspondence with classes or other categories, *Interests*, 57 f.

[65] Gerd Theissen has given a typical example of this type of criticism in his essays
"Theoretische Probleme," *Studien*, 66-71, and "Zur forschungsgeschichtlichen Einordnung," *Studien*, 25-30.

One could mention other examples as well: Arnold Gehlen's idea that social institutions and human needs are connected only via commitment to ideas, in Helmut
Schelsky (ed.), *Zur Theorie der Institution*. Dusseldorf, 1970, 23); Karl Mannheim's and
Theodor Geiger's ideas about "world views" or "mentalities" being the connecting link
between social basis and different ideologies (Klaus Berger, "Wissenssoziologie und
Exegese des Neuen Testaments," *Kairos* 19, 1977, 124-133), 128; Peter Munz's suggestion
that the connection between social forms and religious beliefs are channeled via such
"natural symbols" as Mary Douglas has described (Peter Munz, "The Problem of 'Die
soziologische Verortung des antiken Gnostizismus'," Numen 19, 1972, 41-51).

CORRELATIONS BETWEEN SYMBOLIC AND SOCIAL STRUCTURES   **143**

Peter Lampe has some apposite final remarks on the relationship between social situations and the expressions of faith. That beliefs and theological statements often fit the believer's experiences of social reality cannot be taken to mean that beliefs were "derived" from the social reality or were "projections" of it. Theological changes can always be shown to be dependent on internal, theological, or systematic factors as well! The alternative between a monocausal "social-historical" interpretation of texts and a monocausal "theological" or "traditio-historical" interpretation is a false one. Both are needed because they relate to each other as width and height of a space, and form part of a "three-dimensional" interpretation of texts. In reality theological propositions often have a social function, in two directions: they fill a need of legitimation for a certain behaviour pattern, and they control and shape the behaviour pattern. Social situation and doctrine (tradition, theology) are not statically related as base and superstructure, but influence each other in a dynamic exchange.[66]

The criticism that has been directed in this chapter against attempts to apply the perspectives of the sociology of knowledge on the history and life of early Christianity is not an attack against a whole line of research, and even less against some scholars, but is to be understood as an exercise in accountability. Biblical scholars who use sociological theories and models are in principle fully accountable for them, which means that they must know them, understand them, be acquainted with their critical history, and their fundamental assumptions. Stanley Kent Stowers has formulated this duty of the New Testament sociologist (who is of course also a "historian"):

> The lesson [from the critique of the hidden and value-laden assumptions of Weber's sociology] is that the historian must not only be able to justify and adapt sociological theories to the object of historical inquiry, but must also be able to criticize theories for possible anachronisms, etc. In other words, the historian should fully understand the explanatory significance and implications of a particular theory. . . . To observe or describe requires models, paradigms and conceptual schemes. Thus, the historian of ancient culture cannot evade the self-critical tasks by

---

[66] Peter Lampe, *Die stadtrömischen Christen in den ersten beiden Jahrhunderten: Untersuchungen zur Sozialgeschichte* (WUNT Reihe 2, 18). 2. Aufl. Tübingen, 1989, 347 f. Concerning the problem of causality, see Lampe's distinction between genetic and supportive causality (the latter refers to factors that make the continuation of a certain phenomenon possible), idem 348, and Theissen's remarks on the autonomy of religion in the final note of "Verlassen" (*Studien*, 141 note 79).

claiming to use only traditional historical methods. The models, methods and theories of the social sciences provide new and horizon-expanding opportunities for the historian. At the same time they introduce new complexities, and their use calls for a sustained critical discussion in dialogue with the philosophy of science and history about their use by historians of distant cultures.[67]

No doubt this is raising the demands very high, and it is easy to understand if NT scholars who are interested in using sociology would feel rather put off by being asked for a treble expertise: in exegesis, in sociology, and in the philosophy of science. On the other hand, one could say that, when the fundamental issues concern "human agency, human values, and causality"[68] and the relation between human and divine action, theology and theologians have somehow come into their own again. These are among the type of questions exegetes and theologians set out to find answers to, and concern the core of our intellectual discipline. Diving into the sociology of knowledge and its fundamental assumptions might not be a bad way to approach the problem of meaning and especially the meaning of religion.

---

[67] Stowers, "The Social Sciences," 168.
[68] Ibid., 149.

5 *Finding the Body—*
and Losing the Soul?

Informative but alienating—how handle sociology?

Looking back on the history of biblical studies we can observe that it was by no means an easy transition for biblical scholars to embrace a historical perspective on these scriptures. To treat one's Holy Scriptures just like any other collection of ancient documents and to put critical questions to them about the truth of their assertions must seem to any Bible-believing Christian an act of irreverence. This difficulty is by no means only a thing of the past. I myself vividly remember the mixture of repugnance and curiosity that was my reaction to the welter of critical theories concerning the synoptic problem and the authorship of different biblical documents, which I met in my very first course in theology some twenty-eight years ago—and I see the same in my students. (The reader should be warned that, even if the author is more shockproof now, he is still a conservative, high-church Lutheran student of theology.)

Basically, this kind of difficulty has always accompanied serious theological studies. It was stated in the thirteenth century, for example, that anyone taking up the study of theology would enter into a period of aridity in his or her prayer life. This unavoidable strain results from the attempt at interiorizing a systematic, analytical perspective on your own faith, i.e., to distance yourself from the faith in order to observe it as from the outside, while at the same time it is your heart's innermost treasure and the truth that carries your life.

The believer/theologian's difficulty with historical and sociological studies of biblical texts is greater, however, because here the student is asked to adopt a distance of the second order. The study is not only analytical, rational, and systematic, but pursued under the presupposition that only empirical, observable data can be admitted, or in other words, that God and transcendent causality be excluded. This is not always realized when studying biblical history, because the fundamental presuppositions and explanatory theories behind the study are usually veiled by its descriptive and narrative character. But biblical sociology is a branch of history (cf. chapter 1) where the aGnostic character of historical research is not concealed, but brought to the attention of students, challenging their often theistic perspective.[1]

I think that this is why we can notice the aforementioned, somewhat pained reaction when biblical scholars confront the sociological approach. It seems to many so crass and alien (just as historical or literary methods did a hundred years ago), that they have to ask whether it is at all suited for work on the Bible. Are there not insuperable problems in making use of sociology, which is so obviously a modern type of analysis, on such an ancient material as the Bible? Is not sociology necessarily deterministic and reductionistic in its treatment of supernatural or spiritual phenomena, and therefore apt to distort an empathic understanding of the Bible? What is really the use of sociology in exegetical work?

It would be a mistake to consider such questions and the apprehension behind them as simply the initial resistance to any new and revolutionary perspective, or the unwillingness to confront one's faith with another demanding challenge from systematic rationality. Some of the fears that have been voiced against the introduction of sociology in biblical studies are not well founded, but others are.[2] Although bluntly put, the statement of Daniel Harrington is to the point: "The New Testament writings are religious documents, and sociology has no satisfactory method for dealing with the divine or nonrational element that is so important in religious experience."[3] In order to understand why this is so, we need to take a look at the intellectual tradition of sociology.

The anti-religious bias of sociology
Sociology is not a neutral intellectual technology, which can just be applied to any subject without affecting it. (Whether technology is all

---

[1] An illuminating and interesting discussion of the question concerning these two different perspectives and the "concordat" between faith and reason is given by Robert Morgan, *Biblical Interpretation*, ch. 1, "Interpretation and biblical interpretation" and *passim*.

[2] Cf. Norman K. Gottwald, *The Tribes of Yahweh: A Sociology of the Religion of Liberated Israel 1250-1050* B.C. E. London, 1981, 8-11: Exegetes fear the sociological approach because (a) they think it will undercut the primacy of theology, (b) sociology is so crude and imprecise, (c) it does not fit their middle-class outlook, (d) like all humanists they focus on the individual, unique and concrete, and not—as sociology—on the typical and general.

[3] Daniel J. Harrington, "Sociological Concepts and the Early Church: A Decade of Research" (*Theological Studies* 41, 1980, 181-190), 182 f.

that neutral has been increasingly questioned.) Sociology often has presented itself with the claim of being absolutely scientific and value neutral, all the way since Marx, Comte, and Spencer. To its Enlightenment heritage belongs the somewhat too hasty assumption that once you had thrown the old theologies and philosophies away, you were free to see reality as it really is. No wonder that early sociology, which often criticized religion as neither good nor true, was understood, both by its proponents and its opponents, as an antagonist of religion.[4] This hostile attitude has diminished considerably in our century, but nonetheless this Enlightenment bias is the intellectual tradition that the social sciences are standing in, and it makes the social sciences interpret religion as a human construction, not seldom adding that it *is* nothing but a human construction.[5]

Even after decades of Weberian value-neutrality and Parsonian determination in sociology not to enter any ontological discussions (about the truth of religious or moral opinions), critics can point to the existence of different kinds of bias in sociology. Values enter into the selection of scientific problems, and are ineradicably present in sociological language, because even the most unemotional statements carry "normative freight," which cannot be avoided if sociology is to treat humanly relevant questions at all.[6] The tendency of modern sociological theory is to minimize the part played by cognitive interests in social actions, such as generating and sustaining religious commitments. The religious viewpoint of the actors is registered but not accorded any validity or effect, which is reserved for social factors (level of education, family background, relative deprivation, etc.). Thus the implicit claim of the sociologists is that they understand the

---

[4] See for example Gager,"Shall We Marry Our Enemies? Sociology and the New Testament" *(Interpretation* 36, 1982, 256-265), 256 f. Benton Johnson, "Sociological Theory and Religious Truth" *(Sociological Analysis* 38, 1977, 368-388), 370. For a history of the development of the sociology of religion, see Roland Robertson, *The Sociological Interpretation of Religion,* Oxford, 1972, 7-33.
[5] Cf. the following description of the differing traditions of sociology and theology: "Sociology addresses itself to human events in the historical development of the world; theology to God's creation of man and man's subsequent development in relation to God. The sociological enterprise is horizontal, that of theology vertical. Sociology interprets human experience in terms of the phenomenal realm, theology in terms of the noumenal one. Sociology is compatible with ethical relativism, whereas theology speaks to ethical absolutes. In other words, because of different philosophical assumptions and historical traditions, sociology and theology employ different methods and criteria for analysis, and 'map' their data in radically different ways." Henry Alan Green, *The Economic and Social Origins of Gnosticism* (SBL Diss. Series 77), Atlanta, 1985, 7 f.
[6] Benton Johnson, "Sociological Theory and Religious Truth," 371.

basis of religious belief and action better than religious people do. The sociologist Benton Johnson concludes:

> Sociological analyses of religion imply that religious faith does not arise in response to the 'reality' perceived by religious people but rather it arises in response to the 'reality' perceived by social scientists. . . . Earlier social scientific theories of religion proclaimed that religious ideas are illusions. Modern theory tries to avoid the issue of truth, but in practice it fosters analyses that must appear reductionistic to anyone who takes religious ideas seriously on their own terms. Sociological explanations of religion have the effect of explaining it away. They carry the inescapable implication that religious ideas are not true.[7]

And the theologian Thomas Best puts the same observation this way:

> Sociology as such considers only the human dimension in human behaviour, and systematically eliminates trans-human factors.[8]

We have met the same criticism of sociology in Stanley K. Stowers' demonstration of the sociological tendency inherent in Wayne Meeks' attempts to explain correlations between belief and social situations as the result of latent factors and not of explicit, conscious thinking and planning.[9] This reluctance to let cognitive factors or religious beliefs play a structuring role in the reconstruction of the social life of early Christianity has also been observed by Werner Georg Kümmel in some sociological investigations on New Testament material. He criticizes Theissen for neglecting the content of the beliefs of early Jewish Christians as a decisive factor in their life together, for a one-sided preoccupation with their social situation. And David Verner, whose reconstruction of the social structure of the community behind the Pastoral letters is lauded, is also criticized for simply leaving out the new elements that must have attracted slaves and young widows (who are pushed back socially in these letters), viz., the Christian community of faith. In both cases sociological analysis gets hold of

---

[7] Ibid., 375. "Whether or not social-scientific explanations need presuppose the falsity of religious belief, in practice they invariably do." Robert A. Segal, "The Social Sciences and the Truth of Religious Belief" (*Journal of the American Academy of Religion* 48, 1980, 403-413), 404. Also Margaret M. Poloma argues that sociology has an anti-religious bias, "Toward a Christian Sociological Perspective: Religious Values, Theory and Methodology" (*Sociological Analysis* 43, 1982, 95-108), 99.

[8] Thomas F. Best, "The Sociological Study of the New Testament: Promise and Peril of a New Discipline" (*Scottish Journal of Theology* 36, 1983, 181-194), 192.

[9] See chapter 4 above, the section on commensurability.

new and important aspects of early Christian reality, but seems in-
capable of encompassing in its analysis the faith-dimension that was
unique and existentially important for these Christians themselves.[10]

Is reductionism inevitable?
The question concerning the truth of sociology (and other empirical
sciences) in relation to the truth of religious faith is much too large
to discuss here. (A good starting point would be the above-mentioned
article by Benton Johnson and the discussion he refers to.)[11] However,
some discussion of the problem of reductionism or, as it is sometimes
called, epistemological imperialism, could help to make the relation
clearer.

> Reductionism refers to the procedure of subsuming one model into
> another when both of the models are at the same level of abstraction.
> For example, to explain biology as simply one form of physics, economy
> as one form of psychology, or theology as some form of sociology, would
> be reductionistic. However, to explain sets of data—and not models—
> from the perspectives of biology, sociology, political science, economics
> and the like is not reductionistic. . . . The data set, the range of infor-
> mation remains intact. On the other hand, to equate biblical interpre-
> tation with theology as some systematic theologians do is
> reductionistic.[12]

The idea of "subsuming" is the same as claiming that one's own
conceptual system (model, theory) has a higher ontological status than
others (Bellah), which can be sufficiently explained within the own,
superior system. "These ideas/Your beliefs are nothing but . . ." is the
typical beginning of a reductionistic statement. Such statements are

---

[10] Werner Georg Kümmel, "Das Urchristentum II. Arbeiten zur Spezialproblemen. b.
Zur Sozialgeschichte und Soziologie der Urkirche" (*Theologische Rundschau* 50, 1985,
327-363), 347-49, 361.
[11] One can mention the discussion in the 1970s between Robert Bellah and other
sociologists (especially Anthony, Curtis, and Robbins) concerning "symbolic realism"
and "deep structures"; further Peter L. Berger's sociology of religion (*The Sacred Canopy*)
with its "signals of transcendence" and "relativization of the relativizers" (discussed
by Cairns and Gill); the 1979 Blackfriars Symposium (publ. in Martin—Mills—Pickering
(eds.), *Sociology and Theology: Alliance and Conflict*. Brighton, 1980), essays by Hodges
(1974), Segal (1980), and Poloma (1982); and finally the works of Robin Gill, *The Social
Context of Theology: A Methodological Enquiry* (1975), *Theology and Social Structure* (1977),
and the anthology *Theology and Sociology: A Reader*. Ed. and introd. by Robin Gill (1987).
[12] Bruce J. Malina, "The Social Sciences and Biblical Interpretation" (in Gottwald (ed.),
Bible and Liberation, 11-25), 19. Wayne Meeks has some good remarks on the confusions
and simplifications of theological reductionism in *First Urban Christians*, 4.

not uncommon in biblical studies, although as a rule more implicit than explicitly stated. But one would have to admit that a certain reductionistic tendency is a general quality of historical methods as applied to stories about miracles and other incursions of the transcendental reality.[13]

Bruce Malina, whose definition of reductionism we started with, concedes that social silences are "deterministic" in the meaning that they leave little room for creative activity of God or of humans within their models. But models are only tools for understanding and/or predicting, made for limited purposes. And the limited purpose of social science models is to "seek out generalities, typicalities, and samenesses within human groups. From the social science point of view, human beings are socially determined." But unless used reductionistically, the social sciences do not preclude other avenues of approach to our data set.[14] Obviously, for Malina reductionism is a kind of attitude, an unnecessary arrogance, which the social scientist can step out of when he or she wishes. O. C. Edwards adds that the different levels of description are each valid in its own right, and that they cannot contradict one another, because they function on different levels.[15] Reductionism then would be almost a moral error, a kind of research chauvinism, which thoughtful researchers refrain from.

Alternate epistemologies
No doubt it is true that "sociologists themselves—perhaps more so than the NT scholars who borrow their tools—are becoming increasingly sensitive to the epistemological imperialism inherent in their models," and generally have abandoned the quest for a single causal principle or the grand theory that will explain all social life.[16] And as the explanatory ambition recedes, so does the confidence that this science alone really understands the phenomena of social life, including religious life. But this may be a change that more affects

---

[13] See e.g., Morgan, *Biblical Interpretation*, 134, and Christopher Rowland, "Reading the New Testament Sociologically: An Introduction" (Theology 88, 1985, 358-364), 358.

[14] Bruce J. Malina, "The Social Sciences and Biblical Interpretation," (in Gottwald (ed.), *Bible and Liberation*, 11-25), 20.

[15] O. C. Edwards Jr, "Sociology as a Tool for Interpreting the New Testament" (*Anglican Theological Review* 65, 1983, 431-446), 445. He criticizes Gager for not being willing to allow this kind of multiple, noncontradictory interpretations of biblical phenomena. Cf. on Gager's reductionism also David Tracy, "A Theological Response to 'Kingdom and Community' " (*Zygon: Journal of Religion and Science* 13, 1978, 131-135), 133 f.

[16] Thomas F. Best, "The Sociological Study of the New Testament: Promise and Peril of a New Discipline" (*Scottish Journal of Theology* 36, 1983, 181-194), 189 f.

metasociology, or the outside of sociology, than making any difference to the way sociology is done and must be done. Sociologists may personally become more humble about their profession, but they cannot abandon its fundamental presuppositions and methods without ceasing to be professionals.

Peter L. Berger can serve as an example of what I mean. Berger is a sociologist, who has clearly told his readers that he is a Christian believer and not an atheist. But he considers sociology and theology to be two distinct disciplines, with severely discrete relevance structures. Sociology is and remains an empirical science, caught in historical concreteness and its relativities. It cannot solve the problem of relativity in the sense of arbitrating between conflicting meaning systems in terms of their ultimate truth. Sociology has no choice but to bracket the ontological status of religious affirmations, all of which, insofar as they are properly religious, are beyond the range of empirical availability. In other words it must remain aGnostic.[17] Or even, as the gods are by necessity excluded, atheistic. A sociologist must give sociological, i.e., nontranscendent, nonreligious, explanations to religious facts, even if she outside the profession is a devout believer. She has a metasociological dimension too, which includes a theological relevance structure to which she can migrate. The theological relevance structure contains the sociological one ("the Holy Spirit used Stephanas' feelings of status inconsistency to open his heart for the gospel") and vice versa ("Stephanas' status inconsistency was relieved by believing what Paul told him about Jesus"). This migration between discrete relevance structures within one person is not a kind of schizophrenia, but a matter of daily experience in the lives of modern people.[18]

Robin Gill (who holds doctorates both in theology and sociology) gives a full discussion of these matters, and ends in a position that is rather close to Berger's.[19] He points to the criticism of sociology raised by theologians that the former adopts a thoroughly finite as opposed to a transcendent system of causality, and therefore systematically excludes the operation of God in human affairs. One might answer that the objections of theologians against accepting sociological

[17] Peter L. Berger and Hansfried Kellner, *Sociology Reinterpreted: An Essay on Method and Vocation,* Harmondsworth, 1981, 76, 90, 142.

[18] Ibid., 87 f.

[19] Robin Gill, *The Social Context Of Theology: A Methodological Enquiry.* London and Oxford, 1975; see esp. Chapter 3, "Explanation in Sociology and Theology," 26-39. Further literature is mentioned in note 10 above.

and psychological explanations of how Christianity originated is a case of the genetic fallacy: confusing origins with validity. But Gill points out that this answer is not enough. If John Allegro were right about Christianity having originated as a psychedelic mushroom cult, this would discredit Christianity as a valid religion in the eyes of many Christians.[20] This shows that inner-worldy explanations of such a matter as the origin of one's religion in practise can militate against the faith.

After having discussed and turned down the proposals of John Bowker and Robert Bellah concerning a social science of religion that allows for the truth of religion, Gill ends with proposing a consistent "as-if"-methodology. The sociologist works as if all human interactions have social determinants, even if he or she personally believes that there exists other determinants as well. The theological "as-if" methodology, on the other hand, presupposes that terms like "God" have a referent, and that there exists a transcendent causality.[21]

One might say that this practical solution entails an option for alternate epistemologies: one that allows information from and about God, and will therefore accept and find such information, and another that disallows it and will not find it. The adoption of an "as-if"-methodology is thus not a decision within sociological theory, but within philosophy, more exactly within epistemology. This also means that sociology does not engage directly in questions of ontology, even if its perspective and results will not be left out of such a discussion. David Tracy has pointed out, in his answer to Gager's *Kingdom and Community*, that the acceptance of tough-minded analysis already has a tradition in philosophy and philosophical theology:

> Many contemporary Christian theologians clearly hold to the insistence that, on strictly methodological and inner-Christian theological grounds, personal beliefs cannot be allowed to influence a tough-minded historical or social-scientific analysis of early Christianity into a somehow 'exceptional' (more exactly, tender-minded) analysis of 'Christian origins.' . . . [This position] calls for philosophical analysis of the reinterpreted meanings of historical and hermeneutical and social-scientific meanings. In my view . . . only philosophical analysis can provide the conversation partner needed to provide the sufficient, as distinct from necessary, conditions to assess the religious meanings of the social world of early Christianity. . . . The functional definition of

---

[20] Robin Gill, "Berger's Plausibility Structures: A Response to Professor Cairns" (*Scottish Journal of Theology* 27, 1974, 198-207), 201.
[21] Gill, *Social Context of Theology*, 37-39.

religion employed for social-scientific studies will need to be comple-mented by a philosophical analysis of the meaning and truth of religious claims.[22]

Once again: this discussion naturally leads off into the more hilly regions of philosophy, where we will not follow it. Suffice it to make one final, more practical reflection that follows from adopting the stance of Berger and Gill. Theologians can use sociological analysis as a tool of information, even if they have reservations about the epistemology presupposed by sociology. But they should beware of thinking that sociological data can be fitted just as they are into the-ological explanations. In order to know what the data mean, one must first know the theory behind them. The data are dependent on and shaped by the perspective (epistemology, etc.) inherent in the soci-ological theory, which could be described as a kind of philosophy of society. And it is only at the level of theory that theology can relate to sociology.[23] In other words, neither sociological theory nor socio-logical data are value free, neutral descriptions of reality. They come together, and a historian or biblical scholar has to engage in a "dia-logue" with both together.[24]

The use of sociology in New Testament exegesis

The first conclusion from the survey that has been made in this book is a confirmation of the obvious truth that New Testament sociology is still a young discipline. So many investigations need yet to be done on a number of places, areas, periods, institutions, and texts that have not been analysed. And a variety of sociological approaches wait to be tried out on New Testament materials.

Perhaps the limits of sociological research on biblical material stand out a bit clearer too. Sociology cannot decide historical questions, where evidence is lacking, simply because it is one interpretative approach among others, all of which must have some evidence to

---

[22] David Tracy, "A Theological Response to 'Kingdom and Community' " (*Zygon: Journal of Religion and Science* 13, 1978, 131-135), 132 f.
[23] Helge Aarflot, "Teologi og sosiologi i skjönn eller uskjönn forening? Noen interdis-iplinaere randbemerkninger" (*Ung Teologi* 7, Oslo, 1974, 96-109), 102 f.
[24] Cf. Robin Scroggs' remarks on the necessity "to ask whether that method implicitly or explicitly excludes all dynamic except the immanent social," and the way in which presuppositions concerning ontology are embedded in the sociological method one adopts, idem, "The Sociological Interpretation of the New Testament: The Present State of Research" (*New Testament Studies* 26, 1980, 164-179), 166 f.

work on in order to come up with answers to historical questions. Sociology can no more serve as a gap-filler at the level of evidence than can evolutionary philosophy or Christian theology. On the other hand, it has shown itself capable of generating new hunches and ideas about what to look for, by pointing to fresh comparative evidence and commonalities of social behaviour.[25] One might add the obvious remark that neither sociology nor history in general are sciences that give their practitioners a superior position in judging the truth or value of the social relations or processes they have helped to discover.

Much needs to be learned by biblical sociologists in the way of method, and the sure-footed application of truly cross-cultural social-science models. There are some obvious deficiences in the development here so far. The most obvious one in my opinion is the lack of analytical precision and cross-cultural validity of the most-used sociological model of all: the church-sect typology. One can also observe several cases of the "natural" tendency of a fledgling scientific approach "to adopt one 'favourite' sociologist whose work seems congenial to our material, and productive of dramatic results."[26] Even if life is short, the least an exegete ought to do in the strange terrain of sociology is to familiarize him/herself with what has happened to the preferred idea or model in the scholarly discussion of the sociologists themselves (cf. Cyril Rodd on the weaknesses of the theory of cognitive dissonance as a *sociological* theory). The New Testament student must become fully competent in sociological techniques, to the point of using them from 'inside' the discipline rather than borrowing them as an outsider. As we saw in the preceding chapter this can require even some awareness of and grappling with the philosophical presuppositions of the sociology one is using. This raises the demands on exegetes, as it is very difficult to be explicit about the analytical framework or theoretical underpinning of one's work without understanding it from within.

Perhaps one need not demand so much of all New Testament sociologists, in order to be justified in encouraging them to move from a reactive stance, where they only use ready-made models from sociologists, to an active stance, where they modify and develop these models to be applied to their own data. This necessitates a kind of

---

[25] Norman K. Gottwald, *The Tribes of Yahweh: A Sociology of the Religion of Liberated Israel 1250-1050 B.C. E.* London, 1981 [= Maryknoll, N.Y., 1979], 17.

[26] Thomas F. Best, "The Sociological Study of the New Testament: Promise and Peril of a New Discipline" (*Scottish Journal of Theology* 36, 1983, 181-194), 190 f.

dialogue between the sociological model and the New Testament material, where the exegete's task is to judge whether the model does justice rather than violence to the data. All application of a model or theory in historical or interpretive research underlies the risk of regularizing the bewildering diversity of the source material past the point where one is still looking for inherent generalities and patterns, to where one arrives at harmonization and standardization of the evidence. Sociology is a highly abstract and theoretical type of analysis, and perhaps still retains something of its strongly generalizing, "law-like" character. This can result in a tendency that we have better learnt to master in ordinary historical research, the tendency to "reify" our concepts and models, i.e., regard them as dynamic realities with their own life.[27] Thus a certain experimental atmosphere or even a bit of playfulness in our application of sociological theory and models is to be recommended, but also a real effort at being explicit about what we are doing.

A further conclusion from the discussion of the preceding chapters is a realisation of the fact that sociology often comes with an ontology of its own, which is no necessary part of any scholar's metasociological worldview or understanding of reality. If we simplify a bit by talking of "sociology" and "theology" in the singular, one can state that both these intellectual disciplines raise all-embracing claims to truth. Sociology "explains" theology within its universe, and theology can fit in sociology within its knowledge of divine and human reality. This in itself serves to relativise and refute the epistemological imperialism or tendency to reductionism that is there in both disciplines. This awareness may also encourage the theologian or biblical scholar to coolly insist on the importance of the faith-dimension in the biblical texts (and in understanding the world generally, of course).

> Theology will no doubt be influenced by observations made by other disciplines, but it is now possible to understand religion in ways that combine rational and empirical or descriptive investigation with belief in its transcendent referent.[28]

But the important result from introducing sociology in New Testament studies is, of course, not a greater awareness of the separateness of the two disciplines, nor is it simply a number of fresh hypotheses and historical explanations of the texts. Rather it is the

---

[27] Best, "Promise and Peril," 191-193.
[28] Robert Morgan, *Biblical Interpretation*, 138. Best, "Promise and Peril," 192.

fact that sociology has changed the way we now see and understand the reality of early Christianity. As Wayne Meeks put it, the connotations of the verb "mean" have to be significantly extended. In real life "meaning" is richer and more complex than mere grammatical or semantical analysis can get hold of. Part of the meaning is the way a certain concept or tradition or behaviour pattern made sense of the social experience of those who had and lived with it.[29] The social situation has to be included if we are to understand the reality the texts speak of, and not simply as a kind of "background" that might be useful to know about, but as a dimension of the meaning itself of this text and reality.

> As an encompassing systemic understanding of "social" emerges, it becomes increasingly impossible to restrict sociology to prolegomenon. Sociology demands recognition as a constitutive aspect of all biblical study.[30]

And this is because

> The sociological dimension of early Christian theology is not a peripheral field. It does not have to do only with a few facts—the biography of the author, the traditionality of [his] materials and styles, the functions, effects and claims of writings—but inevitably takes part in the "factuality" of these facts.[31]

We knew this, of course, at least as regards our own contemporary human reality. But sociology has served to open our eyes to the *totality* and full historical presence of early Christianity, in a way that a one-sided historical or theological analysis in fact neglected. Sociology has changed the atmosphere and the type of curiosity of biblical studies, enlarged the historical perspective, and sharpened historical observation. And this deepened understanding of early Christian reality has changed (or will change) theological analysis of the New Testament

---

[29] Wayne A. Meeks, "The Social Context of Pauline Theology" (*Interpretation* 36, 1982, 266-277), 276 f.

[30] Gottwald, *The Tribes of Yahweh*, 15.

[31] "Die soziologische Dimension der frühchristlichen Theologie ist kein Grenzgebiet. Sie greift nicht nur ein in irgendwelche Tatsachen—in die Biographie der Verfasser, in die Traditionalität von Stoffen und Stilen, in die Funktionen, Leistungen und Ansprüche der Schriften—sondern sie nimmt schon immer teil an der 'Tatsächlichkeit' dieser Tatsachen." [my translation] Klaus Berger, *Exegese des Neuen Testaments: Neue Wege vom Text zur Auslegung.* Heidelberg, 1977, ²1984, 218 f.

too. Biblical theology has to be concerned with more than the logic of belief-systems, it also has to grasp the formation and reformation of the Christian community itself, the social embodiment of early Christian faith, in all its revolutionary impact on the life of its believers.[32]

To finish with a viewpoint from theology itself, one could state that this "sociological" broadening of the theoloical task of interpreting the Bible reflects the character of revelation itself, as has been pointed out by Christian theologians. The message of the New Testament is not stripped of all temporal or cultural markers, because it was a message that was received, understood, and accepted by a specific community of men and women, who thought in Old Testament categories (grace, law, sacrifice, wrath, mercy, salvation), and in categories that had been influenced by the contacts between Judaism and the Hellenistic culture.

> When God reveals himself to humans, he does not reveal himself according to his own knowledge, but according to the human spirit, beginning with the simple rules of grammar and language. When this divine communication is realised in a community that calls itself church, it follows in its humanization the laws and rules of the collective knowledge, that any sociologist can observe in human societies.[33]

Pater Chenu, who is quoted here, goes on to point out that sociology cannot restrict itself to the sociology of religious behaviour and leave the sociology of dogma or belief aside. That would be a theological mistake, a separation of what revelation itself has united: divine communication and human community. The meaning of the message from God cannot be fully understood without grasping its embodiment in a living community. There are certainly risks in this enterprise, as the preceding discussion of New Testament sociology has amply demonstrated. But these possible distortions cannot preclude the attempt itself, nor invalidate the conclusion that we will not find the soul of early Christianity without finding the body.

---

[32] See note 29 above.
[33] The Roman Catholic theologian M. D. Chenu, quoted by Roger Mehl, "Bedeutung, Möglichkeiten und Grenzen der Soziologie des Protestantismus in theologischer Sicht" (in D. Goldschmidt—J. Matthes (eds.), *Probleme der Religionssoziologie* (Kölner Zeitschrift für Soziologie und Sozialpsychologie. Sonderheft 6), Köln—Opladen, 1962, 112-122), 120.

Bibliography

Aarflot, Helge 1974	"Teologi og sosiologi i skjönn eller uskjönn forening ? Noen interdisiplinaere randbemerkninger" *(Ung Teologi 7,* Oslo, 1974, 96-109).
Abrams, Philip 1982	*Historical Sociology.* Near Shepton Mallet, 1982.
Alexander, Loveday 1986	"Luke's Preface in the Context of Greek Preface-Writing" *(Novum Testamentum* 18, 1986, 48-74).
Alföldy, Géza 1984	*Römische Sozialgeschichte.* 3. völlig überarb. Aufl. Wiesbaden 1984.
1986	*Die römische Gesellschaft. Ausgewählte Beiträge* (Heidelberger Althistorische Beiträge und Epigraphische Studien, bd 1). Stuttgart, 1986.
Anthony, D., Robbins, T., and Curtis, T. E. 1974	"Reply to Bellah" *(Journal for the Scientific Study of Religion* 13, 1974, 491-495).
Anthony, Dick and Robbins, Thomas 1975	"From Symbolic Realism to Structuralism" *(Journal for the Scientific Study of Religion* 14, 1975, 403-414).
Baasland, Ernst 1984	"Urkristendommen i sosiologiens lys" *(Tidskrift for Teologi og Kirke* 54, 1984, 45-57).
Balch, David L.	see Stambaugh, John E.
Barnes, Barry 1977	*Interests and Growth of Knowledge.* London, Henley, and Boston, 1977.
Bartlett, David L. 1978	'John G. Gager's 'Kingdom and Community': A Summary and Response" *(Zygon. Journal of Religion and Science* 13, 1978, 109-122).
Barton, Stephen C. 1982	"Paul and the Cross: A Sociological Approach" *(Theology* 85, 1982, 13-19).
1984	"Paul and the Resurrection: A Sociological Approach" *(Religion* 14, 1984, 67-75).
Baumbach, Günther 1982	"Die Anfänge der Kirchwerdung im Urchristentum" *(Kairos* 24, 1982, 17-30).
Beckford, James A. 1975	*The Trumpet of Prophecy: A Sociological Study of Jehovah's Witnesses.* Oxford, 1975.
1975	"Religious Organization" *(Current Sociology* vol. 21, No. 2, 1973 [publ. 1975]).

Beidelman, T. O.
1980

"The moral imagination of the Kaguru: some thoughts on tricksters, translation and comparative analysis" *(American Ethnologist 7, 1980, 27-42).*

Bellah, Robert N.
1970

"Christianity and Symbolic Realism" (in Idem, *Beyond Belief. Essays on Religion in a Post-Traditional World.* New York, Evanston, and London, 1970, 236-259).

1970

"Response to Comments on 'Christianity and Symbolic Realism' " *(Journal for the Scientific Study of Religion 9, 1970, 112-115).*

1974

"Comment on 'The Limits of Symbolic Realism' " *(Journal for the Scientific Study of Religion 13, 1974, 487-489).*

Berger, Klaus
1977

Exegese des Neuen Testaments: Neue Wege vom Text zur Auslegung. Heidelberg, 1977, ²1984.

1977

"Wissenssoziologie und Exegese des Neuen Testaments" *(Kairos 19, 1977, 124-133).*

1984

Formgeschichte des Neuen Testaments. Heidelberg, 1984.

Berger, Peter L.
1954

"The Sociological Study of Sectarianism" *(Social Research 21, 1954, 467-485).*

Berger, Peter L. and
Kellner, H. 1981

Sociology Reinterpreted: An Essay on Method and Vocation, Harmondsworth, 1981.

Best, Thomas F.
1983

"The Sociological Study of the New Testament: Promise and Peril of a New Discipline" *(Scottish Journal of Theology 36, 1983, 181-194).*

Blank, Reiner
1981

Analyse und Kritik der formgeschichtlichen Arbeiten von Martin Dibelius und Rudolf Bultmann [Diss. Basel 1978]. Basel, 1981.

Burke, Peter
1980

Sociology and History (Controversies in Sociology 10). London, 1980.

Cahnmann, W. J. and
Boskoff, Alvin 1964

"Sociology and History: Reunion and Rapprochement," in Cahnmann-Boskoff (eds.), *Sociology and History. Theory and Research.* Glencoe-London, 1964, 1-18.

Cairns, David
1974

"The Thought of Peter Berger" *(Scottish Journal of Theology 27, 1974, 181-197).*

Carney, T. F.
1975

The Shape of the Past: Models and Antiquity. Lawrence, Kansas: Coronado Press, 1975.

Clark, Gillian
1985

"The Social Status of Paul" *(Expository Times 96, 1984-85, 110-111).*

Dahlgren, Curt
1982

MARANATA. En sociologisk studie av en sektrörelses uppkomst och utveckling. Helsingborg, 1982.

Deissmann, Adolf
1923

Licht vom Osten. Das Neue Testament und die neuent-deckten Texte der hellenistisch-römischen Welt. 4. Aufl. Tübingen, 1923.

1925

Paulus: Eine kultur- und religionsgeschichtliche Skizze. 2. ed. Tübingen, 1925.

Duling, Dennis C.
1985

"Insights from Sociology for New Testament Christology: A Test Case" *(Society of Biblical Literature 1985 Seminar Papers* 24, 1985, 351-368).

Edwards, O. C. Jr.
1983

"Sociology as a Tool for Interpreting the New Testament" *(Anglican Theological Review* 65, 1983, 431-446).

Elliott, John H.
1981

A Home for the Homeless: A Sociological Exegesis of 1 Peter, Its Situation and Strategy. Philadelphia, 1981.

1985

"Review of The First Urban Christians by Wayne A. Meeks" *(Religious Studies Review* 11, 1985, 329-335).

1986

"Social-Scientific Criticism of the New Testament: More on Methods and Models" *(Semeia* 35, 1986, 1-33).

Engberg-Pedersen,
Troels
1987

"The Gospel and Social Practice According to 1 Corinthians" *(New Testament Studies* 33, 1987, 557-584).

Esler, Philip Francis
1987

Community and Gospel in Luke-Acts. The Social and Political Motivations of Lucan Theology (SNTS Monograph Series 57). Cambridge, 1987.

Filson, Floyd V.
1939

"The Significance of the Early House Churches" *(Journal of Biblical Literature* 58, 1939, 105-112).

Fiorenza, Elizabeth
Schüssler 1983

In Memory of Her: A Feminist Theological Reconstruction of Christian Origins. London, 1983.

Funk, Aloys
1981

Status und Rollen in den Paulusbriefen. Eine inhaltsanalytische Untersuchung zur Religionssoziologie (Innsbrucker theologische Studien 7). Innsbruck, 1981.

Gager, John G.
1975

Kingdom and Community: The Social World of Early Christianity. Englewood Cliffs, New Jersey, 1975.

1982

"Shall We Marry Our Enemies? Sociology and the New Testament" *(Interpretation* 36, 1982, 256-265).

1983

"Social Description and Sociological Explanation in the Study of Early Christianity: A Review Essay" (in Gottwald (ed.), *Bible and Liberation, 1983,* 428-440). [originally *Rel Stud Rev* 5, 1979, 174-180]

Geertz, Clifford
1973

The Interpretation of Cultures. Selected Essays. New York, 1973.

Gill, Robin
1974

"Berger's Plausibility Structures: A Response to Professor Cairns" *(Scottish Journal of Theology* 27, 1974, 198-207).

1975	*The Social Context of Theology: A Methodological Enquiry.* London and Oxford, 1975.
1977	*Theology and Social Structure.* London and Oxford, 1977.
(ed.) 1987	*Theology and Sociology. A Reader.* Ed. and introd. by Robin Gill. London and New York, 1987.
Gottwald, Norman K. 1981	*The Tribes of Yahweh: A Sociology of the Religion of Liberated Israel 1250-1050 B.C.E.* London, 1981 [=Maryknoll, N.Y., 1979].
(ed.) 1983	*Bible and Liberation. Political and Social Hermeneutics.* Maryknoll, N.Y., 1983.
Green, Henry Alan 1985	*The Economic and Social Origins of Gnosticism* (SBL Dissertation Series 77). Atlanta, 1985. [Diss. St. Andrew's University, Scotland, 1982].
Gülzow, Henneke 1969	*Christentum und Sklaverei in den ersten drei Jahrhunderten.* Bonn, 1969.
1974	"Soziale Gegebenheiten der altkirchlichen Mission" (in Heinzgünter Frohnes und Uwe W. Knorr (eds.), *Kirchengeschichte als Missionsgeschichte. Band 1. Die alte Kirche.* München, 1974, 189-226).
Haacker, Klaus 1980	"Dibelius und Cornelius. Ein Beispiel formgeschichtlicher Überlieferungskritik" *(Biblische Zeitschrift N. F. 24, 1980, 234-251).*
Harrington, Daniel J. 1980	"Sociological Concepts and the Early Church: A Decade of Research" *(Theological Studies 41, 1980, 181-190).*
1988	"Second Testament Exegesis and the Social Sciences: A Bibliography" *(Biblical Theology Bulletin 18, 1988, 77-85).*
Hartman, Lars 1978	"Till frågan om evangeliernas litterära genre" *(Annales Academias Regiae Scientiarum Upsaliensis 21, 1978, 5-22).*
1983	"Survey of the Problem of Apocalyptic Genre" (in Hellholm (ed.), *Apocalypticism in the Mediterranean World,* 1983, 329-343).
1988	"Some Unorthodox Thoughts on the 'Household-Code Form'" (Neusner et al (eds.), *The Social World of Formative Christianity and Judaism.* FS H. C. Kee. Philadelphia, 1988, 219-232).
Harvey, A. E. 1979	"Review of *The First Followers of Jesus: A Sociological Analysis of the Earliest Christianity* by G. Theissen" *(Journal of Theological Studies N.S. 30, 1979, 279-282).*
1985	"Forty Strokes Save One: Social Aspects of Judaizing and Apostasy" (A. E. Harvey (ed.), *Alternative Approaches to New Testament Study.* London, 1985, 79-96).

Hellholm, David
(ed.)
1983

Apocalypticism in the Mediterranean World and the Near East. Proceedings of the International Colloquium on Apocalypticism, Uppsala, August 12-17, 1979. Tübingen, 1983.

Hemer, Colin J.
1985

"Review of J. H. Elliott, *A Home for the Homeless*" (*Journal for the Study of the New Testament* 24, 1985, 120-123).

Hengel, Martin
1974

Property and Riches in the Early Church: Aspects of a Social History of Early Christianity. London, 1974.

Hock, Ronald F.
1978

"Paul's Tentmaking and the Problem of His Social Class (*Journal of Biblical Literature* 97, 1978, 555-564).

1979

"The Workshop as a Social Setting for Paul's Missionary Preaching" (*Catholic Biblical Quarterly* 41, 1979, 439-450).

1980

The Social Context of Paul's Ministry. Tentmaking and Apostleship. Philadelphia, 1980.

Hodges, Daniel L.
1974

"Breaking a Scientific Taboo: Putting Assumptions About the Supernatural into Scientific Theories of Religion" (*Journal for the Scientific Study of Religion* 13, 1974, 393-408).

Holmberg, Bengt
1978/80

Paul and Power. The Structure of Authority in the Primitive Church as Reflected in the Pauline Epistles. Lund, 1978 - Philadelphia, 1980.

1980

"Sociological versus Theological Analysis of the Question Concerning a Pauline Church Order," in Sigfred Pedersen (ed.), *Die paulinische Literatur und Theologie.* Århus-Göttingen, 1980, 187-200.

1990

"Sociologiska perspektiv på Gal 2: 11-14(21)" (forthcoming in *Svensk Exegetisk Årsbok* 55, 1990).

Horsley, Richard A.
1986

"Popular Prophetic Movements at the Time of Jesus, Their Principal Features and Social Origins" (*Journal for the Study of the New Testament* 26, 1986, 3-27).

Isenberg, Sheldon R.
1975

"Power Through Temple and Torah in Greco-Roman Palestine," in *Christianity, Judaism and Other Greco-Roman Cults. Studies for Morton Smith at Sixty.* (Studies in Judaism in Late Antiquity 12). vol II. Leiden, 1975, 24-52.

Jeremias, Joachim
1969

Jerusalem zur Zeit Jesu. Eine kulturgeschichtliche Untersuchung zur neutestamentlichen Zeitgeschichte. Göttingen 1923-37; 3. revised ed. 1969.

Jewett, Robert
1986

The Thessalonian Correspondence: Pauline Rhetoric and Millenarian Piety. Philadelphia, 1986.

Johnson, Benton
1977

"Sociological Theory and Religious Truth" (*Sociological Analysis* 38, 1977, 368-388).

Judge, Edwin A. 1960	*The Social Pattern of the Christian Groups in the First Century. Some Prolegomena to the Study of New Testament Ideas of Social Obligation.* London, 1960.
1960	"Die frühen Christen als scholastische Gemeinschaft" (in Meeks (ed.), *Zur Soziologie des Urchristentums.* München, 1979, 131-164). [Originally "The Early Christians as a Scholastic Community" in *Journal of Religious History* 1, 1960/61, 4-15, 125-137].
1972	"St. Paul and Classical Society" *(Jahrbuch für Antike und Christentum* 15, 1972, 19-36).
1980	"The Social Identity of the First Christians: A Question of Method in Religious History" *(Journal of Religious History* 11, 1980, 201-217).
1984	"Gesellschaft/Gesellschaft und Christentum III. Neues Testament" *(Theologische Realenzyklopädie* vol. 12. New York, Berlin, 1984, 764-769).
Kautsky, Karl 1910	*Der Ursprung des Christentums: Eine Historische Untersuchung.* Stuttgart 1910.
Keck, Leander E. 1974	"On the Ethos of Early Christians" in *Journal of the American Academy of Religion* 42, 1974, 435-452. [also as "Das Ethos der frühen Christen" (in Meeks (ed.), *Zur Soziologie des Urchristentums.* München, 1979, 13-36).
Kee, Howard C. 1980	*Christian Origins in Sociological Perspective.* London, 1980.
Kellner, Hansfried	see Berger, Peter L.
Kippenberg, Hans G. 1970	"Versuch einer soziologischen Verortung des antiken Gnostizismus" *(Numen* 17, 1970, 211-232).
1978	*Religion und Klassenbildung im antiken Judäa. Eine religionssoziologische Studie zum Verhältnis von Tradition und gesellschaftlicher Entwicklung.* Göttingen, 1978.
1983	"Ein Vergleich jüdischer, christlicher und gnostischer Apokalyptik" (in Hellholm (ed.), *Apocalypticism in the Mediterranean World,* Tübingen, 1983, 751-768).
Kreissig, Heinz 1967	"Zur sozialen Zusammensetzung der frühchristlichen Gemeinden im ersten Jahrhundert u. Z." *(Eirene. Studia Graeca et Latina* 6, 1967, 91-100).
Kümmel, W. G. 1985	"Das Urchristentum II. Arbeiten zur Spezialproblemen. b. Zur Sozialgeschichte und Soziologie der Urkirche" *(Theologische Rundschau* 50, 1985, 327-363).

Lampe, Peter
1982
"Die Apokalyptiker - ihre Situation und ihr Handeln" (in *Eschatologie und Friedenshandeln: Exegetische Beiträge zur Frage christlicher Friedensverantwortung*, Mit Beiträgen von U. Luz, J. Kegler, P. Lampe, P. Hoffmann (Stuttgarter Bibelstudien 101), Stuttgart, 1982, 59-114).

1989
Die stadtrömischen Christen in den ersten beiden Jahrhunderten: Untersuchungen zur Sozialgeschichte (WUNT Reihe 2, 18). 2. Aufl. Tübingen, 1989.

Lee, Clarence L.
1971
"Soziale Unruhe und Urchristentum" (in Meeks (ed.), *Zur Soziologie des Urchristentums*. München, 1979, 67-87). [Originally publ. in S. Benko and J. J. O'Rourke (eds.), *The Catacombs and the Colosseum*. Valley Forge, Pa., 1971].

Lüdemann, Gerd
1987
Das frühe Christentum nach den Traditionen der Apostelgeschichte: Ein Kommentar. Göttingen, 1987.

MacDonald, Margaret Y.
1988
The Pauline Churches: A Socio-historical Study of Institutionalization in the Pauline and Deutero-Pauline Writings (SNTS Monograph Series 60). Cambridge, 1988.

MacIntyre, Alasdair
1985
After Virtue: A Study in Moral Theory. London: Duckworth 1981, 1985 2. uppl.

MacMullen, Ramsay
1974
Roman Social Relations 50 B.C. to A.D.284. New Haven and London, 1974.

Malherbe, Abraham J.
1983
Social Aspects of Early Christianity. Baton Rouge, 1977, 2. ed. Philadelphia, 1983.

Malina, Bruce J.
1979
"Review of Sociology of Early Palestinian Christianity by Gerd Theissen" *(Catholic Biblical Quarterly* 41, 1979, 176-178).

1981
The New Testament World: Insights from Cultural Anthropology. Atlanta, 1981.

1983
"The Social Sciences and Biblical Interpretation" (in Gottwald (ed.), *Bible and Liberation*, 11-25; expanded version of the same article in *Interpretation* 37, 1982, 229-242).

1985
"Review of the First Urban Christians by Wayne A. Meeks" *(Journal of Biblical Literature* 104, 1985, 346-349).

Martin, D. Mills, J. O., and Pickering, W. S. F. (ed.) 1980
Sociology and Theology. Alliance and Conflict. Brighton, 1980.

McGuire, Meredith B.
1981
Religion: The Social Context. Belmont, California 1981.

Meeks, Wayne A.
1972
"The Man from Heaven in Johannine Sectarianism" (*Journal of Biblical Literature* 91, 1972, 44-72).

(ed.)
1979
Zur Soziologie des Urchristentums. Ausgewählte Beiträge zum frühchristlichen Gemeinschaftsleben in seiner gesellschaftlichen Umwelt. München, 1979.

1982
"The Social Context of Pauline Theology" (*Interpretation* 36, 1982, 266-277).

1983
"Social Functions of Apocalyptic Language in Pauline Christianity" (in Hellholm (ed.), *Apocalypticism in the Mediterranean World (1983),* 687-706).

1983
The First Urban Christians: The Social World of the Apostle Paul. New Haven and London, 1983.

1985
"Breaking Away: Three New Testament Pictures of Christianity's Separation from the Jewish Communities" (J. Neusner and E. S. Frerichs (eds.), *"To See Ourselves as Others See Us": Christians, Jews, "Others" in Late Antiquity.* Chico, California, 1985, 93-115).

1986
The Moral World of the First Christians. London, 1987 [first publ. in USA 1986].

1986
"A Hermeneutics of Social Embodiment" (G. W. E. Nickelsburg - G. W. MacRae, S.J. (eds.), *Christians Among Jews and Gentiles.* FS K. Stendahl. Philadelphia 1986, 176-186).

1986
"Understanding Early Christian Ethics" (*Journal of Biblical Literature* 105, 1986, 3-11).

Mehl, Roger
1962
"Bedeutung, Möglichkeiten und Grenzen der Soziologie des Protestantismus in theologischer Sicht" (in D. Goldschmidt - J. Matthes (eds.), *Probleme der Religionssoziologie* (Kölner Zeitschrift für Soziologie und Sozialpsychologie. Sonderheft 6), Köln - Opladen 1962, 112-122).

Morgan, Robert with John Barton 1988
Biblical Interpretation. (Oxford Bible Series) Oxford, 1988.

Moxnes, Halvor
1988
"Sociology and the New Testament" (in Erik Karlsaune (ed.), *Religion as a Social Phenomenon. Theologians and sociologists sharing research interests.* Trondheim, 1988, 143-159).

Munz, Peter
1972
"The Problem of 'Die soziologische Verortung des antiken Gnostizismus' " (*Numen* 19, 1972, 41-51).

Nickelsburg, G. W. E.
1983
"Social Aspects of Palestinian Jewish Apocalypticism" (in Hellholm (ed.), *Apocalypticism in the Mediterranean World,* 1983, 641-654).

Olsson, Birger
1984
"Ett hem för hemlösa. Om sociologisk exeges av NT" (*Svensk Exegetisk Årsbok* 49, 1984, 89-108).

Osiek, Carolyn, RSCJ 1984 — *What Are They Saying about the Social Setting of the New Testament?* New York and Ramsey, N.J., 1984.

Petersen, Norman R. 1985 — *Rediscovering Paul: Philemon and the Sociology of Paul's Narrative World.* Philadelphia, 1985.

Poloma, Margaret M. 1982 — "Toward a Christian Sociological Perspective: Religious Values, Theory and Methodology" (*Sociological Analysis* 43, 1982, 95-108).

Reicke, Bo 1968 — *The New Testament Era: The World of the Bible from 500 B.C. to A.D. 100.* Philadelphia, 1968.

Richter, Philip J. 1984 — "Recent Sociological Approaches to the Study of the New Testament" (*Religion* 14, 1984, 77-90).

Reis, Ole 1988 — "The Uses of Sociological Theory in Theology— Exemplified by Gerd Theissen's Study of Early Christianity" (in Erik Karlsaune (ed.), *Religion as a Social Phenomenon. Theologians and sociologists sharing research interests.* Trondheim, 1988, 161-178).

Robertson, Roland 1972 — *The Sociological Interpretation of Religion.* Oxford, 1972 [= 1970].

Robbins, T., Anthony, D., and Curtis, T. E. 1973 — "The Limits of Symbolic Realism: Problems of Empathic Field Observation in a Sectarian Context" (*Journal for the Scientific Study of Religion* 12, 1973, 259-271).

Rodd, Cyril S. 1979 — "Max Weber and Ancient Judaism" (*Scottish Journal of Theology* 32, 1979, 457-469)

1981 — "On Applying a Sociological Theory to Biblical Studies" (*Journal for the Study of the Old Testament* 19, 1981, 95-106).

Rohrbaugh, R. L. 1978 — *The Biblical Interpreter. An Agrarian Bible in an Industrial Age.* Philadelphia, 1978.

1984 — "Methodological Considerations in the Debate over the Social Class Status of Early Christians" (*Journal of the American Academy of Religion* 52, 1984, 519-546).

1987 — 'Social Location of Thought' as a Heuristic Construct in New Testament Study" (*Journal for the Study of the New Testament* 30, 1987, 103-119).

Rowland, Christopher 1985 — *Christian Origins. An Account of the Setting and Character of the Most Important Messianic Sect of Judaism.* London, 1985.

1985 — "Reading the New Testament Sociologically: An Introduction" (*Theology* 88, 1985, 358-364).

Russell, Ronald 1988 — "The Idle in 2 Thess 3.6-12: An Eschatological or A Social Problem?" (*New Testament Studies* 34, 1988, 105-119).

Rydbeck, Lars
1967

Fachprosa, vermeintliche Volkssprache und Neues Testament. Zur Beurteilung der sprachlichen Niveauunterschiede im nachklassischen Griechisch. Uppsala, 1967.

Schelbert, Georg
1985

"Wo steht die Formgeschichte?" *(Theologische Berichte XIII. Methoden der Evangelienexegese.* 1985, 11-39).

Schelsky, Helmut
(ed.)
1970

Zur Theorie der Institution. Düsseldorf, 1970.

Schmithals, Walter
1980

"Kritik der Formkritik" *(Zeitschrift für Theologie und Kirche* 77, 1980, 149-185).

Schöllgen, Georg
1984

Ecclesia sordida? Zur Frage der sozialen Schichtung frühchristlicher Gemeinden am Beispiel Karthagos zur Zeit Tertullians (JAC. E 12). Münster, 1984.

1985

"Die Didache—ein frühes Zeugnis für Landgemeinden?" *(Zeitschrift für neutestamentliche Wissenschaft* 76, 1985, 140-143).

1988

"Was wissen wir über die Sozialstruktur der paulinischen Gemeinden?" *(New Testament Studies* 34, 1988, 71-82).

Schütz, John Howard
1975

Paul and the Anatomy of Apostolic Authority (SNTS Monograph Series 26). Cambridge, 1975.

Scroggs, Robin
1975

"The Earliest Christian Communities as Sectarian Movement," in *Christianity, Judaism and Other Greco-Roman Cults. Studies for Morton Smith at Sixty.* (Studies in Judaism in Late Antiquity 12). vol. II. Leiden, 1975, 1-23).

1980

"The Sociological Interpretation of the New Testament: The Present State of Research" *(New Testament Studies* 26, 1980, 164-179).

Segal, Robert A.
1980

"The Social Sciences and the Truth of Religious Belief" *(Journal of the American Academy of Religion* 48, 1980, 403-413).

Skocpol, Theda (ed.)
1984

Vision and Method in Historical Sociology. Cambridge 1984.

Smith, Jonathan Z.,
1975

"The Social Description of Early Christianity" *(Religious Studies Review* 1, 1975, 19-25).

1978

"Too Much Kingdom, Too Little Community" *(Zygon: Journal of Religion and Science* 13, 1978, 123-130).

Smith, R. H.
1980

"Were the Early Christians Middle-Class? A Sociological Analysis of the New Testament" *(Currents in Theology and Mission* 7, St. Louis, 1980, 260-276).

Stambaugh, John E. and Balch, David L. 1986 — *The New Testament in Its Social Environment* Philadelphia, 1986.

Stark, Rodney 1986 — "The Class Basis of Early Christianity: Inferences from a Sociological Model" (*Sociological Analysis* 47, 1986, 216-225).

Stark, Werner 1967 — *Sectarian Religion (The Sociology of Religion.* vol. II). London, 1967.

Stavenhagen, Rodolfo 1975 — *Social Class in Agrarian Societies.* New York, 1975. [Spanish original 1970].

Stegemann, Wolfgang 1978 — "Nachfolge Jesu als solidarische Gemeinschaft der reichen und angesehenen Christen mit den bediirftigen und verachteten Christen. Das Lukasevangelium" (= ch. 3 in Luise Schottroff - Wolfgang Stegemann, Jesus *von Nazareth—Hoffnung der Armen.* Stuttgart, 1978, 89-153).

1979 — "Wanderradikalismus im Urchristentum? Historische und theologische Auseinandersetzung mit einer interessanten These," in Schottroff-Stegemann (eds.), *Der Gott der kleinen Leute. Sozialgeschichtliche Bibelauslegungen. Bd 2. Neues Testament.* München-Gelnhausen, 1979, 94-120.

1987 — "War der Apostel Paulus ein römischer Bürger?" (*Zeitschrift für neutestamentliche Wissenschaft* 78, 1987, 200-229).

Stowers, Stanley Kent 1984 — "Social Status, Public Speaking and Private Teaching: The Circumstances of Paul's Preaching Activity" (*Novum Testamentum* 26, 1984, 59-82).

1985 — "The Social Sciences and the Study of Early Christianity" in W. S. Green (ed.), *Approaches to Ancient Judaism* (Studies in Judaism and Its Greco-Roman Context, vol. 5). Atlanta, 1985, 149-181).

Stuhlmacher, Peter (ed.) 1982 — *Das Evangelium und die Evangelien* (WUNT 28). Tübingen, 1982.

Theissen, Gerd 1973 — "Wanderradikalismus. Literatursoziologische Aspekte der Überlieferung von Worten Jesu im Urchristentum" (*Zeitschrift für Theologie und Kirche* 70, 1973, 245-271; now in *Studien*, 79-105).

1974 — *Urchristliche Wundergeschichten: Ein Beitrag zur formgeschichtlichen Erforschung der synoptischen Evangelien* (Studien zum Neuen Testament 8). Gütersloh, 1974.

1974	"Soziale Schichtung in der korinthischen Gemeinde" *(Zeitschrift für neutestamentliche Wissenschaft* 65, 1974, 232-273; now in *Studien,* 231-271).
1974	"Soziale Integration und sakramentales Handeln" *(Novum Testamentum* 16, 1974, 179-206; now in *Studien,* 290-317).
1974	"Theoretische Probleme religionssoziologischer Forschung und die Analyse des Urchristentums" *(Neue Zeitschrift für Systematische Theologie und Religionsphilosophie* 16, 1974, 35-56; now in *Studien,* 55-76).
1975	"Die soziologische Auswertung religiöser Überlieferungen: Ihre methodologischen Probleme am Beispiel des Urchristentums" *(Kairos* 17, 1975, 284-299; now in *Studien,* 35-54).
1975	"Legitimation und Lebensunterhalt: Ein Beitrag zur Soziologie urchristlicher Missionare" *(New Testament Studies* 21, 1974/75, 192-221; now in *Studien,* 201-230).
1975	"Die Starken und Schwachen in Korinth: Soziologische Analyse eines theologischen Streites" *(Evangelische Theologie* 35, 1975, 155-172; now in *Studien,* 272-289).
1976	"Die Tempelweissagung Jesu: Prophetie im Spannungsfeld von Stadt und Land" *(Theologische Zeitschrift* 32, 1976, 144-158; now in *Studien,* 142-159).
1977	"Wir haben alles verlassen' (Mc. X, 28). Nachfolge und soziale Entwurzelung in der jüdisch-palästinischen Gesellschaft des 1. Jahrhunderts n. Chr." *(Novum Testamentum* 19, 1977, 161-196; now in *Studien,* 106-141).
1977	*Soziologie der Jesusbewegung: Ein Beitrag zur Entstehungsgeschichte des Urchristentums* (Theologische Existenz heute 194). München, 1977.
1979	"Zur forschungsgeschichtlichen Einordnung der soziologischen Fragestellung" (published in first ed. of *Studien,* 3-34).
1979	"Gewaltverzicht und Feindesliebe (Mt 5,38-48/Lk 6,27-38) und deren sozialgeschichtlicher Hintergrund" (first published in first ed. of *Studien,* 160-197).
1983	*Studien zur Soziologie des Urchristentums* (WUNT19). 2., erweiterte Auflage (1. Aufl. 1979). Tübingen, 1983.

1983	"Christologie und soziale Erfahrung. Wissenssoziologische Aspekte paulinischer Christologie" (first published in second ed. of *Studien*, 318-330).
1985	"Review of The First Urban Christians by Wayne A. Meeks" (*Journal of Religion* 65, 1985, 111-113).
1988	"Vers une théorie de l'histoire sociale du christianisme primitif" (*Études Théologiques et Religieuses* 63, 1988, 199-225).
Tidball, Derek 1983	*An Introduction to the Sociology of the New Testament.* Exeter, 1983.
Tiryakian, Edward A. 1985	"Review of The First Urban Christians by Wayne A. Meeks" (*American Journal of Sociology* 90, 1985, 1138-1140).
Tracy, David 1978	"A Theological Response to 'Kingdom and Community' " (*Zygon: Journal of Religion and Science* 13, 1978, 131-135).
Troeltsch, Ernst 1912	*Die Soziallehren der christlichen Kirchen und Gruppen.* (*Gesammelte Schriften* I), Tübingen, 1912.
Tuckett, Christopher 1987	*Reading the New Testament: Methods of Interpretation.* London, 1987.
Venetz, H.-J. 1985	"Der Beitrag der Soziologie zur Lektüre des Neuen Testaments. Ein Bericht" (*Theologische Berichte XIII. Methoden der Evangelienexegese.* 1985, 87-121).
Verner, David C. 1983	*The Household of God: The Social World of the Pastoral Epistles* (SBL Disseration Series 71). Chico, Calif. 1983.
Wallis, Roy 1975	"Relative Deprivation and Social Movements: A Cautionary Note" (*British Journal of Sociology* 26, 1975, 360-363)
Watson, Francis 1986	*Paul, Judaism and the Gentiles: A Sociological Approach* (SNTS Monograph Series 56). Cambridge, 1986.
White, L. Michael 1986	"Sociological Analysis of Early Christian Groups: A Social Historian's Response" (*Sociological Analysis* 47, 1986, 249-266).
Wilson, Bryan R. 1959	"An Analysis of Sect Development" (*American Sociological Review* 24, 1959, 3-15).
1973	*Magic and the Millennium. A Sociological Study of Religious Movements of Protest Among Tribal and Third-World Peoples.* London, 1973.
Wuellner, W. H. 1973	"The Sociological Implications of I Corinthians 1: 26-28 Reconsidered" (*Studia Evangelics*, vol VI. Berlin, 1973, 666-672).
Zimmermann, Alfred 1984	*Die urchristlichen Lehrer* (WUNT 2. Reihe 12). Tübingen, 1984.

Index of Modern Authors